THE IDEA OF
PREHISTORY

GLYN DANIEL AND COLIN RENFREW

THE IDEA OF
PREHISTORY

at the University Press

EDINBURGH

© Glyn Daniel and Colin Renfrew 1988

Edinburgh University Press
22 George Square, Edinburgh

Set in Linotronic Palatino
by Speedspools, Edinburgh, and
printed in Great Britain by
Butler and Tanner Ltd,
Frome, Somerset

British Library Cataloguing
  in Publication Data
Daniel, Glyn
The idea of prehistory.—New ed.
1. Anthropology, Prehistoric
I. Title   II. Renfrew, Colin
930   GN740

ISBN0 85224 532 7
ISBN0 85224 536 x Pbk

Preface to the Second Edition

When it was suggested that this book should be re-issued
it seemed to me right that it should be brought up to date
with two new chapters and I am delighted that my
successor as Disney Professor of Archaeology in the University of Cambridge agreed to do this. Chapters I to VIII
of this book are much as they were when edited for
printing in 1962. Some inaccuracies have been put right
and some infelicities changed. Otherwise they are little
changed from the lectures delivered in Birmingham in
1956–57. Chapters IX and X are by Professor Colin
Renfrew. The list of books for further reading has been
revised by Professor Renfrew and myself.

GLYN DANIEL
St John's College, Cambridge
August
1986

Contents

	Preface	*page* v
	List of Illustrations	viii
I	The Fog and the Flood	1
II	The Beginnings of Archaeological Prehistory .	22
III	The Victorians and Prehistory	41
IV	The Development of Modern Prehistory . . .	60
V	Diffusion and Distraction	79
VI	The Idea of Prehistory in the Study of Language and Race, and in Politics . . .	97
VII	Prehistory and the Historians	115
VIII	Prehistory and the Public	136
IX	The New Archaeology: Prehistory as a Discipline	157
X	Towards a World History	176
	Recommended Reading	205
	Index	214

List of Illustrations

Daniel Wilson	*page* 1
William Stukeley	14
Lord Monboddo	17
Sir Richard Colt Hoare	20
Christian Jurgensen Thomsen	22
Sir Charles Lyell	27
Jacques Boucher de Perthes	34
Sir John Evans	36
Sir John Lubbock	40
Sven Nilsson	41
Heinrich Schliemann	44
Oscar Montelius	47
Gabriel de Mortillet	49
Jens Jacob Worsaae	54
Lewis Morgan	59
Sir Arthur Evans	60
General Pitt-Rivers	64
Sir Flinders Petrie	66
Sir Cyril Fox	70
O. G. S. Crawford	72
Sir Grafton Elliot Smith	79
Gustav Kossinna	97
Gordon Childe	115
Edward Lhwyd	117
Grahame Clark	123
Glyn Daniel	136
Sir Austen Henry Layard	141
Lewis R. Binford	157
Kent Flannery	168
David Clarke	175
Willard Libby	176
C. Wesley Ferguson	179
Gordon Willey	182
Robert M. Adams	184
Hans Helbaek	191
Martin Biddle	194
Colin Renfrew	204

I

The Fog and the Flood

DANIEL WILSON

The first man to use the word 'prehistory' seems to have been Daniel Wilson, in 1851, in the title of his book *The Archaeology and Prehistoric Annals of Scotland.* In the preface to the second edition of this book, published twelve years later, Wilson refers to 'the application of the term prehistoric introduced—if I mistake not—for the first time in this work.' To the best of my knowledge Daniel Wilson was not making a mistake and 1851 was the first time that 'prehistory' was introduced into the English language. The *Oxford English Dictionary* records the stages by which the word came into respectable and general usage. Sir Edward Tylor was using it in his *Primitive Culture* in 1871; seven years later Mr Gladstone is using it, and finally, it becomes a respectable word—*The Times* mentions prehistory in 1888 and *Nature* follows suit in 1902.

1

It is not only in England but on the Continent—in France, Switzerland, Germany, the Scandinavian countries, Spain, and Italy—that, during the second half of the nineteenth century, prehistory came into existence as a conscious and separate aspect of the study of man's past. The word used was naturally not the same; the French spoke of *préhistoire*, the Italians of *preistoria*, the Germans had the word *Vorgeschichte*, while the Danes had the very nice word *oldtid*—old times. And this is of course what prehistory is concerned with; the old or oldest times in man's past—the very earliest moments in that long story of human development which grows in complexity and historicity from the spread of the Roman Empire to the present day.

In England itself the word prehistory was not immediately accepted with enthusiasm. Other names were suggested, of which one was antehistory. Sir John Lubbock seriously considered using this word when he was writing the book that was eventually entitled *Prehistoric Times*, and which, published first in 1865, did so much to popularize prehistory. He wisely decided against this word, and, although it was of course spelled with an *e* and not an *i*, it is fortunate that the name was dropped. Others, in the middle of the nineteenth century, and nowadays, have complained that prehistory was a stupid name, because it was essentially a misnomer; it meant, logically and etymologically, the time before history, and surely, it was argued, there was, strictly speaking, no time in the past of man before he had any history. History was essentially human, unless one referred to natural history. What was prehistory, they argued, but the earliest past of history? This is, I suppose, logically correct; not that logic seems to enter very much into nomenclature; names most often grow up and are not carefully thought out.

But it is true that we normally use the word history in two senses, as when we say the history of man, meaning the whole of man's past, and history *sensu stricto*, when we mean the part of man's past which we know about because he has written down details of it—not necessarily always truthfully or correctly—in inscriptions on stones and tombs, in diaries, state papers, treaties,

2

memoirs, and books. In fact, by history *sensu stricto* we normally mean in usual parlance written history, and I imagine that most people still mean written history when they speak of history. Now it is, of course, prewritten history that we mean when we speak of prehistory, and it was the development of the study of man's past before he began to record it himself in symbols that can now be read, that had come to such a stage a hundred years ago that a special word had to be found for it: the word prehistory.

The whole history of man had, of course, been studied long before Daniel Wilson spoke of prehistory. There is, we must all admit this, a natural, normal, human interest in origins and beginnings. In the world of sixteenth-century German history, the past of man, or universal history, was subdivided according to the four World Empires, i.e., Assyria, Persia, Greece, and Rome—which was to last until the end of the world. This was what is known as the Four Monarchy System. It was, surprisingly enough, philologists and not historians who introduced the idea of ancient, medieval, and modern history; and this is the division we find in *An Universal History from the Earliest Account of Time* produced in London in thirty-eight volumes between 1736 and 1765. What, then, happened in the mid-nineteenth century was that a fourth division was added to the human past, and from then on we have been thinking of history, history in its widest sense, that is—human history—as divided into prehistory, ancient history, medieval history, and modern history. And by the way, when I say 'we have been thinking,' I am afraid I mean people concerned with ancient history, archaeology, and anthropology. It is true that the general public and our universities are only, rather slowly, getting used to the idea of the antiquity of man and the existence of prehistory. Universities have not necessarily been in the van of intellectual progress. In the first of his Ford Lectures at Oxford in 1907 Professor Haverfield said that the Universities—and I think he meant by that phrase at that moment Oxford and Cambridge—had never been interested in archaeology, and that our greatest archaeologists had not been connected with universities. This was so then; it is less so now; but

3

we still have a long way to go before we teach effectively in our British universities the sciences of man. When that time comes prehistory will take its proper place in British education.

But my object is not to fulminate against the neglect of prehistory in our educational system; it is rather to discover what sort of picture people have given at different times in the last century—or more—of man's prehistoric past. It is only too true, as we all know, that history varies with the historian who recounts it, and with the state of development of the subject. We were brought up at school to believe that there were immutable historical facts, and find when we grow up, that they are as mutable as the interpretations of those who write about them, and as varying as the models which those writers assume. So it is with prehistory; the prehistory of man has varied very much with the prehistorian and with the state of development of our knowledge, and with the preconceptions brought to bear on the archaeological record as it is being translated into historical contexts. It is fair, therefore, to speak of Worsaae's prehistory, of Gabriel de Mortillet's prehistory, of Gordon Childe's prehistory, of Nazi and Marxist prehistory. It is with these and other ideas of prehistory that we shall be concerned in these lectures, and also the reason behind the various prehistories—reasons which lie partly in the disposition of the prehistorian—those prejudices and preferences which, try as we may, colour our basic thinking as well as our emotional thought, and whose origin no man can clearly tell—and partly in the state of knowledge of the material which the prehistorian is interpreting. The state of the material record can colour and control the prehistorian's interpretative activities without any consideration of his own preconceptions and predispositions.

We have used the world 'material' advisedly, and we must here be clear at the outset of our discussions what we mean. The material which the prehistorian uses—which he interprets—is, by definition, and by fact, unwritten. It is the unwritten remains of the early past of man, the mute, silent witness of the origins and early development of prehistory—tools, weapons, houses, temples, paintings, tombs, farms, fields, forts, water-

4

mills—in a word it is all archaeological material. It is then, first a record of artifacts, of things made and fashioned by man, and, second, a record of associated features that are not artifacts, such evidence of the flora and fauna that surrounded early man and that he utilized, or his own bones and skin and hair.

The prehistorian is then an archaeologist, indeed has to be an archaeologist, and an archaeologist all the time; so much so that quite often the phrase *prehistoric archaeology* is used synonymously with *prehistory*. Rather too often one finds people—people who ought to know better—who pretend not to understand the distinction between prehistorian and archaeologist, and of course it would only be splitting very thin hairs indeed to say that there was any difference between a prehistorian and a prehistoric archaeologist. But there is an essential difference between prehistory and archaeology; an archaeologist is a person who studies the material remains of the past with the aim of wresting the facts of history from them, and he can work in any period from the Upper Palaeolithic of the caves to the Late Medieval of the Gothic cathedrals or the late nineteenth century of the archaeology of disused railways. Sir Alfred Clapham used to say that archaeology began when living memory ended; many others have said it is much later. Each week—or if we are fortunate, twice a week—we see our domestic refuse being carted off and dumped in municipal refuse dumps—a stratified accumulation of gin bottles and tin cans, broken teacups and rotting cabbage stalks for archaeologists of the future to study. The archaeological record—the material remains of the past—starts yesterday when you throw an empty tobacco tin into the wastepaper basket, or this morning when the roadman was shovelling a broken milk bottle into his cart.

There are of course specialized archaeologists who deal with paintings and houses and ecclesiastical architecture. And there is a very curious tradition which is met with in some parts of the museum world, that splits up the material remains of the past into archaeological objects, antiques, and bygones. Yet an Italian goffering-iron and a seventeenth-century silver tankard are as much archaeology as a La Tène sword or a ruined megalithic tomb. Do not let yourself be confused on this point by books which offer you introductions to archaeology and turn out to provide introductions to prehistory—to a part only of the enormous field which is, properly speaking, archaeology. All material remains are archaeology, but the archaeologist cannot, or should not, usually practice a catholicity in time and space; he must needs specialize and is to be pardoned if he sometimes thinks his specialized interests are the whole of archaeology. It is the archaeologist who specializes in prehistory that is our concern in this book. He has been coming into his own very slowly since Daniel Wilson gave him a name in 1851.

I have said that the archaeologist is concerned in wresting facts of historical meaning out of the intractable material left behind, that he is concerned in creating historical contexts out of the material remains. It was not always so with the student of antiquities. Antiquarian studies began in Western Europe with the renaissance of learning. Sixteenth-century scholars in Italy found and studied the classical civilizations of Greece and Rome not only in literature but in archaeology. At the same time, in England, men like William Camden and Humfrey Lhwyd were studying the visible antiquities of Britain. It may well have been that they were impelled to a study of antiquity by the dissolution of the monasteries and the dispersal of the religious libraries, that they sought in the past for the beginnings of the new and flourishing nation of Tudor England. Whatever was the reason, or the sum total of the reasons, there was in England at that time what Camden called a 'back looking curiousity,' and although he recognized that there were some 'which wholly contemne and avile this study of Antiquity (which is always accompanied with dignity,' he wrote, 'and hath a certaine resemblance with eternity), there is a sweet food of the mind well befitting such as are of honest and noble disposition.'

But for many the attraction of antiquities lay in less philosophical channels. The collectors are among our earliest antiquaries. The Earl of Arundel, the Duke of Buckingham, King Charles I, were all collectors; so was John Tradescant, once gardener to Queen Henrietta

6

Maria, and it is his Closet of Curiosities, popularly known as Tradescant's Ark, which formed the nucleus of the Ashmolean Museum, Oxford. Collecting became something of an obsession, and in his *Polyolbion*, written in 1622, Drayton complains that there was 'nothing esteemed in this lunatique age, but what is kept in cabinets.'

It was the age of the collectors that produced the word *dilettanti*—those who delighted in the arts, and we should not underestimate the aesthetic factor in the development of antiquarianism. The cultivation of taste had a very large influence in the discovery of the past. This aesthetic factor often worked for good in a surprising way. It was Sir William Hamilton's *Antiquités Etrusques, Grecques, et Romaines*, published in 1766–67, that inspired the potter Wedgwood with new ideas, and in recognition of this inspiration the Wedgwood works in Staffordshire still bear the name Etruria.

In 1707 a group of men interested in antiquities and history formed themselves into a club. They used to meet in the Young Devil and Bear taverns in the Strand; and out of this Tavern Society was born the Society of Antiquaries of London, the oldest society of its kind in the world—it received its Royal Charter in 1751—and second in seniority only to the Royal Society among the learned societies of England. But its members were divided as to why they were studying antiquities: were they impelled by the back-looking curiosity, or was it as collectors or as dilettanti that they came to meetings and contributed papers to the Society's journal *Archaeologia*, first published in 1770? One Fellow, Horace Walpole, had no doubts, and fiercely castigated those who had no aesthetic feeling and no discrimination in their study of man's past. The second volume of *Archaeologia* set him off. 'Mercy on us,' he wrote to William Cole, on looking through it, 'what a cartload of bricks and rubbish and Roman ruins they have piled together'; and again, in another letter, 'the antiquaries will be as ridiculous as they used to be; and since it is impossible to infuse taste into them, they will be as dry and dull as their predecessors. One may revive what perished, but it will perish again, if more life is not breathed into it than it enjoyed originally. . . . Bishop Lyttelton used to torment me with barrows and Roman camps, and I would as soon have attended to the turf graves in our Churchyards. I have no curiousity to know how awkward and clumsy men have been in the dawn of arts or in their decay.'

But there were others who had this 'curiousity,' even when they might, as we may now, acknowledge the force of some of Walpole's criticism. There are many of us at the present day who are tormented by, and torment others with, Roman camps and hand axes, Mesolithic flints and megalithic tombs. Is our torment necessary and do we do it because we are still inveterate collectors, at a mature age preferring flints and tombs to the stamps and butterflies of our youth, or are we really and honestly historians? We shall see as we go along what our modern idea of prehistory really is. In the eighteenth century there was no agreement. Then Walpole could call the Society of Antiquaries the 'midwives of superannuated miscarriages,' Edward Balme could say 'the world calls us old women,' and Samuel Foote could have a great success in the Haymarket Theatre in 1772 with a play in the third act of which the Nabob visits the Society of Antiquaries preceded by four black porters bearing the twelve lost books of Livy, a piece of lava from the last eruption of Vesuvius, a box of petrifactions, bones, beetles and butterflies, and a green chamber-pot described as a sarcophagus or Roman urn dug up from the Temple of Concord. These things could happen then, but at this same time a new awareness of the real purpose of antiquarian study was coming into existence. In 1793 the Reverend James Douglas published his *Nenia Britannica or the Sepulchral History of Great Britain.* It was an account of several hundred barrows which he had excavated. Douglas's digging would not pass modern tests, but his purpose in excavation was clear and sound. 'If the study of antiquity be undertaken in the cause of History,' he wrote in his preface, 'it will rescue itself from a reproach indiscriminately and fastidiously bestowed on works which have been deemed frivolous.'

'In the cause of History'; these were Douglas's words and this was the change that was taking place in the late eighteenth and early nineteenth century. The material

8

remains of the past were being studied not by collectors and dilettanti, not because the curious or the beautiful were being cultivated, but by men who were consciously trying to wrest historical facts from the material of archaeology.

In their excavations in Wiltshire, William Cunnington of Devizes and Sir Richard Colt Hoare were trying hard and very consciously to eschew the romantic, acquisitive, or dilettante approach of their predecessors as antiquaries. In 1803 William Cunnington described himself as digging barrows on Salibury Plain 'in the hopes of meeting something which might supersede conjecture.' In his *Ancient Wiltshire* Colt Hoare said, 'we speak from facts not theory. I shall not seek among the fanciful regions of Romance an origin of our Wiltshire barrows.'

Real prehistory began with men like these striving to understand man's prehistoric past from the surviving material remains of that past. But of course there was speculation about man's prehistory, about his beginnings and development before writing, long before prehistoric archaeology began. In a way the theme of this chapter is prehistory before archaeology, and our concern is now with some of the ideas of prehistory that existed before scholars had turned to archaeology as their source. The Greeks, of course, had speculated about early man. In the eighth century BC Hesiod in his *Works and Days* speaks of a time in man's past when bronze had not been superseded by iron. Lucretius in his *De rerum natura* asserted that man first used his nails and teeth, and stone and wood and fire; then copper, and still later iron gained in popularity. The Greeks also had other ideas of Ages and Stages in man's past—the Age of Reason, the Golden Age, the Heroic Age, for example.

The Christian religion provided an answer to speculations about man's early history. God formed man in his own image on the sixth day of creation. Eve was created from one of Adam's ribs and together they were expelled from the park of Eden, bearing Cain and Abel. Adam lived for nine hundred and thirty years. His seventh descendant was Methuselah, who lived to be nine hundred and eighty-two years old. Methuselah's grandson was Noah and it was when this Noah was six hundred years old—almost all the members of this first original family seem to have been extremely long lived—that the Great Deluge of water flooded the earth.From the exact dates provided for these lives many have tried to fix the date of the Flood and of the Creation of Man himself. James Ussher, Archbishop of Armagh, calculated in the early seventeenth century that from the evidence in the Old Testament it was possible to declare that the earth had been created in 4004 BC. These calculations and dates, published in Ussher's *Annals of the Ancient and New Testaments* (1650) were widely accepted; the year 4004 BC was inserted in the margins of the Authorized Version of the Bible where, to quote A. P. White's *History of the Warfare of Science with Theology in Christendom*, it was 'soon practically regarded as equally inspired with the sacred text itself.'

Ussher did not say in what part of the year 4004 BC he thought the creation of man had taken place. Bede in the eighth century, and Vincent of Beauvais in the thirteenth, thought that it must have been in the spring. Others favoured 'September at the Equinox' and among them was Dr John Lightfoot, Master of St Catharine's and Vice-Chancellor of the University of Cambridge, who published his *A Few and New Observations on the Book of Genesis, the Most of Them Certain, the Rest Probable, All Harmless, Strange and Rarely Heard Of Before,* in 1642. Later Dr Lightfoot refined his dating and declared 'heaven and earth, centre and circumference, were created all together in the same instant and clouds full of water . . . this took place and man was created by the Trinity on October 23, 4004 BC at nine o'clock in the morning.' We may perhaps see in these dates and time a prejudice of a Vice-Chancellor for the beginning of an academic year and the beginning of an academic morning, but, at least, Lightfoot did provide an exact and absolute chronology which must have been very comforting.

If you accepted these comfortable dates—and most people did in the late seventeenth and eighteenth century—then the extent of man's prehistory was not long. The civilizations of Greece and Rome had flourished before Christianity, and before them again the empires of the Near East. The Four Monarchy System could easily take up a great deal of the time of man on earth; the time before the four World Empires of Assyria, Persia, Greece, and Rome did not need to be long, and was surely long enough to fit in whatever archaeological remains were shown to be pre-Roman, pre-Greek, pre-Assyrian, and pre-Persian.

But as one moved away from the Four Monarchy area, the gap of time that was prehistory, even on the Ussher-Lightfoot chronology, became larger and larger. In the British Isles there were four thousand yawning years of prehistory before Julius Caesar and Claudius. What was to be put into these four millennia? Or did Britain have no prehistory? The earliest British antiquaries just invented peoples to fill up this early blank in the record of our island story, but their inventions, as was necessary for their successful adoption, bore some relationship to known historical facts outside the British Isles. Sir Thomas Kendrick, in his *British Antiquity* (1950), has given us a splendid summary of antiquarian speculation about British prehistory from the twelfth to the sixteenth centuries, and I have gone over some of these speculations in my 1954 Rhŷs Lecture to the British Academy, *Who Are the Welsh?*

The *Historia Britonum* of Nennius, written in the ninth century AD, gave us a prehistory beginning with Brutus, grandson of Aeneas, settling in Britain in the third age of the world and producing the first regular inhabitants of these islands since the Flood. Geoffrey of Monmouth in the twelfth century made Brutus, Prince of Trojan Blood, land in 1170 BC at Totnes. This Troynovantian prehistory of Britain certainly flourished right up to the sixteenth century in Britain. Men like Sir John Price, Sir Winston Churchill, William Wynne, Daniel Langhorne, and Robert Sherwood in the seventeenth century were all for Greeks and Trojans in British prehistory. Even as late as 1674 the Oxford *Almanack* had Brute heading the list of kings of Britain; two years later he had been replaced by William the Conqueror.

Other antiquaries preferred a more direct Biblical origin to the Trojans and Greeks. One of these was the Reverend Henry Rowlands, Vicar of Llanrhidian in Anglesey, whose *Mona Antiqua Restaurata* was published

11

in 1723. 'Antiquity recordeth and the consent of nations celebrateth the sons of Japhet to have been the first planters of Europe,' he wrote; Britain was 'peopled by these men very soon after the flood.' Seven years before Rowlands wrote these words in English in his Anglesey rectory another Welshman had published a book called *Drych y Prif Oesoedd*—the mirror of the first ages—and here we find a prehistory of Wales beginning in the Tower of Babel and the invasion of Britain by Gomer, the grandson of Noah.

The Phoenicians were canvassed for our prehistory by those who preferred them to Greeks and Trojans, or to Noah and Japhet. John Twyne, Headmaster of Westminster School, died in 1581; his *De Rebus Albionicis Britannicus atque Anglicis* was published by his son nine years after his death. Twyne brought the Phoenicians to Cornwall looking for tin. He argued that the Welsh word *caer* was Phoenician, that Welsh coracles were Phoenician; so was the dark blood of the Silures—even the dress of the Welsh women in the sixteenth century was, according to Twyne, a survival of an old Phoenician form of dress—though it was, of course, a provincial survival of English court dress. Samuel Bochart in his *Geographia Sacra* (1646) and Aylett Sammes's *Britannia Antiqua Illustrata* (1676) were full of the Phoenicians and the civilizing role they played in Western Europe and particularly the British Isles; and there is no doubt that many people at the present day still think of the Phoenicians as having come to Britain and having affected considerably our early civilization.

Other antiquaries preferred the Lost Tribes of Israel to Phoenicians and Trojans, and, in the nineteenth century, the British Israelites excavated at Tara—Royal Tara—in Ireland, searching for the Ark of the Covenant, which they, in all sincerity, believed lay buried there. The Ten-Tribists, like the advocates of the Phoenicians, survive to the present day, and I have often been asked in the Welsh countryside—perhaps my surname has something to do with this—whether the Welsh, and, therefore, of course the ancient pre-Roman inhabitants of Britain, are not really the Lost Tribes of Israel.

But it is unquestionably the Druids who became the

12

most popular explanation of our prehistory in pre-archaeological days. It was the antiquary John Aubrey who floated the Druids into our new historical consciousness, and it was in connection with a monument which is still to many people 'Druidic,' and which suffers at midsummer from visitations of modern out-group cultists calling themselves 'Druids.' I refer, of course, to Stonehenge. King James I became interested in Stonehenge and commissioned Inigo Jones to examine it: he prepared a treatise on the subject in 1620 which was not actually published until thirty years later. He declared that it was a Roman temple. In 1663, Dr Carleton, a court physician, insisted that it was built by the Danes for the consecration of their kings. John Webb restored Stonehenge to the Romans. John Twyne and Aylett Sammes naturally made it Phoenician. Bishop Nicholson made it Saxon. Bolton declared it to be the tomb of Boadicea. 'I come in the rear of all,' wrote Aubrey, 'by comparative evidence to give clear evidence that these monuments [Avebury, Stonehenge, and the like] were Pagan temples; which was not made out before; and have also with humble submission to better judgement, offered a probability that they were Temples of the Druids.' I must go on quoting what he says because, though written in the seventeenth century—John Aubrey's dates were 1626–97—it is most germane to our purpose here of understanding prehistory before archaeology. 'This inquiry, I must confess,' he says, 'is a groping in the dark; but although I have not brought it into clear light, yet can I affirm that I have brought it from an utter darkness to a thin mist, and have gone further in this essay than anyone before me.'

Dr Plot, the historian of Staffordshire and the first keeper of the Ashmolean Museum, believed in the Druids, and so did Toland (1670–1722) who wrote a very odd history of them. But it is William Stukeley who is our arch-Druidist, our arch-romantic, and his Druidomania has been admirably portrayed by Stuart Piggott in his biography of him. Stukeley's books on *Stonehenge* and *Avebury* appeared in 1740 and 1743, and here he made them Druidic monuments. Indeed as he grew older everything was Druidic. Piggott gives a fine account of

WILLIAM STUKELEY

how in 1754 Stukeley visited the Princess Dowager in Kent House to discuss what we know now to be a Late Bronze Age hoard of socketed axes and other tools. They talked of Druids, patriarchal religion, oaks, acorns, and mistletoe, and of Stonehenge. Stukeley returned home carrying a branch of oak picked up in the garden—it was acorn-heavy, symbolic. He passed the house of a friend, Mrs Peirson, and by a servant sent in the oak bough as 'a present from the royal Archdruidess, to her sister Druidess'; and his journal goes on, 'My Lord Archdruid Bathurst ordered me to meet him at dinner.' As Piggott remarks, 'on this wonderful autumn day, everyone was a Druid.'

What I have been saying will, I hope, bring home to you the problem of the antiquaries of the pre-archaeological period. Everything had to belong to something and to something clearly named and historical. One could not confess failure about the early past of man; it had to be peopled by someone, and it did not really matter a great deal whether they were Danes, Romans, Greeks, Trojans, Noah and Japhet, Israelite tribes, Phoenicians, or Druids. They had to be nominate; they had to be named people to whom one could turn confi-

14

ently. Here was no time for the innominate uncertainties of modern prehistory.

Even the Egyptians were canvassed as the progenitors of the British—and this well before the days of Rendell Harris, Elliot Smith and W. J. Perry. Charles Vallancey is a good example of the eccentric antiquaries who cultivated the Egyptians. His dates are 1721–1812; he was an engineer in Ireland and rose to the rank of full general. He wrote on the origins of Irish, which he compared with Kalmuck, Punic, the language of the Algonquin Indians, and later with Egyptian, Persian, and Hindustani. One of his books was called *The Ancient History of Ireland Proved from the Sanskrit Books*. As the writer of Vallancey's life in the *Dictionary of National Biography* says, a little uncharitably, of Vallancey's writing, 'the facts are never trustworthy and their theories are invariably extravagant.' To Vallancey the Egyptians were all over Ireland and Britain; even the great Irish megalithic tomb of New Grange, dating from perhaps 2000 to 1600 BC, was a Mithraic temple. He found an inscription on the walls of New Grange which he declared to be partly Cadmean and partly Egyptian, and read it as '"Angus," the name of an Arch-Druid, or more likely "Anghein," the "Holy Ones."' Poor Charles Vallancey! he was certainly near the broad lunatic fringes of antiquarian thought. But he had one great merit; his work called forth the wonderful parody published in 1790 under the title of *Eymetomena* or *The Antiquities of Killmackumpshaugh*, and for that we must be eternally grateful.

Vallancey had made New Grange Egyptian. In 1735 Thomas Molyneux, Professor of Physick in the University of Dublin, wrote about this remarkable stone tomb. He was very critical of Irish writers who 'deduce their stock from generations near the flood . . . invent antediluvian stories, and a fable of a niece of Noah himself landing in this island.' For Molyneux, New Grange was a *Danes-Mount* 'raised in honour of some mighty prince or person of the greatest power and dignity in his time.' Forty years later New Grange was visited by Governor Pownall. He drew particular attention to a stone with the engraving which Charles Vallancey had curiously translated but which Irish archaeologists in later years, like

15

George Coffey, have thought to be a stylized ship motif. Pownall was sure that it was writing and that the 'characters are evidently neither Irish, Punic nor Saxon.' 'I have persuaded myself,' he goes on, 'that this inscription is Phoenician and contains only numerals,' and was part of a 'marine or naval monument erected at the mouth of the Boyne by some Eastern people to whom the parts of Ireland were well-known.'

But one of the great interests to us in our present inquiry of Governor Pownall is that at the very same time when he is writing in terms of fixed historical named peoples, he also had a wider and more general idea of life in prehistoric times, and was prepared to discuss prehistory in terms of unnamed hypothetical groups of people. In his general account of New Grange published in that very Volume II of *Archaeologia* in 1773 which had made Horace Walpole so cross, he writes this interesting long passage which I must quote *in extenso*:

> This globe of earth hath, according to the process of its nature, existed under a successive change of forms and been inhabited by various species of mankind, living under various modes of life, suited to that particular state of the earth in which they existed. The face of the earth being originally everywhere covered with wood, except where water prevailed, the first human beings of it were *Woodland-Men* living on the fruits, fish, and game of the forest. To these the land-worker succeeded. He *settled* on the land, became a fixed inhabitant and increased and multiplied. Where-ever the land-worker came, he, as at this day, eat out the thinly scattered race of Wood-Men.

Now, here, in Woodland-Men and Land-Workers, is an entirely different kind of prehistory from that which dealt in Trojans and Phoenicians and Egyptians. Where did it come from? It seems to me to be part and parcel of the philosophical speculations about the origins and development of man, language, and society associated with what have been called the Scottish primitivists who flourished in the middle and second half of the eighteenth century, and mainly, as their name suggests, in Scotland. Stuart Piggott has drawn attention to the

16

LORD MONBODDO

appropriateness of that episode in Thomas Love Peacock's *Crotchet Castle* when, at the end of a most convivial dinner, Mr McQuedy repeatedly tries to read a paper which begins 'In the infancy of society . . .' In the eighteenth century Scottish thinkers were interested in the infancy of society, and in the prehistory of man. One who was especially so interested was Thomas Blackwell, who held the Chair of Greek at Marischal College, Aberdeen, from 1723 to 1757.

Blackwell's pupil was James Burnett (1714–99), who took the title of Lord Monboddo when he became a Lord of Session. Monboddo was indeed a strange man; he never sat with his colleagues but always underneath with the clerks. He was an amiable, generous, and kindhearted man; the learned suppers he gave once a fortnight are famous. In 1780 he started visiting London regularly and there often met and talked with George III. He considered the carriage an engine of effeminacy and idleness so went on horseback with a single servant. There is a story of him hailing a coach during a rainstorm to carry his wig, while he continued to walk. Monboddo's great work *On the Origin and Progress of Language* was published in six volumes between 1773 and 1792,

17

and his *Ancient Metaphysics* in another six volumes between 1779 and 1799. It was in these books that he set out the view that the orang-utan was a class of the human species and its want of speech was accidental. He believed, too, that we were born with tails and that it was a world-wide league of quick-witted midwives who had prevented this great truth from being known hitherto.

Lord Monboddo's contemporaries, not unnaturally, thought him most eccentric and treated his views with the utmost derision. He met Dr Johnson during the latter's tour of the Hebrides, at Monboddo in Kincardineshire. Indeed Monboddo has been described by a contemporary as 'an Elzevir edition of Samuel Johnson.' Johnson himself did not like Monboddo and held him and his views in contempt. He said: 'It is a pity to see Lord Monboddo publish such notions as he has done: a man of sense and so much elegant learning. There would be little in a fool doing it; we should only laugh; but when a wise man does it we are sorry. Other people have strange notions, but they conceal them. If they have tails, they hide them; Lord Monboddo is as jealous of his tail as a squirrel.'

Now there are two things of especial interest to us here. First, Monboddo had some interesting ideas, of a general philosophical nature, about the origin and development of man. But the second point of interest is the attitude of Dr Johnson, who thought not only that Monboddo was silly and odd, but that it was wrong and vain and useless to speculate about such things as the origin of man and society.

Arthur Lovejoy has argued, in his discussion of the Scottish primitivists, that Monboddo and Blackwell got their ideas from the medieval notion of an ordained universe of purposeful and unfolding plan—the notion known in the post-medieval world by such names as the Great Chain of Being—a concept in which everything from the lowliest object to man had a place in the framework. Monboddo and the Scottish primitivists conceived a prehistory out of these philosophical speculations. Governor Pownall's Woodland-Men and Land-Workers were part of these philosophical postulates.

Dr Johnson, on the other hand, was sure that such

postulates were absurd. Speaking sharply of Monboddo's views, he said: 'Sir, it is all conjecture about a thing useless, even if it were known to be true. Knowledge of all kinds is good. Conjecture, as to things useful, is good. But conjecture as to what would be useless to know, such as whether men went upon all fours, is very idle.' There is something quite fundamental here; for Dr Johnson there was no prehistory, there *could* be no prehistory. In the words of the late Stanley Casson: 'History to Johnson was recorded history. He could not see further back than the written word. For to him the written word had the value of Holy Writ.' But could Dr Johnson be blamed? Could he really be blamed for saying: 'All that is really known of the ancient state of Britain is contained in a few pages. We can know no more than what old writers have told us.'

What had others to offer? There were the legendary prehistories of the medieval and post-medieval antiquaries, and there were the philosophical speculations of the Scottish primitivists, possibly as remote from reality as the Golden Ages and Heroic Ages of the Greeks. Admittedly there were antiquaries who were trying to wrest some facts about the past from the material remains they studied, but they were not getting very far; indeed from time to time they confessed that they were in despair.

Sir Richard Colt Hoare had set out with high hopes in his investigations of the Wiltshire barrows but, after ten years' work, was forced to confess 'total ignorance of the authors of these sepulchral memorials.' 'We have evidence,' he wrote, 'of the very high antiquity of our Wiltshire barrows, but none respecting the tribes to whom they appertained, that can rest on solid foundations.' Colt Hoare, thwarted from Continental travel, as he declared, 'by the tyrannous Corsican,' had toured Ireland in 1806. In his account of his *Tour in Ireland* published in the following year—and here we are dealing with one of the foremost British archaeologists of his time—'I shall not unnecessarily trespass upon the time and patience of my readers in endeavouring to ascertain what tribes first peopled this country; nor to what nation the construction of this singular monument,' he is writing of New Grange,

SIR RICHARD COLT HOARE

'may reasonably be attributed for, I fear, both its authors and its original destination will ever remain unknown. Conjecture may wonder over its wild and spacious domains but will never bring home with it either truth or conviction. Alike will the histories of those stupendous temples at AVEBURY and STONEHENGE which grace my native country, remain involved in obscurity and oblivion.'

Here was indeed a counsel of despair, and it was felt all over Europe by those who at the end of the eighteenth century and the beginning of the nineteenth were trying to get some ancient history out of what they knew were ancient remains. I always like quoting in this connection a remark made by Professor Rasmus Nyerup, one of the pioneers of Danish prehistoric archaeology. For years Nyerup had been privately collecting antiquities and had formed them into a small museum at the University of Copenhagen, of which he was librarian. But he had been quite unable to classify them in any significant way, confessing that 'everything which has come down to us from heathendom is wrapped in a thick fog; it belongs to a space of time we cannot measure. We know that it is older than Christendom but whether by a couple of years or a couple of centuries, or even by more than a millennium, we can do no more than guess.'

That is where prehistory was at that moment; still at a time of guesses and conjectures—conjecture that will never bring home truth or conviction, the conjecture which Dr Johnson found so idle. The archaeologists, struggling for historical truth, could as yet offer no prehistory—nothing but obscurity, oblivion—thick fog. It was not because they believed in the divine inspiration of Genesis but because of the inadequacy of any other prehistory that learned men even well into the nineteenth century turned to the Genesis account of the Creation, the Fall, and the Flood to explain the origin of man and society, and clutched at the firm dates of Ussher and Lightfoot to give them a secure chronology of the past. The Fall and the Flood of the Fundamentalists would stay as articles of belief until the growth of archaeology and geology gradually penetrated the obscurity and oblivion which so despairingly wrapped in fog the prehistoric beginnings of man. We shall be concerned next with the revolution in thought which took place between 1810 and 1859 and substituted stratigraphical geology and systematic archaeology for the Flood and the Fog of prehistory before archaeology.

II

The Beginnings of
Archaeological Prehistory

CHRISTIAN JURGENSEN THOMSEN

The twenty-third of October is the anniversary of the creation as accurately dated by Bishop Lightfoot. While we realize that many people did not, in the seventeenth and eighteenth centuries, believe in the exact detail of the Ussher-Lightfoot dates, yet the general notion behind them did then condition general thought about man's past. 'Time we may comprehend.' wrote Sir Thomas Browne in the *Religio Medici*, ''tis but five days elder than ourselves, and hath the same Horoscope with the world.' This was in 1635. Time was understood and was short, and this idea of the shortness of man's past and its interpretation in terms of Biblical exegesis was the prevalent way of thought right up to the early nineteenth century. At the end of the eighteenth century there was prevalent what Professor Wood Jones has called 'a most satisfying and spiritually comforting conception of the universe.' The whole universe had been designed in perfection, and there was the perfect Chain of Being, *L'échelle des êtres*, the *Scala Naturae*.

In 1802 William Paley (1743–1805) wrote his *Natural Theology: or Evidence of the Existence and Attributes of the Deity Collected from the Appearances of Nature*, a task in which he endeavoured, as he says in his preface dedicated to the Bishop of Durham, 'to repair in the study his deficiencies in the Church.' He set out to show that man had only inhabited the world for six thousand years, that the world 'teemed with delighted existence,' but had not done so for more than six thousand years, and that it was all a splendid design like a watch, indeed created by God the arch-watchmaker.

In 1833 the Trustees of the Earl of Bridgewater commissioned authors selected by the President of the Royal Society in consultation with the Archbishop of Canterbury and the Bishop of London to write treatises illustrating and elaborating Paley's *Natural Theology* or the thesis clearly expounded therein—Paley has been described as one of the best writers of textbooks that ever existed. These treatises 'designed to prove that the creation story of Genesis was literally exact and that Noah's ark and the Flood were facts of prehistory,' were written by men like Prout and Whewell and Dean Buckland and were published in 1833.

I ask you particularly to remember those two dates; 1802, when Paley's *Natural Theology* was first published, and 1833, the year of the *Bridgewater Treatises*. Two years before Paley wrote, there was published in Volume XIII of *Archaeologia* a short 'Account of Flint Weapons Discovered at Hoxne in Suffolk' by John Frere. The year in which the *Bridgewater Treatises* were published saw also the publication of the third and last volume of Sir Charles Lyell's *Principles of Geology*, the work that really destroyed the Diluvialist geology of the Catastrophists and which was one of the two great formative books in the mind of Charles Darwin as he worked out and developed his theory of evolution.

Three years after the *Bridgewater Treatises*, in 1836, there was published in Copenhagen the first guidebook to the National Museum; it was called *Ledetraad til Nordisk*

Oldkyndighed, and it contained an essay on the early monuments and antiquities of the north, by Christian Jurgensen Thomsen. In this essay he set out the notion of three prehistoric ages of stone, bronze, and iron which had been implicit in his classification and arrangement of the National Museum. It was these three things—the recognition of man's early tools for what they were and their association with extinct animals, the acceptance of a fluvialist geology, and the acceptance of the three ages of man's prehistory, that enabled a systematic prehistoric archaeology to come into existence, for the Fog to disperse, and the Flood to subside.

It is my concern to discuss these three revolutions in human thought that occurred between Paley's *Natural Theology* and Darwin's *Origin of Species*—in the half-century between 1802 and 1859, of which the rough halfway mark is the *Bridgewater Treatises* of 1833 and the *Principles of Geology* (1803–33). Let us begin with geology because the acceptance of stratigraphy and uniformitarianism was fundamental to progress in geology or archaeology.

The Development of Geology

It was the last quarter of the eighteenth century which witnessed the birth of geology as a science, and this period saw a great cleavage between those who insisted on interpreting the record of the rocks in conformity with Genesis, and those who believed in interpreting the record in terms of present-day natural phenomena. If you had to fit in the record of the rocks to the six thousand years allowed you by the Ussher-Lightfoot interpretation of Mosaic chronology, the natural modern normal process of accumulation and change had to be accelerated. There had to be catastrophes, of which, surely, it was argued, the Flood provided one admirable historical example. Hence the cleavage between the Diluvialists and Catastrophists on one hand and the Fluvialists on the other.

Georges Cuvier (1769–1832), the great French geologist and naturalist, universally regarded as the 'founder of vertebrate palaeontology', held that the record of the rocks could be interpreted correctly only by supposing that there had been a series of great catastrophes, not

24

merely one; and that the Noachian Flood of Genesis was a record of one of them. He went further and expressly denied the existence of fossilized man in antiquity; he said that such things just could not be. 'The pope of bones,' as Cuvier was called, had a tremendous reputation in the study of fossils—'the medals coined by creation', as he called them. His reputation was enormous as a naturalist, and enhanced by tales like the famous one of his visit from the Devil—only it was not the Devil but one of his students dressed up with horns on his head and shoes shaped like cloven hooves. This frightening apparition burst into Cuvier's bedroom when he was fast asleep and declaimed: 'Wake up thou man of catastrophes. I am the Devil. I have come to devour you!' Cuvier studied the apparition carefully and critically and said, 'I doubt whether you can. You have horns and hooves. You only eat plants.'

The man of catastrophes believed in a series of geological revolutions. He knew of the stratigraphical evidence that was being accumulated by people like William Smith in England. William Smith (1769–1839), 'strata Smith', as he is often called, was described by William Sedgwick in 1831 as the recognized 'Father of English Geology'. He drew up a table of thirty-two different strata and found different fossils in each of them. He called fossils not medals of creation, but 'the antiquities of Nature', and the first part of his *Strata Identified by Organized Fossils* was published in 1816. Now Cuvier in France did not deny the existence of these layers but said that they were separated by catastrophes which obliterated certain animals and plants and which were followed by new creations. Cuvier died in 1832, at the moment when he was about to be made Minister of the Interior. His disciples and pupils Brongniaert and d'Orbigny carried on his work and drew up a dogmatic system of twenty-seven successive acts of creation and catastrophes.

In England, the Reverend W. D. Conybeare (1787–1857), a geologist who became Dean of Llandaff, postulated three deluges before that of Noah. Adam Sedgwick (1785–1873), who was Woodwardian Professor of Geology at Cambridge in 1818, was also in favour of the

25

Flood, and so was William Buckland (1784–1856). Buckland was a very strange character and anecdotes about him abound—how he ate the heart of a French king in Sutton Courtenay Church, kept an orang-utan in his rooms at Christ Church, and prepared for Ruskin's breakfast an exquisite toast of mice. He seems to have been a very great field geologist; the tale I most like about him is that, lost on a journey on horseback from Oxford to London, he dismounted, bent down, picked up a handful of soil, and said at once, 'Ah, yes, as I guessed, Ealing.' Buckland was appointed Reader in Mineralogy at Oxford in 1813; it has been said that his courses attracted in a high degree the attention and admiration of the University, and very largely contributed to the public recognition of geology as a science by the endowment in 1819 of a Professorship. But by this time Buckland had gone away from Oxford to be Dean of Westminster. In 1823 he published his *Reliquiae Diluvianae: or Observations on the Organic Remains Contained in Caves, Fissures, and Diluvial Gravel and in Other Geological Phenomena Attesting the Action of an Universal Deluge*, and, thirteen years later, his *Geology and Mineralogy Considered in Relation to Natural Theology*. That is what he insisted on—a Universal Deluge, and then held that geology proved it. His 1836 book was a summary of geological knowledge as a proof of 'the power, wisdom, and goodness of God as manifested in creation.'

But, very gradually, a powerful opposition was growing to the Catastrophists and Flood-men. In 1785 James Hutton (1726–97) published his *Theory of the Earth: or an Investigation of the Laws Observable in the Composition, Dissolution, and Restoration of Land Upon the Globe*. He saw in the deposits of sand, gravel, clay and limestone the results of the ordinary deposition of sediments together with organic remains under water, i.e., in the rivers or in the seas, in the same way as this deposition went on at present. He fully recognized that the greater part of the solid land had once been beneath the sea, but formed in an ordinary, that is to say, a non-catastrophic, way. 'No processes are to be employed,' he said, 'that are not natural to the globe; no action to be admitted except those of which we know the principle.' This was the real

SIR CHARLES LYELL

beginning of the doctrine of uniformitarianism. William Smith had not only assigned relative ages to the rocks by noting their fossil contents, but himself argued for the orderly deposition of strata over a long period of time.

But the man who really weighed the scales in this issue, who really proved the case for the Fluvialists against the catastrophic Diluvialists, was Charles Lyell, whose *Principles of Geology* was published, as we have already mentioned, during 1830–33, in three volumes. I quote here the title of his great work, because it is, in itself, a definition of the doctrine of uniformitarianism. The full title was: *Principles of Geology, Being an Attempt to Explain the Former Changes of the Earth's Surface by Reference to Causes Now in Action.* Conybeare, himself a Catastrophist and a Diluvialist, claimed that this work was 'in itself sufficiently important to mark almost a new era in the progress of our science.' Like Darwin's *Origin of Species*, a work which Lyell's book profoundly affected, it was not that the ideas were new; it is that they were set out cogently, clearly, convincingly.

Of course there was considerable criticism when the first volume was published; many leading geologists were against the notion that present conditions were all that one could allow in the past. They may not have wanted catastrophes and floods, but they did think—and it is arguable—that processes might have been more quick in the past than at present. Conybeare said, and was supported by Sedgwick, that these causes 'may have been modified as to the degrees and intensity of their action by the varying conditions under which they may have operated at different periods.' Sir Joseph Prestwich said in 1886 that there was evidence 'that the physical forces were more active and energetic in geological periods than at present.' Lyell himself accepted this point of view gradually; in his third volume in 1833 he said that he had never advocated that 'the existing causes of change have operated with absolute uniformity from all eternity,' although sometimes it did look as if he had done this. It is true that he did change the title of his great work; the title of the eleventh edition of 1872 was *Principles of Geology or the Modern Changes of the Earth and Its Inhabitants Considered as Illustrative of Geology.*

But the change in title was really only a demonstration of a change in emphasis and bias by the extreme uniformitarians. Gradually uniformitarianism had become the way of official geological thinking. Eventually even Buckland and Sedgwick had to abandon their Diluvialist and Catastrophist views. Buckland's former teacher, John Kidd, gave one of the *Bridgewater Treatises*; it was on *The Adaption of External Nature to the Physical Condition of Man,* and was published in 1833, the same year as the third volume of Lyell's *Principles.* It is worth quoting extensively from what John Kidd said.

> Time was also [he wrote], and indeed with the last century, when the shells and other organic remains which are embedded in the chalk and other solid strata, were considered to be the remains and proofs of the Mosaic deluge, and yet at the present day, without any fear of injuring the credibility of the Scriptures, they are admitted very generally to have been deposited anteriorly to the Mosaic deluge. And who will venture to say, in the infancy of a science like geology, that the same change of opinion may not happen with respect to the organic remains of the gravel beds and caverns. . . . By far the greater

number of the organic remains of the gravel, as of the caverns, belong to species not known now to exist.

That was the crux of the matter; the moment you accepted the doctrine of uniformitarianism, in however liberal a form, you immediately drew attention to the fact that long before 4004 BC there existed animal life— 'organic remains in the gravels and caverns, ' as Kidd had said, choosing his words carefully, 'not known now to exist.' That is the real relevance of all this to our present story; it is not merely that uniformitarianism revolutionized scientific thought, or that stratigraphy produced an interpretation of the earth's surface which is fundamental to all archaeology; it is that already human fossils were being found in association with organic remains belonging to species not known to exist at the present. The Flood was disappearing, and the Fog was being dissipated, because here at last was proof of the antiquity of man.

The Discovery of Early Man

I have just said that human fossils were found in association with the remains of extinct animals. These fossils were of two kinds—physical fossils, that is to say, the actual remains of early men, and cultural fossils, that is to say, the remains of tools made and fashioned by man. By definition man is the tool-using and tool-making animal who walks erect, and by definition no animal is human who has no artifacts. Apes can join together two sticks so that they can get at a banana out of their unaided reach, but apes do not make tools. When, therefore, we find fashioned implements we are, by definition, in the presence of men, just as much as if we had found a skeleton which could be classified as human.

Now what we know these days to be humanly fashioned tools of stone had been found centuries before the publication of the *Principles of Geology,* but for long they had been explained away as thunderbolts, fairy arrows, elfshot. Ulisses Aldrovandi in the mid-seventeenth century described stone tools as 'due to an admixture of a certain exhalation of thunder and lightning with metallic matter, chiefly in dark clouds, which is coagulated by the circumfused moisture and conglutinated into a mass (like flour with water) and subsequently indurated by heat, like a brick,' and these rather surprising words were written by a man who has been described as the greatest zoologist of the Renaissance period. Tollius, at about the same time, claimed chipped flints to be 'generated in the sky by a fulgurous exhalation conglobed in a cloud by the circumposed humour.'

Others, however, had already more intelligent views of the nature of stone tools. Mercati, as early as the end of the sixteenth century, had agreed that the so-called thunderbolts were the weapons of a primitive folk ignorant of a knowledge of metallurgy. Sir William Dugdale in his *History of Warwickshire*, published in 1650, declared that these stone objects were 'weapons used by the Britons before the art of making arms of brass or iron was known.' Dr Robert Plot, who was the first keeper of the Ashmolean Museum, said in his *History of Staffordshire* (1686) that he agreed with Dugdale, and later, de la Payrere was giving it as his view that the so-called thunderbolts were really the tools of some early and pre-Adamitic race. The year before the publication of Plot's *History of Staffordshire* a megalithic tomb was discovered and excavated at Cocherel near Dreux in the valley of the Eure. It was the first megalithic tomb ever to be excavated with any semblance of care in Western Europe; it belonged to what we should now call the Paris Basin type of Gallery Grave. Accounts of this excavation were published in 1719 and 1722; what concerns us here is the use and interpretation which these early eighteenth-century scholars made of the polished axes from this tomb. The Abbé of Cocherel had no doubt that the stones were in fact stone tools: he thought they were implements like those used by the American Indians in the early eighteenth century. And Dom Bernard de Montfaucon in his *L'Antiquité expliquée et représentée en figures* (it was published in English translation in 1722) decided that the unburned bodies in the tomb belonged to 'some barbarous Nation, that knew not yet the Use either of Iron or of any metal.' Incidentally there is here a very clear and early idea of the existence of a stone age in the early past of man. We shall mention this realization again

30

later on; at the moment it is the polished stone objects found with the unburned skeletons that concern us.

But the acceptance of the view that stone tools were in fact the artifacts of early man took a very long time to be achieved. In 1766 Charles Lyttelton, Bishop of Carlisle, read to the Society of Antiquaries of London a paper on stone hatchets—it is published in *Archaeologia* for 1773. In this Lyttelton declared: 'There is not the least doubt of these stone instruments having been fabricated in the earliest times and by barbarous people, before the use of iron or other metals was known.' He compared them with examples from France and Mexico, and decided they were Ancient British: 'the most ancient remains existing at this day of our British ancestors,' he said, 'and probably coeval with the first inhabitants of this island.'

That was a fine phrase: 'coeval with the first inhabitants.' It begged one big question: how early were the first inhabitants? The problem came to the forefront when these stone objects, now accepted as cultural fossils of man, were found with organic remains belonging to species not known now to exist. The first find of this kind that we know about was made at the end of the seventeenth century in London; it was made in Gray's Inn Lane by a London apothecary and antique dealer called Conyers. In ancient deposits he found a stone axe and with it bones, which, after much thought, he decided were those of an elephant—but which in fact may very well have been those of a mammoth. Conyers declared that the Ancient Britons of those days had not then known the use of metal and had to use stone tools. His views were laughed at and when his friend John Bagford described this Gray's Inn Lane find in 1715, while he accepted the association of elephant and stone tool, he thought that it was a Roman elephant—a Claudian import.

At the end of the eighteenth century another man faced the same problem and resolutely refused to explain away what he had found. This man was John Frere who on 22 June 1797 wrote to the Secretary of the Society of Antiquaries of London enclosing some flint implements found at Hoxne, near Diss, in Suffolk: his letter is printed in *Archaeologia* for 1800 and is, as Dr Joan Evans said in her *History of the Society of Antiquaries,* 'a landmark in the development of prehistory'. But Frere's views were overlooked for sixty years until discoveries in the Somme gravels and in South Devon proved beyond all doubt the coeval existence of man and extinct animals.

This is what John Frere said of his flint implements: 'If not particularly objects of curiosity in themselves . . . must, I think, be considered in that light, from the situation in which they were found.' They were Acheulian hand axes, as we would now call them, and they were found twelve feet below the surface of the ground in the bottom layer of some undisturbed strata; and here they were associated with the bones of extinct animals. Frere described them, very properly: 'They are, I think,' he wrote, 'evidently weapons of war, fabricated and used by a people who had not the use of metals,' and, he adds, 'the situation in which these weapons were found may tempt us to refer them to a very remote period indeed, even beyond that of the present world'.

The Society of Antiquaries recorded that 'thanks were returned to our worthy member Mr Frere for this curious and most interesting communication,' but it was soon forgotten. It is true that at the beginning of the nineteenth century archaeologists were getting used to the idea that there were such things as stone tools and they were feeling their way towards the idea of a Stone Age in the past of man. But that was not the historical importance of John Frere and his communication to the Antiquaries. His importance was that he realized the significance not only of the tools *qua* tools but of their situation in undisturbed strata and together with extinct animals. 'Objects of curiosity . . . from the situation in which they were found . . . a situation [which] . . . may tempt us to refer them to a very remote period indeed, even beyond that of the present world.'

That remote period *'beyond that of the present world'* was, despite the fact that John Frere's modest yet most percipient remarks were forgotten, coming nearer to recognition as a fact: one of the first facts in a prehistory based on archaeology. In 1828, Tournal, the curator of the Narbonne Museum, published discoveries he had made in the Grotte de Bize near Narbonne, where he had found human bones associated with extinct animals. Actually this was not the first such association to be described. In 1771 Johann Friedrich Esper, a priest, was digging a cave at Gaylenreuth near Bamberg in the German Jura and he found cave bear and other extinct animals associated with human bones. He published his finds in 1774 and asked himself this question regarding the human bones: 'Did they belong to a Druid or to an Antediluvian or to a Mortal Man of more recent times?' and concluded: 'I dare not presume without any sufficient reason these human members to be of the same age as the other animal petrifactions. They must have got there by chance together with them.'

That was it. *Must* have got there *by chance*; there was *no sufficient reason* to think otherwise. Yet the reasons began to accumulate in the second quarter of the nineteenth century. It was not only Tournal at the Grotte de Bize but other French geologists like Christol, Dumas and Pitre. And spurred on by these southern French discoveries, Schmerling worked in the caves at Engihoul near Liège, the most famous of which was Engis. Here he found seven human skulls, many artifacts, some of them associated with the skeletons of rhinoceros and mammoth. 'There can be no doubt, ' wrote Schmerling, 'that the human bones were buried at the same time and by the same cause as the other extinct species.' Nobody believed Schmerling; indeed few bothered to notice his work at the time.

The same fate befell the work of a Roman Catholic priest, Father J. MacEnery, who was excavating in Kent's Cavern at Torquay from 1824 to 1829. Here, in this famous cave, he found the remains of extinct animals associated with flint implements under the stratified unbroken floor of stalagmite of the cavern. He communicated his find to Dean Buckland and other geologists while preparing his discoveries for publication. Dean Buckland insisted that MacEnery was wrong. He said that the Ancient Britons, whose artifacts MacEnery had found in Kent's Cavern, had scooped ovens in the stalagmite and that their implements had penetrated the layer of stalagmite only through those holes. In vain did MacEnery protest that there were no such holes, that no

33

JACQUES BOUCHER DE PERTHES

such ovens had been scooped out; yet out of deference to the views of Buckland, MacEnery abandoned his idea of publishing his discoveries at Kent's Cavern.

At the very time when MacEnery was working in Kent's Cavern, Dean Buckland himself was having trouble in interpreting the finds in the Goat's Hole Cave at Paviland on the Gower coast of Glamorgan. Here he had found the skeleton of a young man—the so-called Red Lady of Paviland—associated with Palaeolithic flint implements. There was no real doubt of the association, but Buckland could not bring himself to accept it—the skeleton, he said, 'was clearly not coeval with the ante-diluvian bones of the extinct species,' and he dated it to the Romano-British period.

Admittedly Buckland was fighting for the Catastroph-ists, and it was not until the battle between the old and the new geology was over that the evidence of the antiquity of man was accepted. The third volume of Lyell's *Principles of Geology* was published in 1833; four years later a customs official of Abbeville, by name Jacques Boucher de Crêvecoeur de Perthes, began col-lecting flints from the Somme gravels. They were roughly chipped flints of the kind which nowadays we call Abbevillian: he called them *haches diluviennes*. In 1838 he showed some of them at Abbeville, and in the next year in Paris; and in that year he published the first of five volumes of his book called *De la Création; essai sur l'origine de la progression des êtres*. His critics laughed at him, but he went on, undaunted, and in 1847 published the first volume of a three-volume work entitled *Antiquités Celtiques et Antédiluviennes*. The title should be noted; his axes were no longer *diluviennes*, they were *antédiluviennes*. He found he could no longer explain the association of human artifacts and extinct animals in the Somme gravels by the Diluvial theory.

Very slowly the French came round to de Perthes' point of view. In 1858 an Englishman, Falconer, visited Abbeville, saw the chipped flints, and thought that Boucher de Perthes' claims were right. He returned to England and told his opinion to Joseph Prestwich and John Evans, urging them to visit the Somme gravels and see for themselves. This they did in the following year.

Meanwhile a new enthusiast had been excavating at Kent's Cavern, Torquay. He was William Pengelly, a local schoolmaster and a private coach, who was fascinated by geology. He found that his work was demonstrating what MacEnery had demonstrated years before but no one had believed, namely that man was contemporary in south Devon with extinct animals. But it was not until a neighbouring cave, the Windmill Hill Cave at Brixham, was excavated that the scientific world was prepared to accept this remarkable south Devon evidence. From the summer of 1858 to that of 1859 Pengelly dug in the Brixham cave; he found flint tools associated with extinct animals in the cave earth 'on which lay a sheet of stalagmite from three to eight inches thick, and having within and on it relics of lion, hyaena, bear, mammoth, rhinoceros and reindeer.' These were careful excavations conducted by William Pengelly on behalf of a committee of the British Association; it was not possible any more to talk about ovens scooped in the stalagmite by ancient Britons. The 'sufficient reasons' demanded by Esper were here.

When John Evans crossed over to Abbeville to visit Boucher de Perthes he wrote in his diary:

SIR JOHN EVANS

Think of their finding flint axes and arrowheads at
Abbeville in conjunction with bone of Elephants and
Rhinoceroses 40 ft. below the surface in a bed of
drift. In this bone cave in Devonshire . . . they have
found arrowheads among the bones and the same is
reported of a cave in Sicily. I can hardly believe it. It
will make my ancient Britons quite modern if man is
carried back in England to the days when Elephants,
Rhinoceroses, Hippopotamuses and Tigers were
also inhabitants of the country.

In a very short while John Evans discovered that what he
could hardly believe had, however hardly, to be
believed. This is what he said at Abbeville:

The flat axes and implements found among the beds
of gravel . . . evidently deposited at the same time
with them—in fact the remains of a race of men who
existed at the time when the deluge or whatever was
the origin of these gravels took place.

Prestwich and John Evans returned to England from
the Somme: on 26 May 1859 Prestwich read a paper to
the Royal Society, and after it Evans spoke of the flints;
on 2 June John Evans spoke to the Society of Antiquaries
and said: 'This much appears to be established beyond

doubt, that in a period of antiquity remote beyond any of which we have hitherto found traces, this portion of the globe was peopled by man.' Later that year, the *annus mirabilis* as it has been called, Sir Charles Lyell as president of the Geological Section of the British Association meeting at Aberdeen said that he was now 'fully prepared to corroborate the conclusions . . . recently laid before the Royal Society by Mr Prestwich.'

The antiquity— the great antiquity—of man was at last accepted; the Flood had gone, the Fog was being penetrated; and prehistory, as the first stage of man's history, was emerging at last. Indeed two years before these solemn pronouncements in London and Aberdeen, prehistoric man had himself emerged. In 1857 the long bones and skull cap of a man-like being was discovered at Neanderthal in Prussia. Schaafhausen, who first described these remains, said that the Neanderthal skeleton belonged to a 'barbarous and savage race' and regarded it 'as the most ancient memorial of the early inhabitants of Europe.' Others disagreed, saying that the Neanderthal skeleton was that of a pathological idiot. But it did not really matter if as yet the anatomical fossils of prehistoric man were accepted; the cultural fossils had been. By 1859 Pengelly in Devonshire and Boucher de Perthes in the Somme had proved the antiquity of man— if you accepted the uniformitarian principles of Lyell, and most people were doing this by the sixties.

Dean Buckland's vigorous refusal to accept the evidence from Kent's Cavern and Paviland was, by the sixties, as outmoded as the Deluge itself, which he had defended for so long. Another flood had swept away the Noachian Catastrophists, the flood of evidence which, from the south of France to the Somme, from Liège to Britain, had demonstrated that man was indeed antediluvian and that the six thousand years from 4004 BC to the present day could not contain his prehistory as it was slowly being revealed in the archaeological record.

The Three Ages of Man

While geologists were disputing the antiquity of man in the gravels of Western Europe, historians and museum curators in Northern Europe were postulating stages in

37

the prehistory of man which at long last penetrated the despairing fog of which men like Rasmus Nyerup and Richard Colt Hoare had complained.

I have already (p.20) quoted the despairing words of Professor Nyerup. Actually, for some while before he wrote them in 1806 there had been hints of how archaeologists could do more than guess at classifying the material remains of the past. More and more people were beginning to recognize the existence of stone tools and to see them as relics of a time when men did not know of the use of metal. They argued on two grounds; first, that people would surely not be so stupid as to use only stone tools, if they possessed more efficient tools of bronze and iron. Secondly they argued from the existence of contemporary savage communities in North America and the Pacific who were in a stone age.

In 1807, the year after he had published a book advocating the formation of a National Danish Museum of Antiquities, Professor Nyerup was made Secretary of a Royal Committee set up 'for the Preservation and Collection of National Antiquities.' The Committee was charged to form a national Museum of Antiquities. In 1816 Nyerup was succeeded as Secretary by Christian Jurgensen Thomsen, who was also made the first curator of the National Museum. Thomsen's first task was to arrange the growing collections in some sort of order; this he did by classifying them into three ages of stone, bronze, and iron. His classification was clearly set out in the guidebook to the National Museum—the *Ledetraad til Nordisk Oldkyndighed* published in Copenhagen in 1836 and translated into English in 1848.

Thomsen's idea of three technological ages or stages in man's material cultural past was soon being used in Sweden, and in Germany, where indeed it may have been independently invented. It was really a very simple idea, when we look back at it now; merely that before he learned the use of metals man had lived in a stone age, and that even when he had learned the use of metals, he first used copper or bronze, and only later learned to deal with iron ores. A simple idea, but one which immediately gave some chronological depth to man's past.

And it was not merely an idea, or a system for museum

classification. Soon excavations in the Danish bogs and the Swiss lake-dwellings afforded stratigraphical proof of the succession of the three ages. As the idea and its stratigraphical demonstration passed to Western Europe archaeologists began to see that the artifacts which characterized Thomsen's Stone Age were different from those found in the Somme gravels, and the Devon caves, and they began to think in terms of two Stone Ages—an earlier Stone Age of chipped stones, and a later Stone Age of polished stone. It was an Englishman, Sir John Lubbock, who coined the words Palaeolithic and Neolithic for these two successive ages; this was in his *Prehistoric Times,* published in 1865. Three years later, in the tenth edition of his *Principles of Geology,* Sir Charles Lyell is using these phrases. Early man was now thought of as living through four historical—or perhaps rather prehistorical—stages: the Palaeolithic, Neolithic, Bronze, and Early Iron Ages.

Of course there was opposition to the acceptance of these ideas. John Kemble, in 1857, said that the Three Age system would 'betray us into grave historical errors' and lead us 'into an historical *reductio ad absurdum.*' Even in 1866 the *Guide to the Exhibition Rooms* of the British Museum refers to the Stone, Bronze, and Iron period 'of the Northern Antiquaries,' and to 'the order corresponding to that of the supposed introduction of such materials into this country.' Thomas Wright, the Secretary of the Ethnological Society, was strongly opposed to the Three Age idea. All bronzes were Roman, he declared: and, as for the Stone Age, 'there may have been a period when society was in so barbarous a state that sticks or stones were the only implements with which men knew how to furnish themselves,' but he doubted, he said, 'if the antiquary has yet found any evidence of such a period.'

But, gradually, this opposition disappeared. By the late sixties prehistory was actually in existence; the word itself, first used in Daniel Wilson's *Prehistoric Annals of Scotland,* soon became current. By 1865 the idea of a prehistory of man was so far advanced that Sir John Lubbock could produce a popular book called *Prehistoric Times,* which became a best-seller.

The Fog and the Flood had at last gone: and in their

place was stratigraphical geology, the antiquity of man, and the belief in the three ages of Stone, Bronze, and Iron. An archaeological idea of prehistory had come into existence.

SIR JOHN LUBBOCK

III

The Victorians and Prehistory

SVEN NILSSON

Sir John Lubbock's *Prehistoric Times* went on being a best-seller for half a century: the seventh edition was published in 1913, a few months after the death of Lord Avebury (as Sir John Lubbock then was), and when I went up to Cambridge as an undergraduate in 1932, mint copies of the seventh edition were for sale on the shelves of Heffers and Bowes & Bowes.

Let us now analyse the sort of idea of prehistory which was being put out between the first and last editions of *Prehistoric Times*—between 1865 and 1913: in a word, to answer the question: what was the Victorian idea of prehistory?

In the first place, it was a notion based on the great antiquity of man, and was firmly based on the acceptance of a very long past for man that could not be cabined and confined within the chronologies set out in the Bible. I

41

realize that Lubbock's *Prehistoric Times* was published when Queen Victoria had been on the throne for nearly half of her long reign of sixty-four years, and that perhaps this chapter should be entitled 'The Later Victorians and Prehistory' rather than 'The Victorians and Prehistory.' From the thirties to the sixties of the nineteenth century the acceptance of the great antiquity of man, as we have seen, was slow. The striking and oft-quoted phrase 'a rose-red city, half as old as time' which John William Burgon wrote in 1845, was not, as I thought as a schoolboy, a flight of poetic fancy. To Burgon, and to many early Victorians, time *was* only six thousand years old, and he literally meant Petra to be half that time in age. Then we must never forget that the Mosaic chronology was accepted by many because they sincerely thought that Moses was separated by only a few generations of oral tradition from Adam and the creation of man and the world. George Rawlinson, in the Bampton Lecture for 1859—that famous year—said in all seriousness that Moses' mother, Jochebed, had probably met Jacob, who could have known Noah's son Shem. Shem, he went on, and there is no doubting his sincerity, was probably acquainted with Methuselah, who had been for 243 years a contemporary of Adam. And Adam was the first man, made on the sixth day after that great day when time began.

Very gradually the early Victorian fundamentalist chronology was replaced by the belief in a remote past for man. On this very issue the first words of Lubbock's *Prehistoric Times* were bold, arresting, clear. 'The first appearance of man in Europe,' he said 'dates from a period so remote that neither history nor tradition can throw any light on his origin or mode of life.' This was only six years after George Rawlinson's speculations about Moses.

James Cowles Prichard (1786–1848) was one of our earliest British anthropologists. He spent the greater part of his life as a physician in Bristol. His two great works are *Researches into the Physical History of Man*, which appeared between 1836 and 1847, and *The Natural History of Man*, which came out in 1843. In the *Researches* he says very clearly: 'Many writers who have been by no means inclined to raise objections against the authority of the Sacred Scriptures . . . have felt themselves embarrassed by the shortness of the interval between the Noachic Deluge and the period at which the records of various nations commence, or the earliest date to which their historical memorials lead us back.' There really was not enough time, Prichard argued, on the short Ussher chronology, for the historical events of the world and for the development of the diversity of the human races. Others argued that the diversity of language demanded a long human past. All these arguments—the archaeo-logical, the argument from physical anthropology, and the argument from language—demanded a long past for man. Gradually, in the face of these arguments, the Vic-torians abandoned the struggle in defence of 4004 BC.

There remained the problem: how old was man? If time was really longer than six thousand years, if the world had a new horoscope, what was man's position in this? Morlot in Switzerland, calculating from the thick-ness of deposits near Geneva, decided that the Stone Age began seven thousand years ago. Gilliéron got to much the same figures elsewhere in Switzerland. It looked as if the Stone Age in Switzerland—and by this Morlot and Gilliéron meant the Neolithic—was at least six to seven thousand years old. Arguments from the thickness and rate of formation of deposits are notori-ously difficult—at the same time as the Swiss calculations were being made a Mr Horner in Egypt calculated that the Neolithic began there thirteen thousand years ago—but they were of some help.

If the Neolithic was so old, what was the age of the Palaeolithic, which lay back of the Neolithic, stretching away to the beginning of man? Sir Charles Lyell was prepared to say that the Somme deposits with their flint implements, mammoth, and hyena were not less ancient than 100,000 years ago; and that the Quaternary Ice Age took 220,000 years. Sir Joseph Prestwich, on the other hand, wanted only 20,000 years for the Palaeolithic, while Gabriel de Mortillet estimated the beginning of the Old Stone Age as 230,000 to 240,000 years. It all was, as Prestwich said, 'a curious and interesting problem,' but not one about which the Victorian geologists and arch-

HEINRICH SCHLIEMANN

aeologists could do more than guess. Geochronology was a product of twentieth-century archaeology and Carbon-14 dating still has far to go. All that was certain in the late Victorian idea of prehistory was that man was old and that his prehistoric beginning went back before the Noachian deluge and before 4004 BC.

The second certainty in the Victorian outlook was that prehistory was no longer a matter of guesswork. It was a matter of scientific deduction; a new discipline which could provide clear and certain answers had arrived. 'Of late years,' declared Lubbock proudly on the first page of *Prehistoric Times*, 'a new branch of knowledge has arisen, a new Science has . . . been born among us, which deals with times and events far more ancient than any which have yet fallen within the province of the archaeologist. . . . Archaeology forms the link between geology and history.'

Others did not share Lubbock's assurance that they had at last discovered the key to the prehistoric past; they felt with Palgrave that 'We must give it up, the speechless past; whether in Europe, Asia, Africa or America; at Thebes or Palenque, on Lycian shore or Salisbury Plain; lost is lost; gone is gone for ever.'

A more hopeful view was being taken by those who found themselves living through a period of great discoveries in prehistoric archaeology. It was only three years after the publication of *Prehistoric Times*, in 1868, that Heinrich Schliemann began excavating in Ithaca, and three years later, at Hissarlik, that he achieved that ambition which had fired him through all his life as a businessman in Russia and America, an ambition first kindled when he saw a picture in Jarrer's *Universal History*. In 1871 he found Troy; and Homer was attested archaeologically. Even if the splendid gold objects from Troy II, which Schliemann's beautiful young Greek wife Sophie smuggled through the Turkish customs beneath her voluminous skirts, are not now thought to be, as Schliemann claimed, the Treasure of Priam, to the world of the seventies of the last century he had, by digging in the ground, made Homer come alive in the dusty hillside of the Troad and later at Mycenae. He had created a fresh chapter in the human past, had himself written prehistory, and demonstrated with overwhelming effectiveness that we must not give it up, that the speechless past could speak, that lost is not lost, that gone is not gone forever.

This of course, as we now see it, is one of the excitements of archaeological prehistory, that the past which seemed forever gone can be brought back by the skilled use of archaeological reconnaissance, excavation, and interpretation. We are now accustomed to learn of whole civilizations being recovered from the speechless past— the Minoan and Harappan are two that come immediately to mind. We are even accustomed by now to recover the faces of the past: the dead in the Scythian barrows at Pazyrik and in the Danish peat-bog at Tollund live again after hundreds of years. But these enormous possibilities had to be learned, and the apprehension by the scholars and public of the seventies that Troy and Mycenae could be made to live again by the spade is one of the great moments of the development of an idea of prehistory.

In 1875 Schliemann came to London and read a paper to the Society of Antiquaries of London on his remarkable discoveries. The discussion was opened by W. E. Gladstone, who had just ended his first term as Prime

Minister and who had himself published, in 1858, a book entitled *Studies on Homer and the Homeric Age*. In this book there was no mention of prehistoric archaeology or indeed of any possibility that anything other than literary criticism could illuminate the problem of Homer. Yet by the time, less than twenty years later, when he is speaking to the Society of Antiquaries, the existence and relevance of prehistory were very much in his mind. 'When many of us who are among the elders in this room were growing up,' said Mr Gladstone,

> the whole of the prehistoric times lay before our eyes like a silver cloud covering the whole of the lands that, at different periods of history, had become so illustrious and interesting; but as to their details we knew nothing. Here and there was a shadowy, an isolated glimmer of light let in. . . . Now we are beginning to see through this dense mist and the cloud is becoming transparent, and the figures of real places, real men, real facts are slowly beginning to reveal to us their outlines.

Now what were these real places, real men, real facts which, Mr Gladstone claimed, were at last appearing by the end of the third quarter of the nineteenth century? They were, very briefly, of three kinds; first, they were facts about the early days of the great known historical civilizations—the early days of Greece and Rome, of Mesopotamia and of Egypt. Secondly they were facts about cultures and civilizations which were hitherto unknown—the Hittites for example and the early civilizations of America. In the third place they were facts about the development of man's culture before the historic civilizations or in areas alongside the historic civilizations.

The framework for the prehistoric culture sequence had been provided by the Danish Three Age system of Thomsen as modified by Lubbock into the Four Ages of the Palaeolithic, Neolithic, Bronze, and Iron Ages. But, gradually, even this framework was too broad and general, and a division of the four stages began to be made. The Palaeolithic was divided into varying stages with names like Chellean, Acheulian, Mousterian, Solutrean, Magdalenian. In Sweden Oscar Montelius divided

46

OSCAR MONTELIUS

the Neolithic into four numbered periods and the Bronze Age into five such. The Iron Age was divided in a variety of ways of which Hallstatt and La Tène were the two best-known divisions, and these were soon widely adopted.

As these divisions and subdivisions were being made, people began to ask: what precisely do they mean? Were they universal, that is to say were they stages of human culture through which everyone passed? Was there a single uniform prehistory of man from the Chellean to La Tène and if so, how did this prehistorical development come about? Just as there had been biological evolution, was there also a natural cultural evolution leading through various stages up to civilization?

It was surely not unnatural in an age which had, with some difficulty, accepted the idea of evolution in the biological world for many to think that cultural evolution succeeded to biological evolution and that when man appeared on the scene, when an animal arrived which made tools— extracorporeal limbs as they have been called—the process of evolution continued. The doctrines of social evolution which Herbert Spencer and others were setting out seemed to provide a clear

47

interpretation of the prehistoric record which the archaeologists were studying.

In 1867 the great international exhibition was held in Paris; for the first time ever in such an international exhibition there were displayed prehistoric collections, mainly in the Galerie de l'Histoire du Travail. These were collections of material from all over Europe and from Egypt. As Gabriel de Mortillet said of these collections, it was the first time that prehistory was able to show itself *'d'une manière solennelle et générale. Eh bien, cette première manifestation a été pour eux un triomphe complet.'*

There was, by the way, no prehistory in the Great Exhibition in Hyde Park in 1851. In response to repeated requests Gabriel de Mortillet wrote a guide to the prehistoric collections at the Paris Exposition of 1867. It was called *Promenades préhistoriques à l'Exposition Universelle.* At the end of this guide he summarized what he thought were the lessons that had so far emerged from the discipline of prehistoric scholarship. He printed them in capital letters as the last words in his book and they were LOI DU PROGRÈS DE L'HUMANITÉ, LOI DU DÉVELOPPEMENT SIMILAIRE, and the third: HAUTE ANTIQUITÉ DE L'HOMME.

About the third of these conclusions there was no doubt. The late Victorians believed in the antiquity of man although they could not agree on an absolute chronology. But there was not really agreement about the other two laws, which had as their keynotes the ideas of Parallel Cultural Evolution and Progress. There were many who agreed with de Mortillet when he declared, passionately, after conducting his tour of the collections in the Paris Exposition: 'It is impossible any longer to doubt the great law of the progress of man.' These were indeed the sort of words which an archaeologist might have been repeating from Herbert Spencer, who in 1850 had been saying, 'Progress is not an accident but a necessity. It is a fact of nature.' It began to look to some as if prehistoric archaeology was confirming the philosophical and sociological speculations of the mid-nineteenth-century scholars. Gabriel de Mortillet, however much his views were influenced by the current beliefs in progress and evolution, was in fact making an observation

48

GABRIEL DE MORTILLET

from the archaeological record. Prehistory, in the idea which many Victorians had of it, was a record of progress and evolution. This was certainly to many the interpretation of the real facts and the real places which Mr Gladstone had seen appearing in his lifetime.

Mr Gladstone had spoken to the Society of Antiquaries in 1875. This was the year in which the Germans began digging at Olympia, a fact which many, and not unreasonably, regard as the beginning of modern scientific techniques in archaeology. This was also the year in which Marcelino de Sautuola began digging in the cave of Altamira in the Cantabrian Mountains of Spain. Five years later Flinders Petrie began excavating in Egypt and the modern period of Near-Eastern excavation commenced. In that same year the daughter of Marcelino de Sautuola walked into the dark inner recesses of the Altamira cave and, lifting her lamp, saw frightening paintings on the roof and ran out to her father, who was excavating outside, crying *'Toros! Toros!'*—'Come and see the bulls.' She had found, by accident, the now famous polychromes on the roof at Altamira and the real fact of Upper Palaeolithic art was with us—not, admittedly, accepted as such by the archaeological world for a

49

quarter of a century, and not, perhaps, really a part of the historical perspective of most people until the years following the sensational discovery of Lascaux in 1940 with its widespread popularization in archaeological and general circles.

As people began to study the naturalistic drawings and paintings of Upper Palaeolithic times that were being discovered in the last third of the nineteenth century, and, as they also began to study the prehistoric record in different countries, they became less and less certain that there was a universal common prehistory of man, and that all was evolutionary progress to a common goal of Victorian complacency. The idea of regression was one which both historians and anthropologists had been discussing for some while. The father of British anthropology, as he has been called, Sir E. B. Tylor, when he wrote his *Primitive Culture* of 1871, said that his aim was to 'sketch a theoretical course of civilization among mankind' which he called 'a progression-theory of civilization,' but even then he was prepared to admit that 'culture gained by progression may be lost by degradation.' When Dr Arthur Mitchell gave his Rhind Lectures on Archaeology at Edinburgh in 1876 and 1878 he was particularly interested in retrogression and regress. He cited the cities of Copan and Palenque and particularly the early glory of Egypt. It was, as Tylor and Mitchell pointed out, the obvious facts of Egyptian decay which Sir Thomas Browne was commenting on when he said of her, 'she poreth not upon the heavens, astronomy is died unto her, and knowledge maketh other cycles.' There it was, in Browne's phrase, and long before Spengler and Arnold Toynbee were trying to elaborate their historical cycles with a wealth of learning and tendentious interpretations. To quote Arthur Mitchell's clear words in the seventies: 'Within the range of history . . . degradations are found presenting themselves both in races which are in the states of high and in races which are in the states of low civilization. In other words savages become more savage as well as the highly civilized. Degradation and development alike occur within the range of history, and, this being so, can there be any sufficient reason for concluding that both have not occurred beyond that range?'

Prehistory was of course dealing with events beyond the range of history. It was reasonable, as Mitchell said, to suppose that it, too, had its degradations and devolutions. But was this merely a reasonable assumption based on an evaluation of history and a late nineteenth-century scepticism about the universality of progress? Tennyson, in *Locksley Hall Sixty Years After*, wrote, in 1886, these oft-quoted lines—

Evolution ever climbing after some ideal good,

And Reversion ever dragging Evolution in the mud.

The question was this as regards prehistory: was it thought that there was degradation and reversion in prehistory just because it existed in history, and in the philosophical preconceptions of the late Victorians? What one has to ask oneself in trying to work out the ideas on prehistory of the late Victorians, and in trying to assess how prehistory affected their ideas if at all, is this: when Gabriel de Mortillet insisted on the picture of technological evolution which prehistory presented, was he making an objective archaeological evaluation which enabled prehistory to confirm the Victorian idea of progress, or was he projecting into prehistory his own widely shared ideas of progress? And, later, was there real archaeological proof of decay and regression in prehistory or was this a late Victorian defeatism projected into the archaeological record?

I regard the discovery of Upper Palaeolithic paintings as of the greatest importance in trying to settle this question, and I need here do little more than touch on the details of the story. In 1864 Lartet and Christy, in a paper in the *Revue Archéologique*, showed that Upper Palaeolithic man had mobiliary art—that engraved and carved bones and stone were found in undisturbed deposits in the Dordogne and the Pyrenees. Gradually the fact that these remote men of the Old Stone Age were artists was accepted. But mobiliary (or home) art was one thing: cave art when first discovered was by no means so easily assimilable. We have referred to the discoveries at Altamira. In 1875 Marcelino de Sautuola had discovered black paintings on the back walls of the cave at Altamira, and then and there had claimed them to be of the same age as the deposits in the cave. Four years later his daughter had found the polychromes and in 1880 de Sautuola published the paintings, claiming them to be Palaeolithic in age. Meanwhile drawings had been found on the walls of the cave of Chabot in the Ardèche. Altamira and Chabot precipitated a tremendous dispute. Many said that Sautuola was an impostor and a fraud, and that he had hired an artist from Madrid to do the paintings. Others said soldiers with nothing better to do had done them when hiding in the cave. Yet some from the beginning supported the claims of Sautuola. Among these was Gabriel de Mortillet who, despite his evolutionary preconceptions, declared: 'C'est l'enfance de l'art, ce n'est pas l'art de l'enfant.'

In 1895 paintings and engravings were found on the walls of a cave at La Mouthe near Les Eyzies in the Dordogne; the entrance to this cave had been found only after Palaeolithic deposits masking it had been removed. The following year animal drawings were published from the cave of Pair-non-Pair in the Gironde and these were partly covered by undisturbed Palaeolithic deposits. The late Abbé Breuil, for long *doyen* of experts on the Palaeolithic, but then a young man, realized the significance of the evidence of La Mouthe and Pair-non-Pair on the authenticity of cave art and set it out in an article in 1901 in the *Revue Scientifique*. In the same year the now world-famous caves of Les Combarelles and Font de Gaume were discovered near Les Eyzies; in the following year all these discoveries were discussed at the Montauban meeting of the Association Française pour l'Avancement des Sciences. A party visited La Mouthe, Les Combarelles, and Font de Gaume and were convinced. Emile Cartailhac, who was at that time the *doyen* of prehistoric archaeology in France, published an article in *L'Anthropologie* entitled 'Mea culpa d'un sceptique,' in which he recanted his earlier disbelief and accepted Upper Palaeolithic art. From the end of Victorian days Upper Palaeolithic art was part of the perspective of prehistory.

The length of time which it took cave art to be accepted by scholars—I do not here refer to the much slower apprehension of it by the general public—was due to the

Victorian conception of progress and of similar development. For there were two things that were soon understood about the remarkable flowering of art during a period of the human past which we would now date from say 30,000 to 10,000 BC. One is that its range in space is restricted to southern France and northern Spain, or so it seemed in the last quarter of the nineteenth century—we know now that examples of it occur in Italy and Sicily, but even so it is still very restricted. And the second is that it came to an end; the fine naturalism, the exuberant virility, the bright colours, the Disney-like humour of these most ancient paintings and engravings belonged to a style which came to an end. Art did not again reach a comparable level of aesthetic performance in Western and west Mediterranean Europe for thousands of years—indeed did not exist at all for thousands of years.

Here was a blow to any idea of prehistory which made the archaeological record the same everywhere, and assumed that there was progress everywhere on parallel lines. It was obvious that, even if everyone in prehistoric Europe had passed through successive stages of stone, bronze, and iron, they had not all possessed artistic ability like those men who had worked at La Mouthe and Altamira and Font de Gaume. Prehistory had to absorb the idea, now perhaps a commonplace to us, of the regional flowering of cultures and to realize that there were cultures, civilizations, societies—call them what you will—in prehistory with different distributions in time and space. It was soon obvious to prehistorians that everyone did not pass through a stage when he painted charging bulls on the roofs of caves, or made great collective tombs of huge megalithic stones, or built multi-ramparted hill forts like Maiden Castle. Prehistory was now becoming a record of cultural achievement set out in parallel columns and not in one evolutionary sequence.

That was the lesson which, very gradually, the prehistorians of the Victorian period were learning, though it was not generally learned until the first two decades of the twentieth century. Yet this lesson, if imperfectly, or rather not universally, learned in late Victorian times, did beg the same old question of cultural origins which

53

JENS JACOB WORSAAE

we have seen was being asked before. If man did not develop in prehistoric times in a natural and uniform cultural evolution, how then did cultural changes and differences come about?

The interesting thing is that this issue had really already been well discussed by the Scandinavian pioneers of the Three Age system, particularly by Thomsen and Worsaae. It is always necessary to emphasize that the concept of the Three Ages as set out in the writings and teaching and museum practice of Thomsen and Worsaae is not primarily an evolutionary one. They did not regard the Three Ages as forming a 'natural' succession in Denmark. Far from it. In his books Worsaae on many occasions explains that the Bronze Age in Denmark did not develop step by step out of the Danish Stone Age; 'the transition is so abrupt,' he wrote in the book translated into English as *The Primeval Antiquities of Denmark* (1849), 'that the bronze period must have commenced with the irruption of a new race of people, possessing a higher degree of cultivation than the earlier inhabitants.' In the same way, he thought, the Iron Age in Denmark was the result of another invasion. The early nineteenth-century Scandinavian archaeologists thus realized clearly that the development of cultural change in prehistory was not by innate organic or super-organic evolution but by the arrival of new ideas from outside—in a word, by diffusion. They even used the word diffusion. 'The universal diffusion of metals could only take place by degrees,' wrote Worsaae. So, from the second quarter of the nineteenth century, we had set out the basic essential idea of the difference in time between the cultures of differing areas. The question now was: how did these new ideas come into an area like Scandinavia—by trade, by the arrival of a small group of people, by invasion, or just by cultural borrowing? And whence?

In his *Prehistoric Times,* Lubbock suggested how a Bronze Age could have come into existence in Northern Europe, and set out the five possibilities which were being discussed in the sixties. First, that it was due to Roman influence, secondly to the Etruscans, thirdly to the Phoenicians, fourthly to a new and more civilized people of Indo-European 'race' coming from the East, who brought with them a knowledge of bronze and overran Europe, dispossessing the earlier Neolithic settlers. The fifth theory, which Lubbock immediately discounted, was the evolutionary one: namely the belief that the earlier inhabitants developed peacefully and gradually on their own into a Bronze Age.

Gradually, the ideas of migrating hordes became popular among late Victorian archaeologists who were reacting from the unilinear idea of progress and realizing that cultural change had to be explained in terms of influence from outside. This problem of interpretation was not confined to the prehistory of Northern and Western Europe. Schliemann's discovery of the civilization of Mycenae posed the question of the origins of the Mycenaeans. To some they were Aryans from the north; to others, Phoenicians; to others, Carians. The Bronze Age origins in Denmark and the origins of Mycenae were all part of the same general problem of cultural origins. Some insisted on a native element in European prehistory: Salomon Reinach was one of these and he castigated those who constantly sought for invaders from the East in his *Le Mirage Oriental* (1893). The great Swedish archaeologist Oscar Montelius, on the other hand, was all for eastern and outside influences and invasions. He strongly argued the *ex oriente lux* theory, especially in his *Orient und Europa* (1899). 'At a time when the peoples of Europe were, so to speak, without any civilization what-soever,' he declared, 'the Orient and particularly the Euphrates region and the Nile were already in enjoyment of a flourishing culture. The civilization which gradually dawned on our continent was for long only a pale reflec-tion of Oriental culture.'

Here, then, was an indication of the long way some archaeologists had travelled since the time of the simple unilinear evolutionists. The travel was in the direction which ultimately led to the hyperdiffusionist excesses of Elliot Smith, Perry, and Lord Raglan that we shall discuss later in this book, and which we shall see are very near to the desires of so many people for a simple explanation of archaeology and history. The Victorians never thought up anything as all-embracing as the Givers of Life of the Heliolithic Civilization of Perry and Elliot Smith, and they had not yet heard of the Sumerians, whom Lord Raglan sees as the master-civilizers of the world; but they did not do too badly with their Aryan hordes. Basic-ally they sought a simple all-embracing solution to the problem of human origins. If this solution could not be one of unilateral evolution, why not, then, a few clear-cut and recognizable invasions?

Even in Rice Holmes's *Ancient Britain and the Invasions of Julius Caesar*, published in 1907, our prehistory is set out in terms of a Palaeolithic succeeded by a Neolithic invasion, then by a Bronze Age invasion, and then an Early Iron Age invasion. All this, in the first decade of the twentieth century, was not very far removed from Worsaae. The truth is that by the end of the nineteenth century prehistoric archaeology needed a fresh impetus, a fresh jerk forward with new techniques of discovery, excavation, and interpretation. The late nineteenth-century prehistorians were really only elaborating the basic concepts which had been hammered out before 1859, and as one looks through the successive seven editions of Lubbock's *Prehistoric Times* produced between 1865 and 1913 it is surprising how little change there really was: and I mean here change in fundamental outlook—there was of course plenty of change in detail and many new discoveries to report.

Indeed one senses in the late nineteenth century a feeling that is attacking many prehistorians at the present day, a feeling of the inadequacy of the archaeological record in giving us a full picture of the prehistoric past. It is perhaps a reflection of this feeling that enabled a virtually non-archaeological prehistory to grow up during the nineteenth century, and it is with this non-archaeological prehistory that I wish to concern myself now. It was incidentally something that had considerable effect on political thought in the twentieth century.

One might say that this non-archaeological prehistory began in the writings of the humanists of the middle and late eighteenth century, such as the Scottish primitivists who were interested in Mr McQuedy's words, 'in the infancy of society,' in Lord Monboddo's views on the origin and progress of language, in Governor Pownall's notions of Woodland-Men and Land-Workers (cf. pp.17ff above). We find similar views in the writings of Sven Nilsson, Professor of Zoology at Lund. His views were originally published in Swedish in 1834 and can be most easily consulted in their translation into English which appeared in 1868. The translator was Lubbock, and the English title *The Primitive Inhabitants of Scandinavia*.

Nilsson, by the comparative study of existing peoples, arrived at a classification of prehistoric man based on the mode of subsistence. There were four stages in his classification: first, the *savage* state—the childhood of the race —when man is a hunter, fisher, and collector of berries and fruits, and you must not think I am going back to Governor Pownall when I remind you that savages are the wild men of the woods—*homines sylvestres*. The second stage, according to Nilsson, was the *herdsman* or *nomad* stage, when hunting was an occasional occupation but man subsisted essentially on the products of his herds. The third stage was the *agricultural*—man the agriculturalist— and the fourth and final stage was *civilization*. Nilsson defined this on the basis of coined money, writing, and the division of labour. Now it is not only the professional archaeologists who had these notions of the development of society in prehistory but also the general literary world. In 1836 we find Coleridge writing that 'the progress from savagery to civilization is evidently first from the hunting to the pastoral stage.'

When Sir Edward Tylor was writing his standard works on anthropology, he fully recognized the Danish system of the Three Ages and fully agreed that the Stone Age was the beginning of man's prehistoric development, but he proposed to distinguish three different stages in the human past and these he labelled Savagery, Barbarism, and Civilization. In his *Anthropology: An Introduction to the Study of Man and Civilization*, which was first published in 1881, Tylor defined what he meant by barbarism; it was a state of culture beginning with agriculture and ending with civilization, which by definition meant writing.

These terms and the use of a non-archaeological prehistory of man were developed by the American anthropologist Lewis H. Morgan in his *Ancient Society* (1877). The subtitle of Morgan's work is particularly interesting: it was *Researches in the Lines of Human Progress from Savagery through Barbarism to Civilization*. Tylor had distinguished three stages; Morgan distinguished seven— seven ethnic periods as he called them, as follows: Lower Savagery from the emergence of man to the discovery of fire, Middle Savagery from the discovery of fire to the discovery of the bow and arrow, Upper Savagery from the bow and arrow to pottery, Lower Barbarism from the discovery of pottery to the domestication of animals, Middle Barbarism from the domestication of animals to the smelting of iron ore (at least in the Old World; Morgan had slightly different criteria for these periods in the Americas), Upper Barbarism from the discovery of iron to the invention of a phonetic alphabet, while his seventh and last stage from writing and the alphabet onwards was civilization.

There are two things to remember about Morgan and his schemes. He was himself a unilateral evolutionist and was working out a progressive sequence of man's cultural evolution. He also firmly believed that this sequence developed naturally in different regions. It is not strange that he, an American, should be so convinced of parallel natural cultural evolution. The expeditions of John Lloyd Stephens and Frederick Catherwood in Yucatán in 1839 and 1840 had discovered the lost Mayan cities of Copan, Palenque, Uxmal, and Chichén Itzá and had precipitated anew the old issue of diffusion versus independent evolution. For a century and a half since the publication of Stephens's *Incidents of Travel in Central America, Chipas and Yucatán* in 1841, the world has been arguing about the origin of Middle American civilization. Jakeman has summarized the modern view on the problem of Mayan origins: 'The evolution of the Mayan civilization in apparently complete independence of the great culture-complexes of the Old World suggests that its separate historical reconstruction may reveal confirmatory parallels for fixing the chief causes underlying the rise and fall of nations, and for determining the laws of human progress.'

While many Old World prehistorians in the twentieth century have not accepted this view, it is not surprising that Lewis Morgan, with the jungle-covered Mayan cities near, should have felt that after all, there might be in human history a natural and inevitable cultural evolution that led perhaps separately in Egypt, China, and Middle America to a civilization of literate cities.

LEWIS MORGAN

IV

The Development of Modern Prehistory

SIR ARTHUR EVANS

Throughout the formative second half of the nineteenth century there was no single and all-pervasive idea of prehistory among the scholars who were, for the first time, seeing prehistory as something that could be obtained by archaeological means. On the contrary, there was a great deal of change of thought. At first, in the full flush of Victorian evolutionary thought it seemed that prehistory was just proving the earlier stages of that long single pattern that led from the beginnings of man through to Victorian prosperity itself, 'the heir of all the ages in the foremost files of time,' as Tennyson himself described it. But then doubts arose, as we have seen. Several development sequences were distinguished, and the phenomena of retrogression and decay were all too apparent if one examined such disturbing things as post-Roman Britain or the end of Upper Palaeolithic art, or the civilization of the Maya. Indeed anthropologists seemed to be turning away from archaeological prehistory and seeking the keys to the prehistoric past in the comparative study of primitive societies.

There were perhaps, however, two things about which everyone was agreed by the first decade of the twentieth century, as far as prehistoric archaeology was concerned. One was the enormous antiquity of man; that had at last become an essential of historical and anthropological thinking, and the Ussher chronology and the Flood had gone forever, except in the fundamentalist tenets of narrow sects and crank religions. Secondly, no one had any doubt, whatever value or interpretation he gave to the facts of prehistoric archaeology, that in the rise of prehistory there had come about a new discipline of great value and importance. It is perhaps strange, this being so, that prehistory took so long to penetrate properly into our universities, and into our awareness and our perspective of the past. That this was so in the last quarter of the nineteenth century no one can have any doubt who reads books, lectures, and papers of that period. I have already quoted what W. E. Gladstone said; in 1871 in his *Primitive Culture* Sir Edward Tylor wrote: 'The history and prehistory of man take their proper places in the general scheme of knowledge,' and three years later, in the preface to his *Cave-Hunting* published the year before, Mr Gladstone declared that he was beginning to see through a dense mist to 'real places, real men, real facts.' Professor Boyd Dawkins said triumphantly that 'archaeology, by the use of strictly inductive methods, has grown from a mere antiquarian speculation into a science.'

That was more than a century ago. In 1874 Boyd Dawkins was congratulating himself and the world in general that archaeology had become a science. Yet if one asks any modern undergraduate to write an essay on the main changes in prehistoric archaeology in the last fifty years he will certainly put very high the fact that it has 'recently' become scientific. And any modern professional archaeologist is always declaiming about the development of scientific archaeology; this always turns out to be the developments he has witnessed or taken

61

part in during the years immediately before his utterance. To a certain extent, and I am not being cynical here, 'scientific' means, in prehistory, modern and recent and anything that is away from the horrid barrow-diggers and muddles of the nineteenth century. Yet this must be the main underlying theme in any account of the development of prehistory between 1900 and the present day—over seventy years between the seventh edition of *Prehistoric Times* and the present that we are discussing now—that it was at last becoming modern and scientific and leaving behind for ever the non-archaeological prehistory of antiquarian speculation.

Indeed, how could one avoid feeling, as the great discoveries were being made from the turn of the century onwards, that one was living at a time when the prehistoric past was really becoming known at last through archaeological means? In the year 1900 itself Arthur Evans began work at Knossos and unearthed the civilization which he named the Minoan. In 1904 Pumpelly and Schmidt were digging at Anau and the world was learning what a wealth of prehistoric story lay buried in the *tells* and *kurgans* of the Near East—or the Near East as it was to archaeologists and the general public before the curious naming of military commands made it the Middle East. In 1906 Winckler began work at Boghazkeui, the old capital of the ancient Hittites. In 1918 Campbell Thompson and Hall were working at Ur and Eridu, and the Sumerians—postulated as early as 1869 by Oppert, and a reality when de Sarzec began work at Lagash—were at last a common fact of prehistory; a fact which became a dramatic and permanent reality to the world at large when Leonard Woolley excavated the Royal Tombs at Ur in 1926. Andersson, five years before this, had discovered Yang Shao Tsun and established the early stages of Chinese prehistory, and in the same year Sahni had begun work in Harappa, and Banerji at Mohenjo-Daro. The next year Sir John Marshall appeared to be bemoaning that it was the misfortune of Indian history that 'its earliest and most obscure pages derive little light from contemporary antiquities'; he had written these words for the first volume of the *Cambridge History of India* before Sahni and Banerji had begun their work.

In 1923 in the *Illustrated London News*, Marshall was announcing that the excavations at Harappa and Mohenjo-Daro had revealed a new prehistoric civilization, and was comparing their discovery with Schliemann's discoveries at Tiryns and Mycenae. In the same year, the same journal, which, since (Sir) Bruce Ingram assumed editorship in 1900, has given a coverage to archaeology which is the envy of the world, was announcing that Howard Carter and Lord Carnarvon had found and excavated the tomb of Tutankhamun.

These were indeed years of heroic discovery—the quarter-century from Knossos to Tutankhamun, from Anau to the Royal Tombs at Ur—and it is amazing, looking back on them, that four were taken up with the First World War, with its senseless cessation of archaeological activities and its tragic slaughter of potential and real archaeologists. These twenty-five years were also a period of amazing change in the methods and aims of prehistory. Indeed it is no exaggeration to say that a revolution took place in prehistoric archaeology during this quarter-century; and if I were pinned in a corner and asked what were really the formative years of prehistory I would say that there were two periods, the first from 1807 to 1859—the half-century between Thomsen and the *annus mirabilis*, and the second from 1900 to 1925—the quarter-century between Pitt-Rivers and the men who in the early twenties revolutionized British prehistory. For there was a great revolution in prehistory in the first quarter of the present century, and it is a revolution which is most clearly seen in the northern countries of Europe and particularly in the British Isles. Indeed it is not extravagant to refer to it as the British revolution in prehistory, just as the great changes that produced the Three Age system in the first quarter of the nineteenth century were a Danish (or Scandinavian) revolution in prehistory.

This 'revolution' which I have dramatically but not sensationally called it, was a series of remarkable changes which had actually started before 1900. The sum total of these changes in retrospect adds up to revolutionary change: 1900 was the year in which General Pitt-Rivers died, and the changes of which we are now speak-

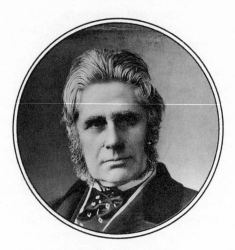

GENERAL PITT-RIVERS

ing began with his own archaeological work. This remarkable man was born Lane-Fox and took the name of Pitt-Rivers when, in 1880, he inherited the Rivers estates, over 29,000 acres of land, including much of Cranborne Chase. Before this, as a professional soldier, he had been concerned with the use and development of the rifle between 1851 and 1857 at Woolwich, Enfield, Malta, and Hythe; he was virtually the creator of the Hythe School of Musketry. He studied the development of firearms and as he did so he found himself arranging collections of types in developing sequences. Himself imbued with the Darwinian notions of evolution, and constantly examining the sequences of firearms and noting their differences, he formulated the idea that all archaeological material, that is to say all the material remains of the past, could be arranged in sequences—in what the archaeologist and anthropologist now call typological sequences.

The idea of typology was not something invented by Pitt-Rivers; it had existed in the work of the early Danish and Swedish archaeologists, and at the same time as Pitt-Rivers was working out his sequences, a man like John Evans was busily classifying and arranging in sequences bronze and stone tools. The collection of tools and weapons which Pitt-Rivers was making soon outgrew his house, and they eventually found their way to Oxford, where a special annex of the University Museum was built to house them.

The Pitt-Rivers collections were arranged not geographically but typologically, and they did not necessarily contain remarkable or beautiful things. He said himself that his collections were 'not for the purpose of surprising anyone, either by the beauty or value of the objects exhibited, but solely with a view to instruction. For this purpose ordinary and typical specimens rather than rare objects have been selected and arranged in sequence.' And in the lectures he gave in London between 1867 and 1874, he kept stressing the need for the study of all material objects of human culture. One of the mainsprings of an interest in antiquarian matters in the seventeenth and eighteenth centuries was the cultivation of taste, the collection and cultivation of the beautiful object which could adorn the cabinet and give intrinsic pleasure as well as, or indeed instead of, being merely a historical document. Gradually, as the nineteenth century had transformed antiquarianism into archaeology, taste and the contemplation of beautiful things were disappearing. As Dr Joan Evans has said, with a tinge of regret with which we can all sympathize, it was Pitt-Rivers who gave the death blow to taste. He finally exorcised taste from archaeology.

Of course, one man himself does not necessarily do these things. He appears to us, looking back at him, as a symbol of change. Flinders Petrie was as much an agent of this change as Pitt-Rivers; his too was an important influence in the exorcising of the ghost of taste. He began his work in Egypt in 1881 and was soon formulating what became the new method in prehistoric archaeology. He insisted on the collection and description of everything found and this was emphasized in his *Methods and Aims in Archaeology* published in 1904. Petrie began excavating in Egypt a year after Lane-Fox had become Pitt-Rivers and assumed control of his large estates. Pitt-Rivers at once began a series of excavations in Wessex; he had dug before and some of his techniques

SIR FLINDERS PETRIE

stem back to Canon Greenwell and William Cunnington. But whatever he had learned from past excavators, he developed and perfected. He had plenty of money and plenty of time, and a long training in military staff methods, survey, and precision behind him. His excavations were well organized, thoroughly carried out; he demanded the highest standards of care from his men. He insisted on the total excavation of sites and substituted this for the old-time technique of digging hopefully during an afternoon into a barrow and looking for a primary burial with a beaker or urn or bronze dagger that would look nice in one's private collection. And he began excavating settlement sites as well as burial mounds.

Pitt-Rivers also insisted on the accurate recording of his excavations and that this record should contain the exact position where everything was found. He made plans and sections, detailed drawings and descriptions of all his excavations, and even made models of the main sites which he dug. There is no doubt that the modern techniques of excavation now practised in Northwestern Europe began in his work on Cranborne Chase between 1880 and 1900, and the four privately printed volumes describing his work achieved a very high standard of archaeological publication. As I have said elsewhere, 'in fifteen years he transformed excavation from the pleasant hobby of barrow digging to an arduous scientific pursuit.' And throughout, he insisted on the study of ordinary objects and of *all* ordinary objects. 'Common things are of more importance than particular things, because they are more prevalent,' he wrote in 1898.

Here, then, right at the turn of the century, was the beginning of a revolution in archaeological technique. Typology, the meticulous examination of sites, the study of the totality of phenomena—these were the things which Pitt-Rivers and Petrie bequeathed as an archaeological legacy to the early twentieth century. Petrie himself went on to practise these techniques until the forties. It was, however, a legacy which was not extensively taken up, developed, and expanded until after the 1914–18 war, and it was developed in Britain mainly by two men, R. E. M. Wheeler and Cyril Fox. In his autobiography, *Still Digging* (1955), Sir Mortimer Wheeler looked back at the moment in 1919 when he began his serious career of excavation:

> Between 1880 and 1900, General Pitt-Rivers in Cranborne Chase had brought archaeological digging and recording to a remarkable degree of perfection, and had presented his methods and results meticulously in several imposing volumes. Then what? Nobody paid the slightest attention to the old man. One of his assistants had even proceeded to dig up a lake-village much as Schliemann had dug up Troy, or St John Hope, Silchester; like potatoes. Not only had the clock not gone on, but it had been set back.

This is Wheeler's crisp verdict. The war of 1914–18 carried away many potential archaeologists. Wheeler himself describes how he was the only one of four university students digging at Wroxeter in 1913 to survive the war, and the sense of isolation which was so apparent to him in 1919. But it is also true that the earlier tradition was carried on to some extent between Pitt-Rivers's death and Wheeler's work at Segontium in 1921 by a few workers such as J. P. Bushe Fox in Wroxeter and Hengistbury Head, James Curle at Newstead in Scotland, and

John Ward in South Wales, as Wheeler himself has recognized. Nevertheless, the work of Wheeler and Fox in the early twenties had the real appearance of a fresh start; they turned back to the Pitt-Rivers traditions, expanded and improved them, and so changed, handed them on to the excavators of the present day. It is not my object here to catalogue the excavations by which Wheeler established his reputation and perfected his technique, but even those who do not know of the beginnings at Segontium and the Brecon Gaer and at Caerleon will know of his excavations at Maiden Castle before the 1939–45 war, at Harappa, Arikamedu, and Taxila in India, towards the end and after the war, and in the sixties at Stanwick. Nor is it my object to do more than mention in passing those who have carried on the traditions of British excavation re-created by Fox and Wheeler in the twenties—men like Ian Richmond, Christopher Hawkes, Grahame Clark, Stuart Piggott, C. A. Ralegh Radford, C. W. Phillips, V. Nash Williams, B. H. St J. O'Neil, and Sean Ó Ríordáin, to mention but a few. Nor do I want to create the impression, because I am emphasizing the British aspects of this story, that the same changes were not taking place in some other parts of Northern Europe—in Holland, Germany, and Scandinavia. It was not, however, happening all over Europe, and we may reflect with pride that the British tradition was a very important element in the re-creation of a new archaeological field technique.

We have, then, a new factor in the ideas of prehistory which have been formulated in the last seventy-five years; the idea that prehistory should not merely be written from archaeological sources but that it should be based on archaeological information which is accurate, detailed, and complete. While the early nineteenth-century excavations were, if not treasure hunts, but very partial examinations of the material, our modern excavations—or at least the best of them—are total and complete examinations of the material.

There are two aspects of excavation: there is the actual surgery of the landscape by pick, shovel, trowel, knife, and scalpel with all the photographic and diagrammatic recording of this operation, and there is then the examination of everything found by every available method—

the analysis of form and material of all the artifacts found, and of all associated material. This analytical aspect of the study of the archaeological material has been one of the major developments since the early twenties and now we are accustomed to have in archaeological reports the findings of specialists who have worked on pollens or on snails, on soils or on grain impressions. Even more exciting has been the development since 1945 of the technique of exact dating by Carbon-14 analysis. This remarkable technique, first discovered by Libby at Chicago as a by-product of research into atomic physics, enables organic substances to be dated in calendar years by the quantity of Carbon-14 they contain. This is a very bad and bald and brief way of describing this amazing technique which has enabled people to date the late Mesolithic settlement at Seamer, for example, to 7500 BC, and the duration of the cultures with which Upper Palaeolithic art is associated as from 30,000 to 10,000 BC.

This is certainly one of the things that must be stressed in trying to see what is really represented by the modern scientific technique of excavation—it is the extraction of every available piece of evidence that can be used for building up the historical contexts of the past, and for that matter even the detailed recording of evidence which in itself at the time does not seem to make sense. It is one of the many remarkable features, for example, of Pitt-Rivers's work that in his notes, excavation reports and models, he recorded information about his excavations which could be used later, and indeed has been used later, by men like Professor Hawkes, to arrive at conclusions which Pitt-Rivers did not or could not have reached. It is often said that all excavation is not only a recovery of the past but to a certain degree a destruction of the past, and in many ways this is true. Everyone who undertakes the surgery of the landscape—which is excavation—has a responsibility to future generations of archaeologists and historians as well as to his own generation. This responsibility is discharged not only by complete and meticulous digging but by complete and meticulous record. It is one of the features of present excavation which vitally affects what ideas we now have of the prehistoric past that we live in a climate of thought

which believes in the highest possible standards of excavational technique and publication.

I have mentioned Sir Cyril Fox as one of those who in the early twenties did so much to re-create in Britain the technique of excavation which Pitt-Rivers had first created. Fox was also a field archaeologist of the first rank. There is often confusion among archaeologists as to what is meant by field archaeology; Sir Leonard Woolley once reviewed O. G. S. Crawford's book *Archaeology in the Field,* and declared with surprise that he had always thought of himself as a field archaeologist until he read Crawford's book and found that he was 'only an excavator!' In the minds of many people there is a dichotomy between the indoors or study or closet archaeologist, and the archaeologist who goes out into the field—the dirt archaeologist as he is sometimes called, the man who gets mud on his boots and sand in his eyes. But the activities of the archaeologist in the field are of two different kinds, as we have already seen: first, excavation which is the surgical aspect of field archaeology, and secondly the nonsurgical or physical aspect of the study of the visible material remains of the past. It is this second aspect to which Crawford was referring when he used the phrase field archaeology as distinct from excavation; this tradition of field archaeology is one which has been built up in Britain over the centuries. It began with exact observers and painstaking travellers to the past like John Aubrey and Edward Lhwyd, and was developed in the late nineteenth century and early twentieth century by men like Williams Freeman, whose *Field Archaeology as Illustrated by Hampshire* was published in 1915.

Crawford and Fox were heirs of this field archaeological tradition, and developed it in various ways, the tradition which produced on the one hand *The Long Barrows of the Cotswolds*, and the megalithic and period maps of the Ordnance Survey; and, on the other, *The Archaeology of the Cambridge Region* and *Offa's Dyke*. This aspect of modern field archaeology has a feature closely akin to what we have been saying about excavational technique. It, too, aims at total information, at the study of the totality of visible archaeological phenomena. When John Aubrey was asked to write about Avebury and Stonehenge he begged to be allowed to defer his work until he had seen all the other comparable monuments in England and Wales. Because of the extension of this idea not only in principle but in practice, we can now study all the representatives of any archaeological category of monument or artifact. If, for example, at the present moment we want to study Stonehenge and Avebury and say, as John Aubrey did, that we can do so only against the background of all other comparable examples of stone circles, we can do so, because twentieth-century field archaeology has brought us to the position where we can view the total pattern of these monuments. The distribution map is one of the main instruments of archaeological research and exposition, but because it is a commonplace of books and papers, do not let us forget what it is trying to do—to accomplish and to demonstrate the totality of information about some archaeological fact, to study the total evidence in space regarding one aspect of the material remains of the past.

I have said that the field archaeologist is concerned with the visible material remains of the past and so he is and was. He is essentially one who plods laboriously

O. G. S. CRAWFORD

over the surface of the ground observing barrows and
linear earthworks and the low grass-covered banks of
long-ruined houses or deserted fields. Williams Freeman, over half a century ago, noted that by the long
shadows of a late summer evening a field archaeologist
on a hill could see earthworks with a clarity denied him
when standing on them; they fell into patterns not visible
on the ground. He once said to Crawford that 'one ought
to be a bird to be a field archaeologist.' The development
of aircraft and of aerial photography during and after the
1914–18 war enabled archaeologists virtually to become
birds. After that war these opportunities were brilliantly
seized by no one so well as O. G. S. Crawford in England.
But air photography not only revealed what Williams
Freeman expected the air archaeologist to observe,
namely shadow marks, but crops and soil marks leading
in a dramatic way to the discovery of sites, in apparently
flat fields, that were totally invisible to the ground
observer. I know of few things more dramatic in archaeological technique than walking over a ploughed field in
spring armed with an air photograph showing the marks
of ploughed-out banks and filled-in ditches on a photograph taken at the height of the growth of the previous

June's corn, and being totally unable to see on the ground these buried ghosts of a prehistoric landscape. Aerial reconnaissance, like the technique of Carbon-14 dating, is one of the most remarkable and surprising advances in the archaeologist's technique in the last half-century or more.

But what do all these technical advances add up to— these scientific techniques, this total excavation, our new typologies, our total field surveys, the distribution maps, and air photography? First and foremost they add up, with all the fresh discoveries that are being made, to an enormous body of facts, and what is more, an enormously complicated body of facts. Nowhere was and is this more directly apparent than in the study of cultural sequences. We have seen that the sequence of cultures became more and more complicated as the detailed knowledge of archaeology developed. And what is more, the sequences appeared to be different in different areas. What was even more complicated was that the old idea of a sequence in a single area was collapsing. A man like de Mortillet had organized an elaborate scheme for French archaeology whose basic feature was successive periods or epochs. If we look at Gabriel de Mortillet's *Formation de la Nation Française,* published in 1897, we get at once a clear idea of the single sequence idea. Here the prehistoric past of man is divided into three ages of Stone, Bronze, and Iron, and these are split up into *périodes,* namely the Stone Age into *éolithique, paléolithique,* and *néolithique,* and the Iron Age, for example, into *galatienne* (the Galatians to whom St Paul addressed an Epistle were, some of us forget, Celts), the *romaine,* and the *mérovingienne.* These *périodes* were in turn split up into *époques;* there is no point in detailing them here, but let us just look at the division of the Palaeolithic. This was split up into six *époques,* namely the Chellean, Acheulian, Mousterian, Solutrean, Magdalenian, and Tourassian. It did look, even if the prehistoric sequences were not the same in neighbouring countries, as though the story were merely one of detailing the epochs.

In the beginning of the twentieth century the whole idea of these successive epochs began to be doubted and the fabric of subdivisions to crumble. In 1909 at the Grotte

73

de Valle, near Gibaja (Santander) in north Spain, the Abbé Breuil and Professor Obermaier discovered a classic deposit of one 'epoch,' namely the Azilian, together with microlithic flints typical of another 'epoch,' the Tardenoisian. After this, archaeologists who had been arguing whether the Azilian came before or after the Tardenoisian could stop arguing. 'After this discovery,' said Hugo Obermaier, 'it could no longer be questioned that the Azilian and the Tardenoisian were contemporary.' But what did it mean if two epochs were going to be contemporary? It meant of course that they were not epochs; that the archaeologists, who, after all, had developed out of being geologists and had for long been thinking in geological terms of time and fossil-directors, had to rethink their basic principles and think in terms of historical time and man.

All this was really the great moment when prehistoric archaeology broke away from the quite understandably inherited conceptions of geology and the natural sciences. The human geographers and anthropologists had for some while been canvassing a new idea with regard to human groupings, and an idea which was to supersede the political idea of nations and tribes. Ratzel in Germany in the eighties of the nineteenth century had been distinguishing what he called 'cultural complexes,' and his pupil Leo Frobenius developed this idea and studied what he called 'culture-circles.' German ethnologists like Graebner, Schmidt, Ankermann, and others gradually extended this idea and soon archaeologists began to see that what they were studying was not a series of epochs but an assemblage of cultures. The prehistorian had been studying the distribution of prehistoric life in time and space; if these distributions and their associations were planned on a graph with space-time co-ordinates, it was found that lenticular-shaped masses developed and to these masses—which are persistent assemblages of material traits—the prehistorian now gave the name 'culture.' This is perhaps an unfortunate use of a more widespread term, and it is an especially limited form of a much wider concept; but, at least from the early years of the nineteenth century through to the 1939–45 war, it seemed a good and a workable concept. The prehistorian had then to readjust his views, and to realize that he was no longer dealing with unilateral sequences but that he was studying the distribution in time and space of the culture (and of necessity mainly the material culture) of different societies.

This new idea took a long time to penetrate into the views of teachers and workers who were imbued with the nineteenth-century ideas of unilateral sequences to such an extent as almost to have given it a religious significance. Perhaps religious significance is the right word to use here. The earlier sequence of Flood and 4004 B C had been exchanged for a sequence of epochs, and to many people in the earlier twenties of this century, this new sequence had attained something of the status of an archaeological fundamentalist doctrine. Compare George Grant MacCurdy's table 'The Chronology of Prehistory' in his admirable book *Human Origins: A Manual of Prehistory,* published in 1924; or Macalister's *Textbook of European Archaeology* (1921); or M. C. Burkitt's *Prehistory,* also published in 1921, with Gordon Childe's *Dawn of European Civilization,* the first edition of which came out in 1925. I have described Childe's *Dawn* as 'not merely a book of incomparable archaeological erudition but . . . a new starting point for prehistoric archaeology.' These words were written in the 1940s and I would not now want to modify them in any way. Here, in 1925, with the *Dawn* was a new starting point in prehistory. Gone was the simple evolutionary cultural sequence. Here was a prehistory studying the complexity of cultures, studying human society in the prehistoric past. Childe's lead was soon followed all over the world by those analysing and writing about prehistory. One might say that one of the main tasks of the archaeological synthesist in the fifteen to twenty years following 1925 seemed to be the elaboration of individual cultures; and for the simple evolutionary sequence we begin to get, instead, Beaker Cultures, Food-vessel Cultures, Passage-grave Cultures, Rinyo-Clacton Cultures, and when suitable geographical or taxonomic names ran out, we reverted to letters and numbers and there appeared Neolithic A and B, and the Iron Age A, B, and C.

The British Isles themselves provide an admirable

example of this process at work. In the times of the earlier synthesists, it was all very easy to understand and to write about. I have already referred to Rice Holmes and his *Ancient Britain and the Invasions of Julius Caesar*: there in the simple synthesis of 1907 the Neolithic race or people introduced the Neolithic, they were replaced by the Bronze Age race or people who brought in metal-working, and eventually by the Iron Age race who introduced the Early Iron Age. But soon there were cracks in this admirably simple structure. Arthur Evans, later to become famous as the discoverer of the Minoan civilization of Crete, published in 1890 in *Archaeologia* his finds of what he described as a Late Celtic urn-field at Aylesford in Kent; he moreover identified the Aylesford people with the Belgae who were in history known as invaders of south-east Britain. In doing this he was of course recognizing a separate culture within the Early Iron Age, and a separate group of invaders within the Three Age invasion pattern of prehistory set out by Rice Holmes and his contemporaries. O. G. S. Crawford, working on distributional and other studies, suggested, in the early twenties, that the Bronze Age was not a single and unitary phase of development and that the Late Bronze Age was a separate culture introduced by a separate group of invaders.

By the late twenties, then, the story of Britain in post-Palaeolithic times was already becoming more complicated than the late-nineteenth-century systematists had believed possible. A Neolithic was succeeded by an Early and Middle Bronze Age culture broken by an invasion which brought in the Late Bronze Age, then a further Early Iron Age invasion which itself contained further separate invasions like the Belgic Aylesford invasion of Evans.

In their *Archaeology in England and Wales 1914–31* T. D. Kendrick and C. F. C. Hawkes set out a complicated picture of cultures and invasions. But our best example of the logical evolution of Childe's ideas is provided by Childe himself in his book *The Prehistoric Communities of the British Isles*, first published in 1940. Here there is set out an amazing sequence of cultures—amazing that is to a person brought up on Gabriel de Mortillet or Rice

Holmes. If we look at southern England alone we find Windmill Hill and Peterborough Neolithic cultures, the cultures of the Collective Tomb Builders, the Beaker cultures, the Wessex culture, the Food-vessel and Cinerary Urn cultures, the Deverel-Rimbury Late Bronze Age people, then Iron Age A 1, Iron Age A 2, Iron Age B, and the Belgae of Iron Age C. Here was indeed complexity and detail, but, one asks, what was happening to man in all this complexity of detail and culture? Was he being forgotten?

One thing was sure. The old idea of a Master Race or a Master Civilizing People was vanishing. As the records of the past become detailed in such a complicated way in each region studied, it was impossible to see one group of civilizers spreading from one region. Rather could one see no more than small-scale and localized movements, such as the Belgae from north-east France and Belgium to south-east England, or the builders of Passage Graves from south-west Spain and Portugal to Brittany, Ireland, and west Wales. Prehistory began to look in the thirties and forties as though it would resolve itself into the exercise of tracing small cultural movements and invasions. The great Master Race had gone, at least in official prehistory, but, as we shall see in the next chapter, it was by no means entirely gone, and I think we shall appreciate that in the hyperdiffusionist theories of Elliot Smith, Perry, and Lord Raglan there is not merely a survival of the old nineteenth-century ideas of master races, not merely a far-reaching conviction that nothing can be invented twice, but a deep-seated desire for a simple story of man's past, and a genuine and not unnatural reaction against the complicated cultural and invasion pattern which was emerging as prehistory in the second quarter of the twentieth century.

The official prehistorians, however, who taught and worked during the period from Childe's *Dawn* in 1925 to the 1939–45 war paid little attention to those who were finding their gradual elaboration of the cultural sequence difficult to master. And we must admit here and now that the detail of prehistory is difficult to assimilate; it is not to be wondered at that the general public sometimes prefer the simplicity of Phoenicians and Druids and

Egyptians to Beaker Folk and Iron Age B.

But, on the whole, I think it fair to say that between 1925 and 1939, the period with which we have been concerned, official prehistorians did not bother a very great deal about what the public could make out of pre-history, or whether prehistory was popular with the public. To them the task was, by scientific excavation, by rigorous comparative study, and by the use of all ancillary scientific techniques possible, to get out the record of the past. And this was not a single unitary record, not the record of the spread of a master race, but a record of hundreds of cultures each varying in distribution in time and space.

Prehistory had become a layer cake but a cake whose layers changed as you turned it round and moved to a different part of the world. Then as you turned the cake you saw that the differently coloured layers, gaily stuffed with the artificial material of past human societies, were in fact not layers but lenticles. But the general analogy of a layer cake is a correct one and when I was an under-graduate and research student before the war it did seem that it was a complicated layer cake that I was studying. Do not misunderstand me; I am not trying to make fun out of this essential phase in the development of pre-history. I am only saying that this was in the thirties the prevalent view of prehistory; just as the Fog and the Flood had been replaced by the unilateral evolutionary sequences of the Victorians, so now, a half-century of new techniques and vastly increased knowledge produced us this gaily coloured layer cake.

We shall see how this layer cake satisfied or dissatisfied those who came to admire and eat it—historians, geo-graphers, anthropologists, politicians, prehistorians themselves. We shall begin by looking at those who deliberately set it aside—the hyperdiffusionists who, by their actions, could almost be said to have set aside also a hundred years and more of archaeology, and gone back to the guesswork of pre-archaeological prehistory.

V

Diffusion and Distraction

We are, at first, mainly concerned with a very great man who was a Fellow of my own College in Cambridge, and who has been described by Warren Dawson, who edited a book of essays that form the biographical record of his life, as 'one of the foremost anatomists and thinkers of his age,' and also as 'one of the outstanding intellectual personalities of his age.' This man, Grafton Elliot Smith, was, and is, the outstanding example of one who fell, as those interested in prehistory are prone to fall, into that extraordinary and interesting intellectual error—the simplistic heresy of hyperdiffusion.

Grafton Elliot Smith was born at Grafton in New South Wales in 1871—the very year in which Tylor published his *Primitive Culture*. Not only because of this coincidence, nor even because Elliot Smith was himself later to write much about Tylor, we must now take a backward glance at this most distinguished figure, father of British anthropology as he has been called, friend of Huxley, Wallace, Spencer, Lyell, Lubbock, and Darwin, whose work we have already very briefly touched upon. Tylor, whose dates are 1832 to 1917, was, to Elliot Smith, 'one of the most significant figures of the Victorian age, ' and he says these words in his essay on Tylor in *The Great Victorians* (edited by H. J. Massingham and Hugh Massingham), and declares that he used these words advisedly because Tylor thought 'the most vital thing in the world is the understanding of human nature.'

Tylor travelled because his health broke down when working in his father's brass foundry. He travelled in Mexico with Henry Christy, the English banker who worked with the French palaeontologist Lartet in the exploration of Upper Palaeolithic sites in the Dordogne. Breakdowns in health have only too often been most detrimental to scholarship : here was one which, together with the stray meeting with Christy, was extremely beneficial to learning. Tylor's interests were turned to anthropology. His first book related to his travels : it was called *Anahuac or Mexico and the Mexicans* (1861). His second was *Researches into the Early History of Mankind,* and it came out in 1865—the year of the publication of Lubbock's *Prehistoric Times*—and was nothing short of epoch-making. It was, of course, primarily a plea for the study of existing preliterate societies but also for the study of the origins of man. 'Civilization,' he wrote, 'being a process of long and complex growth, can only be thoroughly understood when studied throughout its entire range ; that the past is continually needed to explain the present, and the whole to explain the past.' In his *Researches* he fully examined the various views about the origins of civilization and of cultural change. 'Sometimes,' he wrote, 'it may be ascribed to the like working of men's minds under like conditions, and, sometimes, it is a proof of blood relationship, or of intercourse, direct or indirect, between the races among whom it is found.'

Six years later, the year in which, as we have said, Grafton Elliot Smith was born, Tylor elaborated the argument of his earlier book in his *Primitive Culture,* and then, ten years later, in his *Anthropology, an Introduction to the*

Study of Man and Civilization. Tylor's subsequent career need not concern us unduly here. In 1883 he became Keeper of the University Museum in Oxford—the Museum which housed the Pitt-Rivers collections: in 1884 he was made Reader in Anthropology and twelve years later became a Professor—the first Professor of Anthropology in the British Isles.

What is important, here and now, is that Tylor was a great hero to Elliot Smith, and that Tylor himself was a diffusionist. When I say this I must immediately explain how I am using this somewhat tendentious word. There were, in the second half of the nineteenth century, as we have seen, two explanations current as to the origin of the cultural changes which were manifest in the archaeo-logical record, in history, and in the modern world, and these explanations were usually centred over such things as the appearance, in two different parts of the world in the archaeological and ethnographical record, of appar-ently the same cultural features. One explanation was that these features had evolved separately and de-veloped independently. The other was that a feature had spread from one area to another, that it had in fact been diffused—by trade, by the movement of people, or by culture contact. It is these two explanations of culture change that we refer to when we talk of evolution versus diffusion in the study of human cultural development.

There is of course no necessary conflict between these two views; as Lowie said in the twentieth century, look-ing back at the Anthropological Institute in the nine-teenth century, here 'evolution . . . lay down amicably beside diffusion.' As we have seen, the early Scandin-avian archaeologists believed in the possible truth of both evolution and diffusion, and so did Pitt-Rivers. So did Tylor, and you will remember the passage I have just quoted from Tylor in which he mentioned several agencies of cultural change—the like working of men's minds, blood relationship, and intercourse.

The controversy about all this begins when we start to argue about the relative importance of the factors in cultural change, and when we find people manoeuvring themselves into, or pledging, positions in which only one explanation is possible. Adolf Bastian, the German

81

scholar born in Bremen in 1826, is the out-and-out evolutionist who would not believe in diffusion, and a textbook example of such a person. He argued that by a general law the psychical unity of man everywhere produced similar ideas; different geographical environments might produce different responses, and there could of course be contacts in later historic times, but the basic idea was the psychic unity of man and, therefore, the independent evolution of culture. These ideas of Bastian's were a form of super-organic or cultural or social evolution. Others interested in anthropology flew to the opposite extreme and one such early diffusionist was a Miss Buckland who, from 1878 onwards, set out in a series of papers—they have names like 'Primitive Agriculture,' 'Prehistoric Intercourse between East and West,' 'Four as a Sacred Number,' etc.—a most violent and uncompromising hyperdiffusionism. According to Miss Buckland—and this is the key doctrine that is implicit in Elliot Smith and his followers—civilization was *never* independently acquired. It *could* not be and it *was* not. If you read Miss Buckland it will give you a foretaste of Elliot Smith, for she was writing about sun and serpent worship, and the spread of agriculture, weaving, pottery, and metals all over the earth.

Miss Buckland was writing her polemics as Grafton Elliot Smith was growing up in New South Wales and qualifying as a doctor at Sydney. It soon became clear to his chief at Sydney, Professor J. T. Wilson, that Elliot Smith was 'meant for a life-work of scientific investigation rather than for the professional life of a medical practitioner.' He was sent to England, became a Research Student at St John's College, Cambridge, in 1896, and a Research Fellow there three years later. In 1900 Alexander Macalister, the Professor of Anatomy in Cambridge, conveyed to the young Elliot Smith an invitation to become the first occupant of the Chair of Anatomy at the Government Medical School at Cairo. The prime factor in the development of Elliot Smith's hyperdiffusionism was his stay in Egypt, but I think it may well have been Alexander Macalister himself who first interested Elliot Smith in the problems and pitfalls of cultural origins. Of Macalister, Elliot Smith wrote, 'His chief interest is anthropological. If anything delights him more than inventing some new craniometric index it is the manufacture of some cacophonous name to brand it. But he is equally interested in Egyptian history, in Irish and Gaelic literature and archaeology, in the evolution of Ecclesiastical Vestments . . . in the Cambridge collegiate system, in the specific identity of the Egyptian cat, and the progress of the Cambridge Presbyterian Church, among many more or less (probably less) kindred subjects.' This enormous catholicity of interest Elliot Smith admired and practised.

Elliot Smith fell in love with Cairo—'the gayest and most cosmopolitan city on the face of the earth,' he wrote, 'and intensely fascinating.' The fascination was, of course, partly the antiquities which obtruded themselves on the attention of an intelligent, alert, inquiring traveller like Elliot Smith. 'But,' he wrote in 1901, 'I have not quite resisted the temptation to dabble in Egyptology.'

Not quite. The more's the pity. Soon he was involved in the study of ancient human remains from early Egyptian sites and from predynastic sites. He was able to study a chronologically unbroken series of human remains from 4000 BC to 2000 BC and then on to Coptic graves. The result of his complete examination was his book *The Ancient Egyptians* first published in 1911. In 1902 he was referring to 'this sudden burst into anthropology,' but the following year was saying, 'for the next six months I expect to be a slave to anthropology,' and in that year he made his first detailed study of the technique of mummification—a study which according to Warren Dawson was destined 'to have such far-reaching effects.'

What a true comment this was; mummification was the key-point in Elliot Smith's great Egyptocentric hyperdiffusionist doctrine. He believed that the technique of embalming was so complicated in Egypt that it could not have been invented identically, in all its complexity, anywhere else. Whenever, therefore, he came across the practice of embalming and mummification elsewhere he felt himself forced to conclude that it had spread from Egypt. 'Little did I realise,' he wrote in the preface to the second (1923) edition of his *Ancient Egyptians*, 'when I was writing what was intended to be nothing more than a brief interim report . . . that this little book was destined to open up a new view—or rather to revise and extend an old and neglected method of interpretation of the history of civilization.' Eagerly, he took up the diffusionist view with energy and zeal and with much of the ardour of a missionary.

The details of Elliot Smith's career from Egypt onwards are simple: he went to Manchester as Professor of Anatomy in 1909 and to University College, London, in 1919. He died in 1937. At Manchester and London he proved himself as a great anatomist, teacher and administrator. In both these places, as well as wherever he travelled over the world, he also preached his doctrines of the diffusion of culture from Egypt. These doctrines were set out in many books. First his *Migrations of Early Culture* in 1915, then *The Evolution of the Dragon* in 1919, *Elephants and Ethnologists* in 1924, *In the Beginning: The Origin of Civilization* in 1928, *Human History* in 1930, *The Diffusion of Culture* in 1933, to mention the most important statements of his case in book form. He had many enthusiastic disciples: for example Wilfred Jackson, who in 1917 wrote *Shells as Evidence of the Migrations of Early Culture* and Warren Dawson, who wrote *Custom of Couvade* in 1929, but most of all his disciple was W. J. Perry, who was first Reader in Comparative Religion in the University of Manchester in Elliot Smith's time, and then Reader of Cultural Anthropology in London when Elliot Smith moved there.

Perry was in many ways more enthusiastic and intransigent than his master. He wrote *The Children of the Sun* (1923), *The Origin of Magic and Religion* (1923), *The Megalithic Culture of Indonesia* (1918), and a general summary designed for the ordinary reader called *The Growth of Civilization*. This last book was first published in 1924 and was reissued in 1937 by Penguin Books with all the widespread public appeal and wide circulation that such publication acquires. In the brief description on the jacket of the Penguin Books edition, it was said of Perry: 'He is one of the chief supporters of the "diffusionist" theory of the growth of culture.' In an analysis of the growth of this theory he stresses that two things most affected

Elliot Smith: the first, which we have mentioned, was embalming and mummification. The second was megalithic monuments; Elliot Smith had conceived the idea that the pyramids and mastabas of ancient Egypt were the prototypes of the megalithic monuments that are found, in a very wide diversity of form, all over the ancient world. Elliot Smith could not believe that mummification and megalithic architecture could have been invented more than once and he, therefore, concluded that both 'practices' had been diffused from ancient Egypt.

He then began to see most of the elements of all culture as originated in Egypt, and defined a culture-complex of about thirty centuries ago which spread 'like an exotic leaven'—the words are those of Elliot Smith and Perry—over the world, taking with it civilization. This original Egyptian civilization was the Heliolithic or Archaic Civilization; Elliot Smith and Perry saw small groups of people setting out, mainly by sea, from Egypt and colonizing and civilizing the world. These merchant venturers of five thousand years ago were 'the Children of the Sun.'

But why, some people asked, did they set out on these extraordinary world travels? The answer given by Elliot Smith was in terms of the Givers of Life formula, and we had best give it here in his own words. 'In delving into the remotely distant history of our species,' he wrote in *The Evolution of the Dragon,* 'we cannot fail to be impressed with the persistence with which, throughout the whole of his career, man . . . has been seeking . . . for an elixir of life to give added "vitality" to the dead . . . to prolong the days of active life to the living, to restore growth and to protect his own life from all assaults, not merely of time but also of circumstance.' These world travellers were then, according to Elliot Smith and Perry, looking for elixirs, for what they called collectively 'givers of life.' They set out from Egypt and reached almost everywhere. There was no civilization before Egypt, at least no civilization that was not derived from Egypt. Elliot Smith immediately crossed swords with ethnologists in America because to him the Central American civilizations were certainly derived from Egypt. Everything started in Egypt—everything. When he was once

85

asked what was taking place in the cultural development of the world when Egypt was allegedly laying the foundations of civilization, he answered at once, 'Nothing.' Perry's comment on this statement is flabbergasting in its naïveté and ignorance. 'The accumulation of fresh evidence during the twenty-odd years that have since elapsed has tended to confirm the essential accuracy of what was then an astonishing generalization.' Those are Perry's very words; at least we can be in agreement with the phrase 'astonishing generalization.'

We do not want to spend too long in discussing the authors of this pan-Egyptian hyperdiffusion theory. Elliot Smith and Perry really abandoned any pretence at scientific method. They did not evaluate the evidence and arrive at a theory. Elliot Smith had been swept away by Egypt, he had been convinced by mummies and megaliths, his theory was formed and everything was squeezed into this theory—circumstances of time, place, and function were brushed aside with airy condescension. Lowie is not a whit too sharp, not an iota too cruel when he says of the astonishing development of the Elliot Smith theories: 'Here there is no humble quest of the truth, no patient scrutiny of difficulties, no attempt to understand sincere criticism. Vehement reiteration takes the place of argument. . . . Everything is grist for his mill, everything is either black or white. . . . In physical anthropology Elliot Smith controls the facts hence, right or wrong—his judgments command respect while in ethnography his crass ignorance darkens counsel.' Nor is Lowie too severe when he refers to 'the unfathomable ignorance of elementary ethnography' displayed by Elliot Smith and Perry. In a lecture on *Conversion in Science* which Elliot Smith gave in 1928 at the Imperial College of Science—it was the Huxley Memorial Lecture—he said this: 'The set attitude of mind of a scholar may become almost indistinguishable from a delusion.' He was not, quite naturally, thinking of himself when he wrote this sentence, but this is unfortunately just what had happened to him. He had acquired a set attitude of mind with regard to the Egyptian origin of all culture, and it had become a delusion.

To us at the present day it is a distraction to look back

at this pan-Egyptian diffusionist delusion but its significance is much more than an amusing sidelight on the
development of ideas of prehistory. For the Elliot Smith-
Perry school were not alone in their search for a simple
all-embracing solution. Elliot Smith died in 1937. Two
years later Lord Raglan published his *How Came Civilization?* Raglan corresponds in his essential philosophical
basis with Elliot Smith and Perry. He does not believe in
the possibility of inventions being made twice. Let us
quote his views:

> No invention, discovery, custom, belief, or even
> story is known for certain to have originated in two
> separate cultures. . . . The natural state of man is a
> state of low savagery . . . towards that state he
> always tends to revert whenever he is not checked,
> or forced in the opposite direction, by that unex-
> plained, but highly artificial localized and spasmodic
> process which we know as the progress of civiliza-
> tion. . . . Savages never invent or discover anything
> . . . many of the principal discoveries and inventions
> upon which our civilization is based can be traced
> with considerable probability to an area with its
> focus near the head of the Persian Gulf, and such
> evidence as there is suggests that they were made by
> ingenious priests as a means of facilitating the per-
> formance of religious ritual.

Lord Raglan allows a great civilizing process to take place
in the sixteenth century AD but this is only the second
time in man's whole history, and his general conclusion
remains that 'civilization then, far from being a process
that keeps going on everywhere, is really an event which
has only happened twice.' Raglan has done little more
than substitute Sumeria for Egypt, and this is also what
Heine-Geldern has done, and nervously realizes he has
done, in the number of *Diogenes* devoted to the work of
Toynbee.

Now why does the world tolerate this academic rubbish from people like Elliot Smith, Perry and Raglan?
There are many reasons. First there is a deep-seated
desire for a simple answer to complicated problems.
That is why the earlier pre-archaeological prehistorians
clutched at the Trojans, the Phoenicians, the Lost Tribes

of Israel, the Druids, and, let us particularly not forget in this present context, the Egyptians. The Ancient Egyptians as the saviours of the world were invented long before Elliot Smith was made Professor of Anatomy in Cairo. And this simplistic easy solution to prehistory is still something which people hanker after. I have little doubt that the cult of Atlantis at the present day is a part of this, and the sale of books explaining how all civilization came from the vanished island of Atlantis, or Mu, or Lake Titicaca, or Heligoland is a proof of it. These theories are still widely canvassed at the present day and the books dealing with them sell well, and one is always being asked about Atlantis and Titicaca just as one is asked about Phoenicians and the Lost Tribes of Israel.

It is often said by professional archaeological scholars that we should not concern ourselves unduly with what is, after all, only one aspect of the rather large lunatic fringe of prehistory, that we have far better things to do advancing the true path of knowledge and accumulating by archaeological means the basic facts to be distilled out of prehistory, and that most of these extraordinary books giving single origins to man's civilization in one great movement or event or spread of culture-heroes are beneath contempt. There is much in this, but here we *are* concerned with the ideas people have or want to have about prehistory, and there is no doubt that many have had and want to have the simple solutions of an Elliot Smith, a Raglan, a Bellamy, or a Spanuth. This is not merely because, as I have said, there seems a deep-seated desire for a simple all-embracing explanation but because the gradual elaboration and complication of the archaeological record has begun to bewilder people. It was all right in Victorian times when you could read Lubbock's *Prehistoric Times* or in Edwardian times when you read Rice Holmes's *Ancient Britain and the Invasions of Julius Caesar*, all right when the prehistoric past of man seemed an easily assimilable tale of Palaeolithic, Neolithic, Bronze Age and Early Iron Age, but not all right when you began to read the complicated story which prehistorians offer at the present day with its extraordinarily complicated sequences of cultures in different areas. Look for example at any chart at the end of Childe's

Dawn of European Civilization or of Christopher Hawkes's *Prehistoric Foundations of Europe*, at the chart at the end of Stuart Piggott's *Neolithic Cultures of the British Isles*, and you may well be pardoned if you recoil from the complicated archaeological constructs which seem to have replaced the simple succession which the Victorians so gladly elaborated into the not so complicated succession advocated by de Mortillet and which was set out by MacCurdy in his *Human Origins* and Burkitt in his *Prehistory*.

It is then, we suggest, as part of a desire for a simple all-embracing solution, and as part of a reaction from the complexity of the archaeological record, that we should look at the distractions of this hyperdiffusionism which beset the fringes of our discipline from Miss Buckland to Mr Bellamy.

It needs emphasizing here that the error lies in the simplistic hyperdiffusion of the one-centre school, just as the Victorian unilinear system of cultural evolution was an error. Neither diffusion nor evolution itself as an explanation of cultural change is an error; the error has lain in the extravagant interpretation of cultural change in terms of only one of these explanations and that taken to obsessional extremes. In the new prehistory which was coming into being in the twenties diffusion was the accepted explanation of cultural change in archaeology. The man who was perhaps most responsible for slowly and surely putting across a modified diffusionism was Gordon Childe in his *Dawn of European Civilization* (1925), his *Danube in Prehistory* (1929), and his *Bronze Age* (1930). In these books we see developing the climate of the new prehistory which carefully builds up the details of the succession of cultures in each area and sees cultures or elements of cultures spreading from one area to another. This diffusionism is not open to the charges levelled —and very correctly—at the hyperdiffusionist school, namely that it neglected all semblance of scientific methods.

In our own modern prehistory the Childe and Childe-derivative archaeologists are working in the best traditions of scientific method. Before two cultural objects or traditions are compared it is made certain that they are functionally and formally identical. It is one of the great confusions of the Elliot Smith-Perry school of hyper-diffusion that they never made sure that the objects they were comparing were functionally and formally identical; they rashly compared the Pyramids of Egypt with the Pyramids of Central America, monuments which are admittedly superficially identical, without realizing that while the Egyptian pyramids were tombs, the American pyramids were great temple platforms on the top of which religious rites were performed. The diffusionists of the new prehistory do not make these mistakes; they compare only cultural features which are formally and functionally identical and only derive the one from the other if such a historical process can be shown to be chronologically, geographically and historically possible.

Let me take as an example of the modified Childe diffusionism of the twenties, which had become standard archaeological theory in the thirties and forties, the megalithic tombs of Western Europe. In the nineteenth century the likenesses between megalithic tombs from Denmark and the Orkneys to Iberia and the Mediterranean were appreciated, but there then seemed only one of two possible explanations for these likenesses. The first was that these monuments had come into existence naturally in different areas as part of the natural cultural evolution of man. The second view was that there was a great megalithic master race which spread from one centre—Denmark itself was sometimes canvassed, and at other times it was some unspecified area in the east Mediterranean—indeed at the present day the general view is to talk in fairly vague terms of an Aegean or Minoan-Mycenaean cultural spread. We have already seen how Elliot Smith and Perry took over this idea of a megalithic race which became part of their pan-Egyptian colonial movement.

But when one gets down to detailed analysis of the spread of megalithic tombs in the western Mediterranean and Western Europe, one sees that no one facile explanation will suffice. In the first place megaliths do not represent a single unitary movement but contacts along the same routes over many centuries. Many scholars at the present day would date the first passage graves of Ireland and Brittany to the middle of the third millennium BC, but it is equally clear to many who look at the decorated entrance slab at New Grange that it must be compared with the spirals and lozenges on the blocking slabs at Castelluccio in Sicily, the Hal Tarxien slabs in Malta, and the designs on the shaft-graves at Mycenae—all evidence of contact across Europe in the sixteenth or fifteenth century BC. Secondly, even if one allows initial movements of people with a basic tomb type and a basic custom of collective burial, that basic tomb type is probably a rock-cut tomb; megalithic architecture may have arisen independently in the west Mediterranean in several places, Malta for instance and southern Spain and southern France. Tomb types in these separate areas developed often along parallel lines.

There has been in recent years an even greater revolution in the generally accepted modified Childe diffusionism. Northern antiquaries have for a long time classified the megalithic tombs of Denmark, Sweden, and Germany into three successive groups: first, the *dos* or *dysse* usually confusingly translated into English as 'dolmen'— a word used in English in a very wide variety of ways; secondly the passage grave; and thirdly the long stone cist. Now while at first it was argued that these three stages represented a simple evolutionary sequence in Northern Europe, the later diffusionist view was that each stage represented a movement from some part of Western Europe and the west Mediterranean. The last stage, characterized by the long stone cists, was thought, for instance, to have spread from the Paris basin somewhere between 1600 and 1400 BC and this is still a possibility; the second stage, characterized by passage graves, was, and indeed still is, seen as part of the spread of passage graves in Western Europe between 2500 and 1500 BC. The first stage, that characterized by *dosar*, *dysser*, or *dolmens*, was less easily explained but there were vague parallels to these monuments in Western Europe—various archaeologists pointed hopefully, if a little uncertainly, at the polygonal dolmens of Portugal and the rectangular dolmens of the Pyrenean area. But now as the result of detailed researches by Professor Becker of Copenhagen we see the tombs of this first stage as something quite different, as the translation into megalithic architecture of earth graves that existed in Northern Europe before; what is more, Professor Becker reminds us that these first-stage megalithic tombs are not collective tombs at all and never contained more than a few burials. It now looks as though we must accept the independent origin of some megalithic architecture in Denmark.

Very gradually we are entering on a new mid-twentieth-century stage in our ideas of the interpretation of prehistoric change: indeed after the distractions of the hyperdiffusionists and the fairly generally accepted reasonable doctrine of the modified diffusionists we are back to one of the Victorian positions when, said Lowie, as I have already quoted, 'evolution . . . lay down amicably beside Diffusion.'

There is now, then, a very considerable change going on in the view which people are beginning to have and express about the nature of cultural spread and change in prehistory. Yet some would say that while we may be forced to modify our views in detail on some points, the over-all picture would appear to be something like this: that the elements of a higher food-producing civilization came into existence in the Near East in and around what Breasted called the Fertile Crescent, and that the elements of this culture-complex spread all over the world, not of course diffused by a master race, but by varying peoples in varying stages. Perhaps there were two great stages, the earliest of which was called by Childe the Neolithic Revolution of, perhaps, ten thousand years ago, and the second the Urban Revolution of five thousand years ago, which produced urban literate communities in Egypt and Mesopotamia. This was the picture painted in Gordon Childe's *What Happened in History?* and *Man Makes Himself,* and in the series of books written by H. J. E. Peake and H. J. Fleure called *The Corridors of Time.* The first volume of *The Corridors of Time* was published under the title *Apes and Men* in 1927, and the tenth and last volume, called *Times and Places,* in 1956; Peake had himself died in 1946. Now Peake and Fleure were not Elliot Smith-Perry diffusionists; indeed Peake used to say with a twinkle that he found it difficult to look at the world through a Perryscope. But the Peake and Fleure books, on which my generation of archaeologists was brought up, admirably demonstrate the modified Childe diffusionism of the twenties and thirties.

Let me quote from the preface to the last volume, *Times and Places*:

> It has been the writers' belief in compiling the *Corridors* that south-west Asia was the region in which man made the great step forward from dependence on hunting and collecting to food-production by cereal cultivation; and to this the keeping of domestic animals was soon added. While there may have been small attempts at cultivation begun independently elsewhere, and there were probably several more or less independent beginnings of the domestication of animals, the spread of food-production from south-west Asia and Egypt and its consequences remain major features of the story of mankind.

Now this is very true, but how 'major' is another story which Peake and Fleure omit entirely from their ten-volume essay down the corridors of time, and this omission is deliberate and planned. 'The Americas,' they write, 'with their largely distinct problems have not been included in the survey.' But the problem of prehistory is the problem of the prehistory of man, not the prehistory of the Old World. We find the same refusal to study the American evidence in Gordon Childe's *What Happened in History*? Yet the story of New World cultural origins is of paramount importance to our study of Old World cultural origins.

The Western World learned about the Americas for the first time in 1492, when Christopher Columbus discovered America when looking for the Indies. The subsequent explorers of Central America 'succeeded in doing,' to quote Carleton Coon's words, 'something every archaeologist dreams of, which is to step backwards in time . . . they marched into an Early Metal Age civilization comparable in many respects with that of Egypt in late Predynastic or early Dynastic times, and that of earliest Sumeria.' Since then historians and archaeologists have wanted to find out how this civilization came into existence and what relation it bore to the civilizations of the ancient world. The Spanish found themselves in the New World face to face with the Aztecs of Mexico who met them in battle with composite weapons of obsidian blades set in grooved wood, and the Maya of Yucatán, Guatemala, and Honduras who built elaborate temples and pyramids and who had no metal at all except a few gold and copper ornaments, and the Incas of Peru who had complicated networks of roads like the Roman roads, suspension bridges of rope, and domesticated animals—the llama, the alpaca, and the guinea pig. All these three native American civilizations—Aztecs, Maya, and Incas—were based on agriculture. And both the Aztecs and Maya, as well as other American Indians in Mexico, could write; they had a pictographic script which they wrote on deerskin books.

How had all this come about? Of course Christopher Columbus was not the first European to visit America. Leif Ericsson got to Greenland and Vinland in AD 1001. It is not suggested that Leif Ericsson introduced the elements of higher civilization to America, but it has been the fashion to suggest that someone did do this, and, of course, particularly the fashion by those who could not bring themselves to believe that anything could be invented or discovered on more than one occasion. While there has been a fashion, there has been no agreement on who brought (or was thought to have brought) the higher civilization to America. To some they were Phoenicians or the Lost Tribes of Israel, to others Welshmen like Madoc or Irishmen like St Brandon, to others Negroes from Africa, Japanese, Polynesians, or people from the supposed and supposedly sunken continents of Atlantis, Lemuria, or Mu—or of course if you were looking at prehistory through a Perryscope, it was brought by the ancient Egyptians themselves. It is really the old problem that we discussed in the first chapter; we are back in the legendary epoch of prehistoric research.

That may be so, but in studying American cultural origins we are engaged in what is almost a controlled laboratory experiment. That is why American prehistory is so important to the prehistorian working in Europe or the Near East or India. We are now in a position to give objective answers to American prehistoric chronology—

94

answers based first on dendro-chronological researches but latterly on Carbon-14 analysis. The Carbon-14 dates in the Bat Cave in New Mexico show that American Indians were growing maize by 4000 BC. Further comparative analysis and study shows that almost every cultural element in the New World can be explained as of purely local growth. There are still some puzzles—the gourd, cotton, the sweet potato and Indian corn are among them—but on the whole the story as it looks at this moment is that about 10,000 BC man came to America, probably across a dry Bering Straits, and that by 5000 BC all of the New World except the Eskimo country was occupied. By 4000 BC agriculture had begun in the New World and in due course these early agricultural communities developed into the Urban Civilizations of Central America; and at the moment it looks as though this development happened in America without any contact of a serious nature from abroad. It was in fact a tale of independent cultural evolution.

If this was so in America, we now ask, why not elsewhere in the Old World? Rice cultivation probably developed independently in south China when wheat and barley were being cultivated in the Near East and maize in America. Indeed it is probably true that we have been creating our own difficulties to a certain extent, and inventing the problems of diffusion versus local evolution by conceptualizing certain ideas. Agriculture and civilization are two such ideas; we talk about the origins of 'agriculture' and discuss whether 'it' started in the Near East and spread from there to China, India, and America when all the time what we should be talking about is the discovery of the cultivation of wheat and barley in Egypt, Palestine, and Iraq, of rice in eastern India and south China, and of maize and squash in Central America. We have created our own problems by grouping together all these material advances in culture under one word 'agriculture'. And it is to a certain extent the same with 'civilization.' We describe civilizations in Egypt, Sumeria, the Indus Valley, China and Central America and ask how they came into existence, flourished, and decayed, and what was their genetic interrelationship—without perhaps realizing that because all these societies had writing and cities and a high skill in metal-working they are not necessarily connected.

It would seem, then, that we have travelled a long way from the earlier diffusionists to our present very modified diffusionism with its recognition of the real existence of independent evolution; perhaps that long way had to involve the distractions of the hyperdiffusionists. I said in the previous chapter, that the development of the prehistoric record had brought us to a stage where we were studying the development of cultures in time and space, that we were studying a gaily coloured layer cake. The first concern of prehistoric archaeology was the study of the chronological and spatial position of these layers. It was also, secondarily, the study of their inter-relations if the time-space positions permitted such inter-relationships; this study, which after all is the only way in which we can begin to understand cultural change and its complex mechanics, is one we should undertake without any preconceived ideas of diffusion and independent invention.

We should approach this study of cultural origins and change at the present day with the lessons of American prehistory very much in mind, for here it does seem that man developed from the Mesolithic food-gathering savages of the end of the Ice Age through to the literate urban communities of Central America without significant contacts observable in the archaeological record from the Old World of Europe and Africa, on the one hand, or Asia and Indonesia on the other. If there is one lesson more than any other which mid-twentieth-century research is forcibly injecting into our idea of prehistory it is that of the independent development of prehistoric American culture. The news of the early dating by Carbon-14 of the first American agricultural communities has come like a tremendous blast of cold wind blowing down the corridors of time where walked scholars who seemed to have arrived at a fixed picture of world prehistory and cultural origins in terms of Neo-lithic and Urban Revolutions in the Near East.

VI

The Idea of Prehistory in the Study of Language and Race, and in Politics

GUSTAV KOSSINNA

We have seen how prehistoric archaeology came into existence as a new perspective of the human past—as an extension backward of ancient history and forward of geology—and how by the second quarter of the twentieth century prehistory had developed its own expertise, both in methods and results. The main result seemed to be a gaily coloured layer or Neapolitan cake which changed as one turned the cake round. This was the complicated space-time cataloguing of cultures. We have also seen that the first task of the prehistorian seemed to be the listing and definition of these cultures, and his second the study of the nature of their inter-relations. I hope we have seen, too, that, as the twentieth century advanced, no simple explanation in terms of independent cultural evolution or of diffusion unilaterally from one centre was really acceptable, but what was and is acceptable is the notion that the development of cultures in prehistory (as in historic times) is a complicated process in which independent evolutionary forces and outside influences both play important parts.

It was not surprising that, as prehistoric archaeology developed, scholars should begin to say that it seemed to be becoming an arid discipline of cultural listing, or a sort of archaeological cultural chess. The question was asked, Was the prehistoric archaeologist going to tell us no more about the prehistoric past than the lateral and vertical moves on a three-dimensional chessboard? Was all we were going to get out of research in prehistory a catalogue of changes in material culture? These questions were asked particularly sharply by archaeologists interested in the findings of neighbouring disciplines —of geographers, anthropologists and historians themselves interested in this aspect of the human past. There were also the language scholars, the linguistic palaeontologists, and others who were themselves concerned in certain aspects of very early human history.

Let us take first the linguists and the physical anthropologists; they were concerned with the facts of language and race and were asking how their conjectural history of language and race fitted in to the record of prehistory, and also what new and definitive answers prehistory could give about the origins of language and race.

Now language is a cultural feature of man, but it only becomes apprehended by the archaeologist who is studying the material culture of man when it becomes material, i.e., when it is written down on coins, stones, or books. We are here concerned with prehistoric times— the times when there was no writing on coins, stone and books: we deal with preliterate times, so that one might say that, *ipso facto*, the prehistorian cannot tell anything about the spread and diffusion of languages. The prehistorian cannot answer you when you say, 'When was the Celtic language introduced into Great Britain?' Or, more specifically, 'Is it true that the Q-Celtic languages now surviving in Irish, Scots Gaelic, and Manx were introduced into the British Isles before (or long before) the P-Celtic languages which survive in Welsh and Breton, and survived until recently in Cornish?'

It is unfortunately not quite so simple as that. If as prehistorians we could wash our hands of linguistic equations and problems we would be happier: if we could just say, well, no language survives from any prehistoric culture so we can tell you nothing, all would be well. As it is we cannot do this. The great family of languages variously referred to as the Aryan, Indo-European, or Indo-Germanic languages came into existence somewhere between Eastern Europe and the Himalaya, somewhere north of the Turkish-Armenian-Iranian mountain barrier, perhaps on the plains of Hungary, the Ukraine, or Turkestan. The speakers of this basic Indo-European language and its derivative languages, like Sanskrit, Celtic, Slav, Greek, Latin, and the rest of them, spread out from this area all over Europe and southwest Asia and into India, where Aryan-speaking peoples (here the noble caste actually called themselves Aryas) overran and destroyed the urban Bronze Age literate civilization of Harappa and Mohenjo-Daro. It is often argued that the material culture of these Aryan speakers ought to be identifiable and that we should be able to say of a collection of tools and weapons, here are the material remains of the Aryans.

There is a great difficulty here. An invasion of people as seen in a sudden change in the material culture of a region does not necessarily betoken a change in the language spoken. The reverse is often true: a new language may be introduced into a country and there is no apparent evidence for the appearance of new people as shown by new material cultural traits in the archaeological record. The Norman Conquest of England and Wales, on the one hand, and the conquest of Brittany in the fifth and seventh centuries A D by settlers from southwest England and Wales are good proofs of these statements. We do not speak Norman-French in England although there is plenty of archaeological evidence of the material culture of the Normans in England; the Breton language is a version of Old Welsh or Old British but there is hardly a trace in the material culture of fifth–seventh-century Brittany of the arrival of these new speakers from Britain. It is very difficult to argue correlations for invading cultures in linguistic terms and the archaeologists who say

99

that the Beaker Folk spoke Q-Celtic or the Late Bronze Age invaders of Britain spoke P-Celtic are extending possibilities into facts and treating very tentative hypotheses as proven.

But do not think that what I am saying is a counsel of despair. Let us look at the Iberian peninsula. Here at the time of the Roman conquest were tribes, mainly in the north and northwest, who spoke Celtic languages; these people must have come into Iberia from outside France, and if there is to be an archaeological component to these people it cannot be any people before the urn-field invaders of the late Bronze Age and early Iron Age—people who came into Spain between 850 and 600 b c and the distribution of whose material remains agrees quite well with that of the Celtic place-names and Celtic tribes of Spain. Here in Iberia is a legitimate and valuable correlation that can be made between the archaeological invasions of the prehistorian and the facts of the student of languages. In Spain we can go a little further. Here there exists a language—Basque—unlike any other in Europe; it must have been there before the arrival of the Indo-European speakers who introduced Celtic into Iberia. If this was so, and it is difficult to argue any other case, then Basque must be the survival of a Bronze Age language spoken in Spain and south France. We cannot go any further than this but it is not impossible that Basque was the language of some of the Neolithic Chalcolithic tomb builders of southwest France and north Spain in the early second millennium b c.

We cannot really go so far as this, and indeed seldom can we go so far as we have done in Spain. We cannot for example say who introduced the Q-Celtic language into Ireland or who really introduced the Greek language into Greece or the Italic tongues into Italy. This is quite naturally one of the frustrations of prehistory—one of the very many frustrations—or should one say that it is one of the defining limitations of prehistory?

The same sort of problem is found when we come to deal with the problems of race. Race to the anthropologist is a group of people with physical characteristics in common—inherited physical characteristics that is—and though we may not agree with this or that classification

100

of race, we do not, without any training in the mysteries of physical anthropology, have any difficulty in distinguishing the Nordic type with its tall stature, blue eyes, fair hair, and fair skin, from the Bushman with his kinky hair, black skin, short stature and steatopygia. Any ordinary political cartoonist quite untrained in measuring heads and working out cephalic indexes has no difficulty in drawing a Negro and a Chinese as different racial portraits. The various races of man developed in the last few thousand years, and it is reasonable to suppose that in the past, that is to say in the remote prehistoric past, when human groups were not in such close contact with each other as in later phases of history and were mating from the same sort of stocks, geographical groups of people were more racially pure than they are at the present day. If this is so, then, it has been argued, cannot the cultures of the prehistorians be given some more semblance of reality by a description of the physical appearance of the people? Can we not in the earlier phases of prehistory equate physical types with cultural groups? Can we not say that the so-called warrior cultures of Northern Europe—the people who buried their dead in single graves with battle axes in the second quarter of the second millennium BC—were created by people who belonged to the Nordic type?

There is inherently here a methodological difficulty, and an obvious one like that involved in the tracing backwards of language groups. It is that the fleshy parts of our prehistoric ancestors do not survive; the hair, eyes, and skin on which so much of racial classification is based and by which we ourselves so easily describe racial types, do not survive. Very rarely are we given special clues: the bodies in the Danish peat-bogs like Tollund preserve for us the oldest examples of flesh in prehistory, and the older bodies from the Danish tree-coffins of the Bronze Age are also of some value in determining racial types.

There are also representations of human beings in early art but they give us little in the way of racial characteristics to go on until we come to the Egyptians who in the nineteenth dynasty decorated the walls of the royal tombs with representations of four races of mankind, namely the Eyptians themselves whom they painted red, the Asiatics whom they painted yellow, the Southerners or Negroes whom they naturally represented black; and a fourth type, the Libyans, Westerners, or Northerners, whom they represented as white with blue eyes and fair beards. Even this information, imprecise though it is, goes back only three thousand years.

A second factor which vitally affects any attempt we make to take man's racial history back and to equate aspects of it with archaeologically derived facts is that it is not only the fleshy parts that do not survive; sometimes nothing survives at all. Whole skeletons—bone as well as the mantle of flesh—may disappear in acid soils, and the moment cremation became a general custom, as it was, for example, extensively in the Middle and Late Bronze Ages in Britain, we were left with nothing at all to assist our study of the physical remains of man except a heap of ashes. It is, then, not really possible to say a great deal about the physical types of early man, but we can make a few useful generalizations. The type of person normally found in megalithic tombs in Northwestern Europe, for example, has a skeleton not far removed from that standard in the so-called Mediterranean race. This is not a surprising fact in reality, when we consider that most of the builders of these tombs spread up into Northern and Northwestern Europe from the Mediterranean. This may be as far as we can go; and yet, perhaps, not quite—the population of Ireland, for example, is probably most extensively derived from that of the megalithic builders and it is tempting on this ground and on the identity of the megalithic builders skeletally with the present-day Mediterranean race to see their bones clothed with a sallow skin, their eye-sockets filled with dark eyes, and the tops of their long heads covered with black hair.

The existence of this Mediterranean type in our Neolithic and Chalcolithic communities of megalithic and non-megalithic types in the British Isles is quite beyond dispute and it contrasts very markedly with the Beaker type found in inhumed single graves of the Early Bronze Age in Britain—tall, strongly built types with robust, squarish faces.

Thus far we can go in correlating the facts of archaeology and physical anthropology; no further than in the correlation of facts of archaeology and linguistic history. And, as we think about it, we see that it is not really very far. Race, language, and culture are, as we well know in the modern world, separate ways of classifying and grouping men. The Jews, for example, were until recently a detribalized nation bound together at least in part by religious ties; they were a cultural unit not necessarily speaking the same language—though they preserved Hebrew as a liturgical language, and Hebrew in a much modified form in Judaeo-German or Yiddish—and not necessarily belonging to the same race although people in Western Europe, whose only acquaintance with the racial types of the Middle East was through seeing Jews, thought they did form a racial group. When we see, as in this example of the Jews, how very clearly it is impossible to equate racial, linguistic, and cultural groupings in modern times when we have very full documentation to assist us, we see it is a hopeless task to try to do it in prehistoric times when we have no written sources, when we have to judge language facts by later distributions of place-names, and our physical types are often skeletons or jars of ashes from funeral pyres.

The idea of prehistory which we must now have with regard to the early spread of races and languages must essentially, except in a few rare cases, be separated from our ideas of cultures. We must alas, for the most part, keep the builders and bearers of our prehistoric cultures speechless and physically neutral. This may seem an unsatifying conclusion. And so it is; but then much of our prehistory is unsatisfying and difficult, tantalizingly meagre and sketchy. We can appreciate this and accept the limitations of prehistory along with its excitements. But what is good enough for you and me—this hard scholarly doctrine—was not good enough for the politicians and propagandists who, in the recent past, have been using the facts or apparent facts of prehistory to confuse the public.

They have done this because the facts could so easily be grafted on to the apparent facts of racism. Now racism of course is something very different from race. To quote the late Ruth Benedict's neat statement on racism: 'Racism is not, like race, a subject the content of which can be scientifically investigated. It is like a religion, a belief that can be studied only historically. Like any belief that goes beyond scientific knowledge it can be judged only by its fruits and by its votaries and its ulterior purposes.' Racism is the dogma that one race, or one ethnic group for that matter, is superior, other races or groups inferior, and that indeed the superiority and inferiority is something congenital, something to which people are condemned or blessed by nature. It is of course a comforting and comfortable doctrine for those said to be the superiors. It is, also of course, entirely wrong; it is a form of racial modern superstition. Some of us remember vividly how racism was made a principal basis of German policy. But all this started long before Nazi politics.

The classic statement of racism is that of Comte de Gobineau, who between 1853 and 1857 wrote his *Essay on the Inequality of Human Races*. Gobineau was a Frenchman and he was really developing the ideas of Boulainvilliers—the Comte de Boulainvilliers—who argued that the nobles of France, the survivors of the feudal aristocracy, were the remains of the Germani, the Teutonic barbarians who had overrun the Roman Empire, while the populace of France was of quite a different racial clay. The populace were the old Gallo-Roman stock of France; racially Mediterranean and linguistically Celts. They were, according to Boulainvilliers, destined to racial inferiority as the Franks were to racial superiority. The Comte de Gobineau—and I always feel that it is not insignificant that these doctrines were being developed by two members of what was supposed to be the racially superior element in France—developed Boulainvilliers' ideas. He taught that the hope of the world, not merely the hope of France, lay, and indeed always had lain, with the fair-haired Teutons; and he was now calling these people *Aryans*. It was the current fashion to call them this, and what he meant, of course, though imprecisely, was what physical anthropologists would, at the present day, call the Nordic race.

Perhaps I should re-emphasize here that there is nothing imprecise and nothing wrong in the idea of the

Aryans; it is a precise linguistic term, in origin and in present usage linguistic. It is the extension of this linguistic term to include racial characteristics—those of the Nordic race—that was the first confusion; and the second that these Aryan-Nordics were superior, were the leaders of the world. It was not meant to be a succession of confusions in the Comte de Gobineau's writings; far from it. He was not engaged in deliberate confusions; he was merely unable to think straight about these matters. But it was meant to be a confusion by the time it became an accepted part of Nazi policy, because its progenitors and advocates did not want to think straight, nor want their deluded followers to think straight; and after all nobody who bothered to analyse the Nazi-superiority-Aryan-Nordic myth and then to think of the fair-haired Teutons could come to any flattering conclusions about the racial affinities of many of the German political leaders from Hitler downwards.

The really interesting thing about the Comte de Gobineau is that he was not preaching a nationalist doctrine of racialist prehistory. His theme was international, was pan-European in scope. He dedicated his *Essay on the Inequality of Human Races* to George V of Hanover, and this is what he wrote himself about the whole problem:

> Gradually I have become convinced that race overshadows all other problems in history, that it holds the key to them all, and that the inequality of people from whose fusion a people is formed is enough to explain the whole course of its destiny. I convinced myself at last that everything great, noble, and fruitful in the works of man on this earth in science, art, and civilization derives from a single starting point; it belongs to one family alone, the different branches of which have reigned in all the civilized countries of the universe.

Gobineau was, as indeed all out-and-out racialists preaching about a Master Race must be, a hyperdiffusionist—in many ways like the hyperdiffusionists we spoke about in the last lecture, such as Miss Buckland, Sir Grafton Elliot Smith, W. J. Perry and Lord Raglan. But the cultural hyperdiffusionists demanded a master people; Gobineau's was a Master *Race*. He had divided the world into the Whites, Yellows, and Blacks; his 'fair-haired Teuton-Aryans' were the only representatives of the White Race and he was therefore forced to classify the Alpines of Central and Eastern Europe as Yellow, or of Yellow extraction, and the Mediterraneans as of Black extraction! Of course Gobineau was writing in the early 1850s before the publication of *The Origin of Species*, and well before the development of scientific physical anthropology with its accurate measurements and classifications.

Gobineau was a Frenchman but the Germans were not slow to adopt his racial views, or a modification of them. Richard Wagner found Gobineau's work excellent and popularized his writings in Germany. The Gobineau Vereinigung was founded in 1894: and five years later Wagner's son-in-law Houston Stewart Chamberlain published his *The Foundations of the Nineteenth Century*. It was actually published in German at Munich that year; the English translation appeared in 1911. These two large volumes made Gobinism a cult and an important cult in Germany. The Kaiser read them aloud to his sons, had them distributed to officers of the army, and directed that they should be displayed in bookshops and in public libraries throughout Germany. Chamberlain's book went through edition after edition and without any doubt whatsoever became part of the underlying unconscious assumptions of the German nation—or of a large part of it.

Houston Chamberlain had to operate and propagate his racialist doctrines at a time when a great deal was becoming known about physical anthropology, and he could not go on insisting that the Master Race was one of tall, blonde, fair-skinned, blue-eyed giants. So they were just called Teutons, but they were not Teutons in the strict sense of people who spoke a Teutonic language: there were Celts and Slavs also in this 'single pure stock' which were the original great ones, the really chosen people: but some were brunette and broadheaded and others blonde dolichocephalics. But as his doctrines were accepted and developed there was a steady shift away from even a prejudiced and confused physical anthropology; in the end it was all a *mystique*—a *mystique* of the

106

Great German Race versus the rest and particularly against the Jews, that, following Houston Chamberlain, were confusingly called Semites. Now it is true that Hebrew is a Semitic language, but there are many other Semitic languages, notably Arabic. The use of the phrase Semitic in a pejorative sense was part of the denigration of the Jews as anti-Master-Race people. We can see how far Houston Chamberlain had himself gone towards this racialist *mystique* when, for example, he says: 'Whoever reveals himself German by his acts, whatever his genealogical tree, is a German,' and again, 'One can very soon become a Jew . . . it needs only to have frequent intercourse with Jews or to read Jewish newspapers.'

Small wonder, when one reads ridiculous sentences like this, that though *The Foundations of the Nineteenth Century* was received with such signal honour in Germany it remains 'among the most confused, pretentious and over-written books that racism has produced.' Small wonder, too, that the Nazis took over these ideals which the Kaiser had read aloud to his sons. *Mein Kampf* absorbed them, and liked getting round the obvious difficulties of physical appearance in German leaders by the Chamberlain trick of 'a German soul in a non-German body.' How far we have got from physical appearance if we begin talking about souls.

Even so there were difficulties; the German opposition to Communism meant that the Slavs had to be dropped out of the Master Race stock of the chosen people; and after the Rome-Berlin axis was invented, it too had to be given a racialist basis and the Mediterranean race had to be looked at a little more charitably, although a great deal of emphasis could be and was laid on the Germanness of northern Italy.

I have deliberately taken the main development of racialist theory from Gobineau to Chamberlain and on to Alfred Rosenberg—the ideologist of Nazism. Rosenberg was born in 1893 in Estonia, then a part of Russia: he joined Hitler, Röhm and Hess in Munich in 1919 in the nascent Nazi party. In editing the party newspaper, *Völkischer Beobachter*, he drew on the ideas of Chamberlain and on *The Protocols of the Learned Elders of Zion*, a nineteenth-century fabrication concerning a supposed Jewish

107

plot for world domination. According to him the Germans were racially pure and were descended from a Nordic race that derived its character from its environment which was a pure, cold, semi-Arctic continent, now disappeared! The Germans, the only descendants of this pure ancient race were entitled to dominate Europe: their enemies were Russian Tartars, Semites (which included Jews), the Latin peoples and the Roman Catholic Church. These ridiculous travesties of cultural history, as set out in his speeches, were published under the title of *Blut und Ehre* (1934–41). At the Nürnberg trials Rosenberg was adjudged a war criminal and hanged in 1946.

Because I have emphasised Gobineau, Chamberlain and Rosenberg, this must not be taken to mean that it was only the Germans who had this exaggerated racialist Master Race myth at the basis of their thought. It existed also in America, and the best and classic example of American racialists was Madison Grant—the man who in 1917 produced his remarkable book *The Passing of the Great Race*. The thesis of this book is a very simple one, and there is hardly any need to mention at this stage who the great race was—it was our old friends the Nordic Teuton leaders, and Madison Grant said very outspokenly: 'The amount of Nordic blood in each nation is a very fair measure of its strength in war and its standing in civilization.' So far, so good, the Gobineau French and German racialists might say, but as they read on through *The Passing of the Great Race* they had to exclaim 'but no further,' because Grant's thesis was that the Germans and French of today were the descendants of the peasants, and that the Great Race of Nordic Teuton leaders had left Europe and were now in America. Even in 1917 Madison Grant was prepared to insist uncritically that the majority of Americans were Nordic; he declared that that moment was the chance for America to capture the glorious position of leadership which Europe had lost. Henry Fairfield Osborn, the *doyen* of American archaeology and anthropology at that time, wrote a preface to Grant's book in which he said that what America should do was to prevent 'the gradual dying out among our people of those hereditary traits through which the principles of our religious, political or social foundations were laid down and to stop their insidious replacement by traits of less noble character.' Other American racialist books were even more inept, preaching the patriotic duty of Nordic racial hygiene.

We had something of this kind, but the other way round, in England, where it became a denigration not a praising of the Nordic-Teutons. There were ancient historians who saw the Germans in 1914 as 'what they were fifteen centuries ago—the barbarians who raided our ancestors and destroyed the civilization of the Roman Empire.' But no one was a patch in this matter on the German racialists, who harnessed prehistory to their racial-mad chariot and did so because they felt somehow that history must be, or must be made to be, on their side. 'The one and only thing that matters to us,' Heinrich Himmler is supposed to have said, 'and the thing these people are paid for by the state, is to have ideas of history that strengthen our people in their national pride.' And here of course prehistory, where we really know so little and guess so much, came into its Germanic own.

In 1939 courses in prehistoric archaeology were given in no less than twenty-five German universities, and archaeological research was lavishly supported by the Nazi State. Professor Hermann Schneider of the University of Tübingen writing in 1939 said this: 'The year 1933 witnessed the victory of an attitude towards the history of the culture of Germany which gave to the Germanic element of all that is German a significance previously unthought of. The best of what is German is Germanic and must be found in pure form in early Germanic times. Archaeological research thus found itself faced with the pleasant task of examining and reconstructing the real essence of Germanic life and customs.' These were the words of a Professor at Tübingen; if a Professor alleged this much, how much more were politicians ready to employ racialism and derive support for their doctrines from the prehistoric record. Himmler said: 'Prehistory is the doctrine of the eminence of the Germans at the dawn of civilization.' Here we have naked and unashamed the political view of prehistory.

It might well be thought that such a doctrine could hardly be sustained for long even in Nazi political circles, merely by constant reiteration. But there were unfortunately not lacking prehistorians who would supply necessary information for supporting these doctrines. The best —or worst—exponent of this political idea of prehistory was Gustav Kossinna. His dates were 1858–1931: he began as a philologist and then turned to prehistory. In 1895 he set out his views on prehistory in a lecture at Cassel. In 1902 he was appointed Professor of German prehistory in the University of Berlin, and held this post until he died nearly thirty years later.

German interest in the German national past dates back to the same time as the first stirrings of British interest in the British past. Camden's *Britannia* was published in 1587, and at the same time the same back-looking curiosity in a new nation state was operating in Germany. In 1615 Philip Cluver (1580–1623) published a large book called *Germania Antiqua*: its aim was to assemble everything that existed in classical writers about the ancient Germans. At this time the Germans were depicted as rude barbarians and also at this time, as in England and France, there was little or no effort to interpret the ancient Germans from a study of their material remains. This had to wait in Germany as in England and France for the geological and antiquarian revolutions of the second quarter of the nineteenth century. Actually two Germans at this time, Danneil and Lisch, seem to have hit on the Three Age system independently of the Danes.

The nineteenth century saw great development in German archaeology but, at first, in the field of classical and Near-Eastern archaeology. A branch of the German Archaeological Institute was set up in Athens in 1875 and in that year excavations began at Olympia under Ernst Curtius. They occupied the six winters of 1875–80, cost £30,000, and the expenses of the last winter season were borne by the Emperor William. Later, from 1899 through to 1914, the Germans, led by Koldewey and Andrae, were excavating at Babylon and Ashur. These latter were most thorough and efficient excavations which revealed stratigraphic succession of occupations and effected the total clearance of town sites. Nor should we forget that Schliemann though not an official German archaeologist—and indeed himself proud of his American status—was by birth and upbringing a German; although his earlier excavations were much criticized, his later work under the guidance of Dörpfeld was very good. Certainly in the last quarter of the nineteenth century the Germans were coming into their own as archaeologists.

But Kossinna complained that the new German archaeology was concentrating on classical lands and was, therefore, prepared implicitly or explicitly to describe the Germans of antiquity as poor barbarians. He complained that the Berlin Academy of Sciences welcomed representatives of Egyptian, Greek, Roman, and Oriental antiquity but no one dealing with German prehistory. He further complained that the organization of museums in Prussia made the museum of German prehistory appear as of less importance than the collections illustrating Hottentot and Papuan life. He kept insisting that this was wrong and kept quoting the historian Sybel's doctrine that 'a nation which fails to keep in living touch with its past is as near to drying up as a tree with severed roots. We are today what we were yesterday.'

Kossinna deliberately set out to prove the importance and greatness of the Germans through prehistory. He inflated chronology so that everything seemed to have started in Germany and spread out from the superior Germans to the inferiors all around. He was quite certain about the megalith builders, for example, and had them moving out from Germany all over the ancient European and Mediterranean world. We can laugh at these fantasies of Kossinna at the present day; but he was serious about them, and they were seriously taken up by German racialists who readily accepted the apparent proof provided by prehistory of the antiquity and superiority of the Germans.

Other countries have supplied similar examples of the use of early history and prehistory for political ends. Mussolini had great illuminated maps by which the Roman Empire gradually enlarged from Rome to its fullest extent under Trajan. Then the illumination went out abruptly and, as Professor Grahame Clark remarks: 'The observer waited in vain who hoped to see unfolded successive stages in the decline and disintegration of the Empire; the lights went out abruptly and the process of growth began anew.' And these prehistoric political tricks continue; a few years ago I saw in Madrid maps of the Iberian colonization of Europe and it was some while before I realized that I was looking at a distribution map of Beakers dating from say 2000 to 1800 B C.

I have given you some examples of the use of a false idea of prehistory in recent politics; the best example was of course in Germany, where a perversion of prehistory was crossed with racialism and anti-Semitism. The Nazi regime did not last long enough for us to have maps deriving all civilization from the Germanic north, but this might have been arranged in time. As Hitler himself said: 'There is no such thing as truth. Science is a social phenomenon and like every other social phenomenon is limited by the benefit or injury it confers on the community.'

Let us now turn briefly to Russia. Here since the revolution the possibilities of archaeology have been pursued by the N. Y. Marr Institute of Material Cuture, a research organ of the Academy of Sciences of the U S S R. Now one of the avowed functions of the Research Institutes of the Academy of Sciences of the U S S R is to 'organize and lead the struggle against pseudo-scientific theories and trends in the various fields of knowledge,' and the late Professor A. M. Tallgren of Helsinki has told us how this struggle has disposed of the archaeologists whom he knew in the twenties. In his survey of Archaeological Studies in Soviet Russia, Tallgren said sadly and cynically after giving a long list of his liquidated archaeological colleagues: 'How rich humanity must be if it can dispense with such good men.' Now, of course, these men were being disposed of so that a particular brand of prehistory could be taught in Russia, and there is no confusion or shame or uncertainty about the Russian desire to do this, as there was none in Nazi Germany. Stalin himself said that the significance of historical ideas lies in the way they hamper the development and progress of society. He was saying in another way Engels's words: 'Men

112

make their own history.' To a certain extent this is true, and my predecessor as archaeologist in giving the Josiah Mason Lectures, Gordon Childe, said roundly and frankly: 'It is just no good demanding that history shall be unbiased.' Childe himself was praised in Soviet archaeological circles. In his *The Crisis in Bourgeois Archaeology*, Mongait says:

> contemporary bourgeois archaeologists . . . are the vanguard of reaction, against which we lead and will continue to lead a bitter struggle. . . . Bourgeois archaeology, like history, is distinguished by extreme idealism (A. Goldenweiser). The English historian Collingwood goes even further . . . and Daniel follows after Taylor. . . . There are also progressive scholars who are friends of our country and who understand very well the universal significance of our science. . . . One of these is Gordon Childe; Childe has not yet succeeded in overcoming many of the errors of bourgeois science. But he understands that scientific truth is in the socialist camp and is not ashamed to call himself a pupil of Soviet archaeologists.

We have already referred to the work of Lewis H. Morgan and how he set out a series of ethnic periods leading from Lower Savagery to Civilization. What is important is to realize that Engels was enormously influenced by Morgan. He summarized Morgan's ethnic periods in his *Origin of the Family* (1884) and there declared in a statement which of course cannot be sustained for a moment that 'Morgan is the first man who with expert knowledge has attempted to introduce a definite order into human prehistory.' At first the Russians liked the system of ethnic periods but it was not readily usable as a classification of archaeological material, and in the twenties of this century the Russians, like everyone else, were using the Thomsen system of the Three Ages of Stone, Bronze, and Iron. In the 1930s they abandoned this and began to speak of three grades of society, namely pre-clan society, clan society, and class society. Efimenko said that pre-clan society was represented by what we would call the Lower Palaeolithic. The rest of the Palaeolithic and the rest of prehistory was mainly clan society; first, the matriarchal clans which were alleged to be Upper Palaeolithic and Mesolithic, then a transition to patriarchal clan organization beginning with the Neolithic and from then on a steady decline to class society—what was called 'the period of the disintegration of the clan.'

I want to say only two things about all this. First, that it is a deliberate going back to the psychic unity of man, to the ideas of natural, social, or supra-organic evolution. No diffusion was allowed at all. Secondly it was a hypothetical system of cultural evolution which when devised was then imposed on the archaeological material. We have seen how the first ideas of prehistory were pre-archaeological and how an archaeological idea of man's early past was developed painfully over the last hundred years. We have seen how responsible scientists like Elliot Smith rejected the idea of archaeological prehistory as unsatisfactory, and how politicians rejected prehistory based on archaeology because it did not suit their ends, and replaced it by an invented prehistory based on premises like the superiority of the Germans or the natural evolution of society from pre-clan through clan to class.

I hope you are beginning to see what a great choice there is for you in ideas of prehistory. To misquote Engels, you see that men make their own prehistory. What a choice lies in front of you at present! You can have a Russian Marxist prehistory, a German chauvinist prehistory, you can have Elliot Smith and his Egyptians, or you can ever bury your head in the sand and sigh for the good old days of the Phoenicians and the Druids, or, emerging from the past, pay your subscription to the Atlantis society or buy books on Tiahuanaco. Or you can, with as little prejudice as any man can bring to any problem, try to see what the prehistoric record does tell, and what at this moment we should try to evaluate as the lessons of the prehistory of man, what as historians we do now think of man's earliest history.

VII

Prehistory and the Historians

GORDON CHILDE

I have attempted to trace, albeit in very summary fashion, the way in which prehistory as an academic discipline and a branch of learning came into existence in the last hundred and fifty years, and to discuss the different ideas of prehistory which have been held at different times—before and after the development of archaeology as a deliberate technique of studying the material remains of the past. This development, which put an end to legendary or mythological prehistory—to prehistory based entirely on speculation—did not rule out the possibilities of prehistory which, while using archaeological methods like distribution maps and the comparative study of material remains, yet flourished with such a disregard for facts as virtually to revert to mythology and to the days of pre-archaeological prehistory.

I now want to consider what has, in fact, been created

by a century and a half of archaeological investigation and prehistorical research. In the first place a branch of learning, an academic discipline, has been brought into existence and one which, as we shall see in the last chapter, has at the moment surprisingly great claims on the interest of the general public. What is this branch of learning? What does it try to tell us? What does it tell us? What are its relationships to kindred fields of study like human geography, sociology, anthropology, history? And what is the relevance of its teachings, its conclusions, its perspective of the past to us as private individuals, as political individuals, and as educationists? These are some of the questions about the nature and relevance of the idea of prehistory that I am now proposing to discuss.

First, of course, a word about the eternal question which besets everyone who sets out to discuss the nature of any branch of learning; is it a science or not? In the end it is all a matter not of absolute values and ultimate decisions but of terminology and definitions. We ourselves have made these terms science, the humanities, the arts, the human sciences, and whether a new branch of learning which we as scholars have created, developed, and defined falls within any of these terms depends on how we define them—how we define them now and how we have defined them in the past.

Originally science meant all knowledge and in the seventeenth century when the Royal Society, which we nowadays regard as the stronghold of 'science', came into existence it comprised all knowledge. It certainly dealt not only with what we should now call the natural sciences but with the material remains of man, and in its early days counted as members men like John Aubrey and Edward Lhwyd, who were antiquaries. Yet they were polymaths and Lhwyd himself wrote about asbestos and fossils as well as about New Grange and Cornish and Breton. And there was nothing odd in the early days of the Royal Society in a Fellow of my own College in Cambridge, Martin Lister, reading papers to the Royal Society both on zoology and on Roman remains. A liberal polymathy comprised all these interests. Aubrey, Lhwyd, Lister did not call themselves scientists.

116

EDWARD LHWYD

When Sir Isaac Newton became president of the Royal Society he discouraged an interest in the material remains of the past and the Royal Society began to confine its interests to what we now call the natural sciences, to the study of nature, and to exclude the study of man's culture. Here began or was first formalized the distinction between the study of nature and the study of man—between the sciences and the arts, or between the natural sciences and the human sciences. The arts or humanities, by definition, deal with man as a cultured animal, in fact the only animal with culture, with a transmittable body of ideas, customs, beliefs and practices dependent on that main agent of transmission, language, and in the last few millennia of his existence, that other main agent of cultural transmission, the written word.

It is beyond dispute that by practice in school examination and university degree system and in general paralance we distinguish between the natural sciences (or the natural and physical sciences) and the humanities (or the arts or the human sciences). It is also beyond dispute that this distinction is not only one of subject-matter but of fundamental principles; the natural scientist hopes to find laws which are immutable and which are indeed the ultimate facts of the natural world. The scholar who devotes himself to man and his works may hope, and may piously declare that he aims, to find laws of a similar nature. But this he never does unless general statements, like 'Man is a religious animal,' or 'Man is a historic animal' (meaning that no known societies exist in which there is no religion and no awareness of the past) are thought to be general laws.

There are then two customary ways of using the word science; it can mean knowledge or it can mean knowledge of nature. There is of course a third way in which we use the word science or particularly the adjective 'scientific.' That is as applied to method. We speak of the scientific method when we mean the use of principles of collecting evidence, deduction, experimentation—but these have by now become so much a general part of the methodical exploration of all knowledge that we sometimes find people thinking the scientific method is no more than just common sense.

When, then, we are asked, 'Is prehistory a science?' we are really being asked one of three questions, namely, 'Is prehistory a part of knowledge?' and 'Is prehistory concerned with nature?' and 'Is prehistory scientific in its method?' The answer to the first and third questions is in the affirmative, but to the second the answer must surely be no. Prehistory deals with man and not with nature and is not part of the natural sciences: it is part of human not natural history. It comes, of course, very close to the natural sciences and indeed is the bridge between geology and history. It deals a great deal with periods of time, the Pleistocene and Holocene, which are the concern of the geologist and natural historian, and uses a great number of techniques which belong to the natural and physical sciences, such as Carbon-14 analysis, fluorine analysis, the petrological analysis of stone, the metallurgical analysis of metals, to mention only a few of these analytical techniques.

The prehistorian is dependent for a great deal of his information about the biome of early man, the vegetation in which a society flourished, the plants they collected or grew, the animals they hunted or reared, on expert advice from zoologists and botanists; and it is a prerequisite of the training of a prehistorian, more especially if he is going to concern himself with the long millennia of human development comprised by the terms Palaeolithic and Mesolithic, that he should be thoroughly grounded in the natural sciences which serve him. It is also true that in dealing with the Lower Palaeolithic cultures the prehistorian is little different from the Pleistocene geologist who is studying the fossils of horse or hippo in the same deposits. The cultural fossils may appear little different from the organic fossils in the technique required for their discovery and study. But Acheulian hand axes are cultural fossils and the product of the human mind and human craftsmanship. The scholar who studies Neanderthal man's bones is a natural scientist while he who studies Neanderthal man's artifacts is a historian, however little cultural material he has to work on. This break in the study of man grows as the complexity of the archaeological evidence grows. We would not today confuse the specialist who studies our bones with the man who studies our crafts or culture. We should not make this confusion in prehistory because in the very remote past the cultural and the physical records are so thin and one scholar can be master of both. Prehistory is then a humanity; it is the earliest phase of historical study. It is part of history and those who would call it science are using the word science in a very special way. Prehistory is part of human history and, therefore, suffers from all the problems inherent in historical method—the difficulty of evaluating evidence, the inability of writing without some form of bias, and the constantly changing picture of history according to the changing ways and ideas and preconceptions of historians.

But it suffers from far more difficulties than those which beset the writer of history, difficulties based mainly or entirely on written records. The main difficulty is that by definition prehistoric archaeology is dealing with pre-written sources only; so that all prehistory is anonymous. We do not know the name of the architect of Stonehenge, or of the man whose body was recovered from the Tollund peat-bog in Jutland and whose noble features look calmly at us across twenty centuries. We do

119

not know the names of the communities or societies whose material culture we study and classify as cultures. This is why prehistory reads with such difficulty to so many people, with its Beaker people and its Long Barrow men not to say its pieces of archaeological algebra like Iron Age I (*a*) i. And the difference between pre-written and written history goes much deeper than names and the absence of names. It is this more fundamental fact that from preliterate sources we know and can know only a part of the total culture of these preliterate societies. Prehistory not only deals with anonymous societies grouped into divisions of its own devising; but it is inevitably mainly concerned with the material cultural aspects of these anonymous societies. This is, as I have said, inevitable from the nature of the archaeological source, for what survive from prehistoric times are stone tools, bronze weapons, hut foundations, tombs, field walls, and the like. We are accustomed to speak of the imperishable ideals of a society, but the prehistorian is witness to the sad fact that the ideals perish, and it is the cutlery and chinaware of a society that are imperishable. We have no way of learning the moral and religious ideas of the protohistoric city dwellers of Mohenjo-Daro and Harappa but their drains, their brick rubbish shutes, and their terra-cotta toys survive.

It is in the fact that the prehistorian seems to be concerned mainly with varieties of houses and tombs and cutlery and safety pins that many have found the greatest criticism of the subject. Prehistory would appear to be concerned, some have argued, with the non-essentials of human life: 'We do not wish to know,' say these critics, 'about the types of safety pin used by the Early Iron Age farmers of France, or the details of tomb construction adopted by the metal prospectors of 2000 BC in Western Europe; we want to know the essentials of these societies—how they lived, what they thought, what were their ideals and illusions.'

Now there is some truth and much distortion in this view of prehistory. Prehistory is not concerned only with types of safety pins and tombs; it uses these and other facts to build up a picture of prehistoric life—how food was obtained, what sort of villages and farms existed, what were the crops and field systems and animals, what were the types of burial custom. Certainly prehistory concerns itself with the types of life of prehistoric societies. But equally certainly it does not speak about the spiritual, mental, and moral culture of these societies. It cannot speak of the social organization or the religious beliefs of prehistoric society, and this is a fundamental limitation of prehistory. When prehistorians speak of the ideas and ideals of men before writing, they are making guesses—intelligent guesses by people best qualified to make them, but nevertheless guesses.

Some prehistorians have attempted to break through this limiting factor by using two methods of special, and to my mind doubtful, validity. The first is the use of ethnographical comparisons, and the second is the acceptance as fact of hypothetical evolutionary systems. Let us discuss the use of ethnographical parallels first. Balked by the absence of detail in prehistory, or so it must seem as one looks at the limitations and intractability of the surviving archaeological material, some prehistorians have turned to surviving preliterate societies, namely the present-day primitive societies studied by the anthropologist, which only just miss being classified as prehistoric. These archaeologists seek in these existing societies a guide to the way of life of our prehistoric ancestors. A good example of this is provided by W. J. Sollas in his *Ancient Hunters*, first published in 1911.

To a certain extent the use of these ethnographical parallels is fair and just. The prehistorian can understand the nature of the prehistoric artifacts he studies only by comparing them with those used by modern primitives. But some prehistorians, not content with inferring the function of prehistoric artifacts from the identity of form between prehistoric and modern artifacts, have gone further and have assumed that the identity of form between the artifacts of modern preliterates and of prehistoric societies means not only probable identity of function in material culture, but also identity in the social structure and mental and spiritual beliefs of the two societies being compared. Surely this assumption is most fallacious: because the Magdalenian folk of south France have certain parallels in formal material culture with the

Eskimo, we cannot argue that they have the same economic organization, marriage customs, or beliefs about the after-life. It is not even reasonably probable that the same form of artifact should imply the same kind of economic organization, let alone social structure, or mental and spiritual culture; and this inherent improbability is borne in on one the more one studies the variety of social and mental culture that exists at the present day among the so-called primitive communities of the world. In a word, as Ehrenburg has put it, 'it is a delusion to think that "experimenting" with the so-called primitives of yesterday and today provides scientific material for prehistory and history.'

I am not saying that by trying to understand the life of the Tlingit and Haida in British Columbia, for example, or of the Bushman Hunters of South Africa, one does not get a better view of the inside of food-gathering communities in the past than if one confines one's viewpoint to modern twentieth-century food-producing cultures in southern England; nor am I saying that the technology and spiritual life of preliterate societies do not give us hints and suggestions of great value in the interpretation of prehistoric artifacts. The same is true of the study of modern folk cultures, as Professor Grahame Clark has often insisted, but again it gives only suggestions and hints, and cannot be used deterministically. Ethnographic determinism is as dangerous as any other determinist doctrine; we cannot say, for example, that because the Tasmanians when they were discovered, described, and destroyed in the nineteenth century were formally Palaeolithic, that they are a complete guide to the ideas and beliefs of all Palaeolithic communities. And the same is very true of the food-gathering communities which in a general way we can compare with the Palaeolithic and Mesolithic hunting-fishing communities. Indeed there is a tremendous variety among the beliefs of hunting communities; compare the rich and leisurely British Columbians with their *potlatch* economy and their fine woodwork and blankets on the one hand and the Tasmanians on the other.

The real point here is that, quite apart from our present problem, there is no coincidence between the material

122

GRAHAME CLARK

and non-material aspects of culture. Indeed why should there be? And if we once accept this, it is clearly useless to expect the moral and mental culture of modern primitives in the same or apparently the same state of material culture as some prehistoric primitives, to give us a real or true guide to the moral and mental culture of the prehistoric society.

If ethnography does not help us in reconstructing the total picture of prehistoric societies, what can we turn to? I have already referred to the evolutionary systems of cultural development which were being proposed in the nineteenth century. Spencer, Tylor and Jevons suggested stages in the supposed religious evolution of man, while Bachofen, McLennan and Morgan suggested stages of social evolution. I have already spoken of Morgan's ethnic stages and how they were approved of by Engels and how Marxism has made use of these fallacious evolutionary systems. The interesting thing, for our immediate purpose, is that some prehistorians have accepted these evolutionary sequences as of equal validity with the sequence of technological stages associated with Thomsen, and it is from these equations that we find the Neolithic Age being spoken of as one of primitive communism, the Bronze Age as seeing the beginnings of private property, and so on. Now all this is a process of hypostasization; of treating proposed evolutionary sequences as facts, and of forgetting that all the nineteenth-century cultural evolutionary sequences, like the sequence proposed by Soviet archaeologists for pre-clan, clan, and class society, are merely schemes, ideas, and projects. They may be right, but they are invalid as a source for the mental and spiritual life of prehistoric man—as invalid, though as suggestive, as our ethnographical parallels.

But there is this difference between ethnographical parallels and hypothetical systems. The facts of the ethnographical parallels are accurate; it is merely using them as deterministic parallels that is wrong. But the 'facts' of the supposed evolutionary cultural sequences of man are not necessarily facts at all; these sequences are mainly the result of nineteenth-century evolutionary thought and a belief that cultural or supra-organic evolution must necessarily follow physical evolution, and which arranged all social and cultural phenomena in such sequences. It is easy to set out baldly the basis of this nineteenth-century thought: monogamy and monotheism were the practices and the virtues of the nineteenth century, and the extremes from these practices, namely polygamy or promiscuity and animism, were necessarily what the earliest men thought and practised. Of course, subsequent anthropological work has shown that many of these alleged early stages in belief and practice just do not exist, and that their arrangement in sequences is pure hypothesis.

We are then driven back from modern primitives and the schemes of historical anthropologists to the hard archaeological facts. How hard are they, and how exciting can we make our modern story of ancient man? We must repeat that our only source for information on prehistoric times is archaeology. In the Josiah Mason Lectures which Professor Gordon Childe gave in Birmingham in 1947–48, and which were published in his book *Social Evolution* in 1951, he asked how far it was legitimate to infer non-material facts about prehistoric man from the material remains that survive. I do not want to go over the ground he trod so well in dealing with this question, but let us put the question in its crudest form like this. When we look at the great paintings in the hillside of Lascaux are we really able to say that they were done for purposes of sympathetic hunting magic? When we see the great stone tombs in France with their carved goddess figures, can we say that these are the tombs of chieftains who imposed their beliefs on an impoverished population? When we find two people, a man and a woman, buried in the same grave, does it mean suttee or murder, or that they both died at the same time through some disease? Let us look at this archaeological problem in a different way. If one day—which God forbid—my own University City of Cambridge is reduced to uninhabited ruins, and no written records survive of its life, the ruins will shows several rectangular buildings like King's College Chapel, many cinemas, the Examination Schools, and public buildings like the Corn Exchange which was until recently used mainly as a skating rink. The archaeologist of the future, if he has no written or epigraphical sources, will surely lump together all these rectangular buildings as 'public ritual buildings,' and, in a way, so they are whether they be College chapel, skating rink, or cinema. One thing will puzzle the archaeologist and that is the ruins of the Church of St Sepulchre, one of the four round churches of Britain. This too would clearly be a ritual or cult building; it is obviously not a tomb or a house. Perhaps the archaeologist of the future would distinguish two cultures in Cambridge, one having long rectangular buildings and the other having round buildings. Within the justifiable limits of exaggeration to emphasize a point, this is just the sort of way, uncritically, that archaeologists might work.

Now let us look at Gordon Childe's conclusions. Here are his words:

> In certain circumstances, and always with reserve, archaeology can provide some indications as to the form of government and of the family, the recognition of rank, the distribution of the social product and the practice of war. It is never likely to be able to tell us anything about the administration of justice,

the penalties needed to enforce it, nor the contents of any laws, the way in which descent rather than the inheritance of property is determined, the effective limitations on the powers of chiefs, or even of the extent of their authority. The content of religious belief and the nature of the prestige conferred by rank are irretrievably lost.

I have deliberately quoted at length these words by one of our most distinguished prehistorians, whose mind was so agile and nimble that he took an almost perverse delight in archaeological experimentation—in turning upside down theories which the orthodox (including himself of a few weeks or months or years before) taught and wrote about. He himself in his *Scotland Before the Scots*, admittedly a wicked experiment in archaeological interpretation, did not practise the reservations which he laid down in his Mason lectures. These reservations are right ones, and it follows from our acceptance of them that not only is the record of the prehistoric past limited, not only can we not answer so many of the questions which the interested public ask, but also that it is impossible to equate any of the theoretical stages of cultural evolution with archaeological stages. Let me say one thing about this again: when I wrote of the work of the Russians and the application of archaeology to their schemes of pre-clan, clan, and class society, I did not mean that the schemes were necessarily wrong; merely that it was wrong to pretend that the record of prehistoric archaeology proved these schemes. The unfortunate fact that must be faced is that prehistoric archaeology does not tell us so much of what we want to know as historians of man about man's early life.

And here perhaps we come to the very nub of an extremely important and interesting problem. Why do historians in a general way pay so little attention to this fourth division of the study of the human past; while recognizing ancient history why do they not give more recognition to prehistory? Just take a look at any of our short histories of this country from Trevelyan through Feiling and Arthur Bryant to Winston Churchill; in all of them all we get about pre-Roman Britain is a short curtain-raiser and we are moved hurriedly and with relief on to the Romans with their names and dates and inscriptions and good historical habits. Let me quote the words at the end of George Trevelyan's introduction to the beginnings of British history:

> The study of the Mingling of the Races in Britain, ending with the advent of the Normans, covers a thousand years of history very dimly descried, succeeding to many thousands more of archaeological twilight. The era of Celt, Saxon and Dane is like Macbeth's battle on the blasted heath. Prophecy hovers around. Horns are heard blowing in the mist, and a confused uproar of savage tumult and outrage. We catch glimpses of giant figures—mostly warriors at strife. But there are ploughmen, too, it seems, breaking the primeval clod, and we hear the sounds of forests crashing to the axe. Around all is the lap of waves and the cry of seamen beaching their ships.

These words were originally written in 1926 but they are still relevant. Historians are taking a long time to integrate prehistory into their general view of man. There are many reasons for this. First, the material of prehistory is, as we have seen, difficult and different. Secondly, it is often tantalizingly inadequate and refuses to provide the answers to so many problems we ask. In the third place, I think many historians are still suspicious of some of the preoccupations and ideas of prehistoric archaeologists.

It has seemed to me that one of the reasons why prehistory was not more immediately accepted by historians as part of their general story was that the prehistoric archaeologists were sometimes apparently suspect because of their association with geographers. I mean here nothing, of course, rude or derogatory about geographers, nor that the geographer has not a role and function in the study of prehistory. Indeed the geographer has very important, interesting and vital roles. There are endless definitions of the scope and nature of geography—almost as many as there are Professors of Geography—but what everyone is agreed about is that the geographer in the modern convenient arrangement of fields of study is concerned with the face of the earth, and is perhaps at his finest when he is describing small areas of the earth's surface, when he is engaged in regional geography. Here the geographer is doing what the good historian does when he takes a small period of time in an area and tells us all he can about the historical context of the space-time area so defined. Similarly the geographer is at his best in giving us geographical contexts; he tells us for example what the face of Brittany looks like and describes the features of that rugged sea-girt countenance—the mountains and rivers, the driving rains and thick sea-mists, the harbours and the sardine and tunny fisheries, the isolated granite farmsteads, the long cold meadows. In any geographical context there are natural and cultural features to the landscape, and if we analyse the cultural landscape we will find that it is of two kinds—the living and functional cultural landscape, and the dead, fossil, cultural landscape. The geographer, as he describes his region or chosen area, as he analyses the man-made features of the face of the earth and constructs his geographical context, is constantly coming up against the dead and the dying—prehistoric earthworks, Roman villas, Norman *mottes*, dead and decaying towns, deserted villages, nineteenth-century disused railways. All these things he sees as he describes the living towns and villages and farms and factories of the landscape. The geographer then shares the non-functional cultural landscape with the archaeologist, and the barrows and banks and ditches of pre-Roman Britain are as much his concern in one way as they are the concern of the pre-historian in another.

We surely do not need to labour this point, but let us take just one example: Dartmoor. The geography of Dartmoor must most necessarily be concerned with the dead aspects of the landscape—the cultural fossils of the period generally referred to as from the Early Bronze Age through to the Roman Conquest—a period of some fifteen hundred years from which survive stone rows and circles, megalithic tombs, field pounds, huts and smelting sites. The geographer must needs know about all this if he is ever to read accurately the face of Dartmoor, and so must the prehistorian if he is trying to reconstruct historical contexts and understand why and

128

how people lived on the moor in the pre-Roman centuries. The geographer and the prehistorian meet in the map. Prehistory is vitally concerned with the distribution of the material remains which survive from the prehistoric past; indeed this is the first of its two techniques of interpretation—examining an antiquity or a culture in space and time. Space means the map, and the distribution map has been a key feature of archaeological interpretation, research and exposition for nearly a hundred years.

But the geographer does not study one element of the cultural landscape alone: he sees it as part of the total landscape made up of natural and cultural features. Very gradually this geographical approach to prehistory became popular. Antiquities and cultures were studied not merely distributionally on a blank map of Europe but geographically on a map of soils, rocks, climate and vegetation, and in relation to these facts of physical geography. The German geologist Gradmann did this in 1898 and as a result argued that prehistoric settlement was virtually confined to open country—country of a steppelike character—and this of course included the loess lands. In England O. G. S. Crawford began preparing maps of antiquities and studying them against the background of prehistoric vegetation, or, rather, the postulated background of prehistoric vegetation; his maps of *Neolithic Wessex* and *Roman Britain* are perhaps the best known examples of this work.

In 1916 two geographers working at the University College of Wales, Aberystwyth, namely H. J. Fleure and W. E. Whitehouse, argued that from distributional studies alone one could say that prehistoric man lived on the hilltops and only gradually moved down into the valley bottoms. Of course there is some truth in this. We know how in the early period of Roman occupation the conquered Ancient Britons moved from hillforts like St Catherine's Hill and Maiden Castle to lowland settlements like Winchester and Dorchester. But Fleure and Whitehouse made this a general law: the law of the Early Valleyward Movement of Population in Southern Britain, and as a general law it began to look dangerous, and deterministic, and unhistorical. In 1923 Sir Cyril Fox published his *Archaeology of the Cambridge Region* and showed how the pattern of settlement had changed in relation to the natural vegetation; he was able to show that what Fleure and Whitehouse had observed in Wales was a specialized instance of the real trends in British prehistory, namely the shift from primary to secondary areas of settlement, from light easily worked soils to the hard, difficult, waterclogged, clayey soils; that it was a Welsh mountain version of a general principle. Indeed, Mortimer Wheeler has cynically described the work of the Aberystwyth geographers as a doctrine 'naturally popularized by a school of able and eloquent geographers working in a mountain environment.'

Following on his studies in East Anglia, Fox tested his thesis in relation to England and Wales as a whole, and we see his ideas set out in *The Personality of Britain*, first published in 1932. Here Fox combined the ecological-distributional ideas of people like Gradmann and Crawford with the ideas of positional geography developed by Halford Mackinder in his *Britain and the British Seas* and the 'personality' idea of the French geographers. But it began to savour rather strangely of geographical determinism; prehistorians and historians began to get suspicious. They began to get more suspicious when other prehistorians referred to Fox's interesting and suggestive conclusions as 'Fox's laws.' In the revised fourth edition of *The Personality of Britain* he says, 'The further a continental society is from the Mediterranean the more barbarous it will be,' and confesses that he was driven to study the geographical factor in prehistory because he was looking for a unifying force to take the place in preliterate days of the individual factor in historical days.

But should we assume that the geographical factor is any more powerful among preliterate societies in the prehistoric past than it is in historic times; should we underestimate the personal factor in prehistory just because the persons are nameless? I do not want to take up any more space here in discussing the validity of the ideas of geographical determinism in prehistory: most people today would say that there were no mandatory geographical laws in prehistory, as in history, except the obvious extreme mandates of climate and natural

resources. These when stated baldly are obvious plati-
tudes—it is clear that the climate and resources in the
South and North poles have not made those areas centres
of population and cradles of civilization. It is equally
obvious that a bronze industry cannot originate and
flourish naturally or easily in an area where copper and
tin do not exist. My concern here is to suggest that these
geographical ideas of prehistory arose and flourished for
a while and did something to make prehistory suspect to
the formal historians; it became to some of them for a
while something like historical geography, emphasizing
a facile and inaccurate explanation of a series of facts
which might not be explicable at all. The historians then,
in their approach to prehistory, have had to get over
their dislike of the geographical determinist bias.

They have also had to get over their intrinsic dislike of
the over-advocacy of the importance of prehistoric archaeology, of the school of scholars who said in all good
faith that a sherd of decorated pottery was worth all
Herodotus, or that 'to the peoples of the world generally
. . . Palaeolithic man has more meaning than the Greeks.'
They have also had to get over the way in which men
trained in the methods and results of prehistory have
extended their studies to include the whole of history
and produced books which seemed to put the study of
written history into an unimportant position *vis-à-vis* prehistory. Admittedly, as the American anthropologist
Lowie has said, written history is 'only the final scene of
a lengthy drama,' and it is surely impossible for thinking
people today to study history by studying only written
history; that would be, as Charles Letourneau said half a
century ago, like trying 'to reconstruct a book from its
last chapter.' But a prehistorian like Gordon Childe goes
too far in the opposite direction when he calls a book that
deals mainly with prehistory and protohistory, *What
Happened in History?* and we see the same sort of problem though not in such a degree in Carleton S. Coon's
The History of Man (published in America as *The Story of
Man*). Nevertheless, books such as these and the writing
of prehistory as a whole have done a great deal to jerk
modern historians into a new universalist outlook.
World or Universal History existed in the sixteenth cen-

tury, but it gradually became more and more specialized and detailed, particularly since 1881 when Pope Leo XIII opened the Vatican archives and, in England, since 1886, when Sir Henry Maxwell Lyte became Director of the Public Record Office. A new and detailed form of history developed, sharply described by Geoffrey Barraclough as 'that devoted worship and admiring contemplation of its own navel which has made many otherwise not unsympathetic observers ask whether the measurable results justified the immeasurable expenditure of effort.' Whether this be true or not, we must agree with Butterfield when he says that 'Universal history has ceased to hold a prominent place in our interests presumably because it spreads the mind over so wide an area that the knowledge can hardly avoid becoming too thin. '

I shall comment again on the view that the knowledge becomes too thin; here let me underline the phrase 'spreads the mind.' Is that not really what we want historians and prehistorians to do as well as to concentrate on the intricacies of nineteenth-century Germany or the construction of Stonehenge, and is not that why we welcome H. G. Wells's *Outline of History*, Gordon Childe's *What Happened in History?*, and Coon's *The Story of Man* even if we criticize them in detail? Here is the broad sweep which we need. To quote Barraclough again: 'The crying need today is not for specialization, which means fragmentation, but for integration and this requires not simply specialized knowledge but the general historical understanding of the course of European and indeed extra-European history.'

There has been one recent historian who revived universal history and tried to make historians look at the world other than as a Western European world. I refer to Professor Arnold J. Toynbee, but his conclusions and his basic thesis do not recommend themselves to a prehistorian. His basic thesis, as I understand it, is that we can distinguish a certain number of complicated societies which he calls civilizations with their cities, technologies, and religions, and that we can study them in isolation from their past and their contemporary civilizations and we can see them behaving as living organisms.

Let us look very briefly at Toynbee in relation to the

problem usually referred to as that of the birth of civilization. Archaeological research has shown that the earliest
traces of civilization—that is to say societies with writing
and a city life—are found in Egypt, Palestine, and Mesopotamia. We know now that writing, urban life, and the
arts of metallurgy were invented in one centre or in
several centres in what Breasted called the Fertile Crescent. Now, of course, it is vital to Toynbee's thesis to
study the origin of the oldest of his civilizations in the
Near East. This he does, and these are his conclusions:
he attributes the origin of civilization to the desiccation of
the Sahara and represents this desiccation as a challenge
to be overcome. He makes the valleys of the Nile and the
Tigris-Euphrates not delectable as do the geographical
prehistorians like Peake and Fleure, but horrible jungle
swamps—another challenge to be overcome. Toynbee
then says that six things happened to man as the Sahara
dried up and became a desert: first, some people stayed
there and perished; secondly, some people stayed where
they were in the Sahara, mastered the challenge of the
environment, and evolved a nomadic way of life; thirdly,
some went south and retained their old way of life,
becoming the Dinka and Shilluk. In the fourth place,
some people went north, according to Toynbee, and
became the Neolithic agriculturists of the European continent—although Toynbee does not tell us how these
folk discovered agriculture on the way along a route
where cereals do not occur wild. Fifthly, there were those
who plunged into the jungle swamps of the Near East
and met this challenge by inventing civilization; and
sixth and last, there were those who plunged across the
sea and made the Minoan civilization.

The real tragedy of Toynbee's writing on the origin of
civilization is that here is a distinguished historian with a
flair for universal history who somehow failed to understand the archaeological record. Instead of using his
great gifts towards the acquisition and synthesis of knowledge to provide us with the universal history we so
much wanted in the middle of the twentieth century, he
confused the early history of man with his predeter-
mined patterns, and thus further discredited universal
history and the study of prehistory in the eyes of

specialist historians.

In concluding our discussion on these matters I must make two confessions. First, prehistorians have been rather slow to popularize their work. The lead given by Lubbock's *Prehistoric Times* in 1865 has not been followed until very recently. You may find this a strange statement of mine and may think that the railway bookstalls disprove it any day. It is true that there are books on how the archaeologist works and the method and limitations of prehistory, but, to the best of my knowledge, there does not exist a book setting out impartially, authoritatively, and simply the prehistory of Europe. We still await a good book telling the public what went on in Europe before the Roman conquest and while such a gap exists in the literature how can one blame the Toynbees of the world for displaying an ignorance of prehistoric matters?

Secondly, prehistory has only recently become consciously a historical discipline and realized that its job is writing history and not classifying antiques. We have a great backlog of scholarship to make up here because the excavators and museum curators still naturally tend to think that the work of archaeology is virtually over when they have dealt with it. There is, to my mind, a great danger here—the danger of a new antiquarianism in archaeology. I am not in any way decrying excavation, which is the surgery of the fossil landscape and the essential prerequisite of any archaeology, nor museums, which are the Public Record Office of the prehistorian. But I am saying that we too often pay lip service to prehistoric archaeology and declare it to be the discipline of writing history from archaeology, without perhaps writing any history ourselves. The description of artifacts was one stage in the development of prehistory: the description of cultures was a second. A half a century ago we could have Grahame Clark saying that 'the science of archaeology might well be defined as the study of the past distribution of culture traits in time and space,' and Gordon Childe defining the task of prehistory as 'largely devoted to isolating . . . cultural groups of people tracing their differentiations, wanderings and activities.' These were true statements but prehistory was then still in a stage on the way to the historical study of prehistorical times. In his *A Study of Archaeology*, W. W. Taylor urges that the prehistorian is not concerned with listing cultures but in studying culture, not in delimiting regional variations of little importance within a historical context but in studying the context as a whole. As Brøndsted has said, 'the goal of archaeology is the history of culture.'

And to that goal we now move slowly and surely. A really notable stage in that movement was represented by Grahame Clark's *Prehistoric Europe: The Economic Basis* (1952). In this book the individual and unimportant varieties of material culture are gone; gone too is the microtomic specialization of industry and culture. Here we are looking at the development of man's economic life in prehistoric Europe portrayed on a broad canvas. Here, at last, is prehistory as the historians—or at least the economic historians—understand it. And here at last is one pattern of the future of prehistory

VIII

Prehistory and the Public

GLYN DANIEL

In *The Times* of London for 19 July 1956, there appeared a curious little paragraph amusingly headed by an intelligent sub-editor, 'Judicial Archaeology.' This is what the paragraph said:

> During the hearing in the Chancery Division at the Royal Courts of Justice of a war damage case concerned with Buildings in the City of London, Mr. Justice Vaisey told Mr. Harold Williams Q.C. 'There is nothing more interesting than the investigation of the history of old sites. This very building in which we are now sitting was built on the site of a very old farm, and the actual site of the well which was used for watering the cattle is in the building.

The report did not tell us any more—what Mr Williams said in reply, nor is it relevant to our present purpose. What is relevant and interesting here is Mr Justice

Vaisey's first sentence: 'There is nothing more interesting than the investigation of the history of old sites.' You must admit that this is a forthright and sweeping declaration.

A few days before I read this rather unusual report in *The Times* I had been reading a review in the *Antiquaries Journal* by my Cambridge colleague Miles C. Burkitt, who had been teaching prehistory in Cambridge for over thirty years and who in 1921 produced the first book in the English language to be called *Prehistory*—some seventy years after Daniel Wilson first used that word. In this review Mr Burkitt said, 'prehistory at present is popular,' and we cannot disagree with this brief alliterative doctrine. I had for some while a close connection with archaeological broadcasting, and from the existence and continuance of archaeological programmes on radio and TV, from the large audiences they attract, from the most extensive and interesting correspondence they promote, it is abundantly clear that prehistory is popular at present in Britain, that the public like prehistory, want prehistory, and often prefer prehistoric archaeology to many other subjects. Indeed in an unguarded moment at a College Feast in Cambridge I heard Sir Ian Jacob, then Director-General of the BBC, say that the two popular things on television seemed to be archaeology and show-jumping.

You will all have heard of the German Kurt Marek who wrote under the pseudonym C. W. Ceram and the success of whose book *Gods, Graves, and Scholars* is by itself a proof of the widespread popularity of prehistoric archaeology. In his second book, translated into English under the title of *The Secret of the Hittites*, Ceram says: 'The British were, and are, fascinated by archaeological questions as are no other people in Europe'; and the number of books on archaeology pouring from our presses surely emphasizes this point of view.

Here surely is a curious state of affairs and it is worth analysing and discussing. Why is prehistory, which was not in existence as an organized discipline or a branch of learning a hundred years ago, a popular subject today? Is it due, as some have said, kindly or unkindly according to how you interpret their remarks and the adjectives

137

they choose, to the existence of a small group of people who have found it easy and amusing and profitable to put archaeology across by the means which success in this great new educational and entertainment medium of television apparently demands, namely panel games, documentary films, personality promotion? There is some truth in this and I would be guilty of a very false modesty if I tried to deny that radio programmes like *The Archaeologist*, and television programmes like *Animal, Vegetable, Mineral?*, *Buried Treasure* and *Chronicle* had not contributed a great deal to the present popularity of prehistory. But the interest was there before: the agencies of mass communication have, as I believe they can do with any branch of learning, widened the audience in quality and multiplied it enormously in size; but archaeology was an attraction and prehistory was popular long before Marconi invented the wireless and Sir George Barnes the Third Programme.

In the year (1956) when Penguin Books celebrated their twenty-first anniversary we tended to think that popular education was a very recent thing; but this is not so. The British Association for the Advancement of Science was founded in 1830–31 and its primary and principal purpose was the dissemination in the widest possible way of scientific knowledge. In 1851, at its Ipswich meeting, it admitted Ethnology as a distinct section, and during the period 1840–70 many contributions on prehistoric archaeology appeared in the Geology and Ethnology sections.

Thirty years before the foundation of the British Association, George Birkbeck of Glasgow had started the first course of lectures which developed into the first Mechanics' Institute. The London Mechanics' Institute was founded by Birkbeck and Brougham in 1826 and in the second quarter of the nineteenth century these Mechanics' Institutes were very important in disseminating knowledge to the lower middle classes. G. M. Young has argued that the work of the Society for the Diffusion of Useful Knowledge and the Literary, Scientific and Mechanics' Institutes was mainly literary, and was concerned with, for example, the Bible and its commentaries, Milton, the economists, philosophers and historians;

science, he said, apart from phrenology, 'for want of apparatus, did not much affect the workman: the culture of the self-educated man was still literary.'

This may be true of physical science, but geology and the geological beginnings of archaeology were certainly finding their place in the work of these institutes. Let us take William Pengelly as an example. Pengelly was a private tutor at Torquay who was fascinated by archaeology; he had an overmastering passion for geological research. He explored Kent's Cavern in 1846 under the auspices of the Torquay Natural History Society, and later under the British Association for the Advancement of Science. He superintended the excavations at Windmill Hill, Brixham, from 1858 to 1859, which convinced many people of the authenticity of the antiquity of man. He himself, as well as being an original worker, was most keen on popularizing his finds and his first success as an expositor was in the Torquay Mechanics' Institute. Wherever Pengelly lectured, whether to the Mechanics' Institute at Torquay, or to the Sciences Lecture Association in Glasgow, and on whatever subject—Kent's Cavern, the discoveries on the Somme, the caves at Mentone—his audiences were large and enthusiastic.

The *Encyclopaedia Britannica* first appeared (in three volumes) between 1768 and 1771 in Edinburgh; and the *Chambers's Encyclopaedia* (completed in 1868) by the Edinburgh firm of W. R. Chambers, who had already published *Chambers's Journal* since 1832, the *Educational Course*, and the *Miscellany of Instructive and Amusing Tracts* begun in 1845 and completed in twenty volumes 'to furnish innocent entertainment mingled with correct information and instruction.' In 1844 Robert Chambers's *Vestiges of Creation* had been published anonymously; in its way it was comparable to Wells's *Outline of History* published in 1920 and Carleton Coon's *The Story of Man* published in 1954. Special mention should be made here of T. D. Fosbrook's *Encyclopaedia of Antiquities and Elements of Archaeology* published in 1822, 1823 and 1825.

At the same time as the Mechanics' Institutes and the *Encyclopaedias* were being born, the upper middle classes were being instructed in geology and archaeology by the *Spectator*, the *Gentleman's Magazine*, and the *Athenaeum*.

John Mitford became editor of the *Gentleman's Magazine* in 1824 and filled it with antiquarian and archaeological information and discussion. It was thought to be quite natural in the middle of the nineteenth century that a man interested in antiquarian pursuits should subscribe to the Society of Antiquaries and the *Gentleman's Magazine*. The *Magazine* itself published articles with a clear idea of why and what antiquarianism was: in the issue for 1829 we read:

> It is not the business of an Antiquary merely to decipher, transcribe and to pile document upon document, extract upon extract. . . . The judicious Antiquary has higher views than these: it is . . . to draw strong conclusions out of minute facts which have escaped the general eye. . . . Without the exertion of a conjectural spirit, guided by sober caution, the Antiquary would indeed be little better than a heaper up of old bills, inventories, ballads, a dealer in verdigris and iron rust, or a collector of . . . bricks, stones, tiles and pipkins. . . .

Especially notable in the *Gentleman's Magazine* were the Antiquarian Notes edited for it by Charles Roach Smith.

In 1846 W.J. Thoms began a series of articles in the *Athenaeum* under the pseudonym of Ambrose Merton. These articles, to which he gave the title 'Folklore,' dealt with all kinds of antiquarian subjects; they were so popular and caused such a great deal of correspondence that Wentworth Dilke, then editor and part proprietor of the paper, suggested to Thoms that he should start a special journal to deal popularly with the study of antiquities. The result was *Notes and Queries*, the first number of which appeared in November 1849.

There was no doubt that the public were interested in prehistory and early man, whether their interest sprang from natural science and geology or from something which can only be described baldly as the 'romance of excavation.' Certainly the romantic story of excavations in the Near East was a very clearly compulsive interest for the public at large. And, when one looks back at the story of archaeological discovery—what splendid and exciting things had happened—Botta finding Nineveh, or thinking he had found it (he was really digging at

SIR AUSTEN HENRY LAYARD

Khorsabad—Dur Sharrukin, Sargon II's city), Layard finding the palace of Sennacherib at Kuyunjik with its great library of cuneiform tablets, Rawlinson hanging over the cliff face at Behistun taking paper squeezes of the trilingual inscriptions engraved in 516 B C on the order of Darius Hystaspes, or that great moment in 1855 when the country boats and rafts, which were carrying downstream all the finds made by Oppert, Fresnel, and Thomas in south Mesopotamia and the two hundred and forty cases of material from Khorsabad and from Ashur-bani-pal's palace at Nineveh, were maliciously capsized by Arab brigands at Kurnah, at the head of the Shatt-el-Arab.

Austen Henry Layard began digging at Nimrud in 1845 and he worked there from late in that year until mid-1847. Here he discovered the palaces subsequently identified with the Assyrian kings Ashur-nasir-pal, Essarhaddon, and Shalmaneser III. It was from these excavations that the British Museum has obtained some of its most priceless treasures—the huge winged bulls, the sculptures of Ashur-nasir-pal, and the black Obelisk of Shalmaneser III. In 1847 the *Morning Post* published dispatches from its correspondent who visited Layard's work at Nimrud. Layard thought he had identified Nineveh in the remains at Nimrud just as Botta thought he had done at Khorsabad. When he returned to England he published a book entitled *The Monuments of Nineveh*, but also a popular account of his excavations, *Nineveh and Its Remains*. This was in 1848 and 1849. This popular account—surely the earliest and one of the most successful of archaeological best-sellers—was very widely read. It became an instant success; in a letter Layard mentioned that eight thousand copies were sold in one year, 'which,' he added 'will place it side by side with Mrs Rundell's *Cookery*.' This book was published by John Murray, who had also published Dennis's *Cities and Cemeteries of Etruria* and Fellows's *First and Second Excursions in Asia Minor*. A year or so later Murray's produced the first series of books for reading in the train: they were for sale in the new bookstalls which W. H. Smith had been opening. Among the first half-dozen titles was an abridgment of *Nineveh and Its Remains*; the title was *A Popular Account of Discoveries at Nineveh*. Could there by any clearer proof that in the nineteenth century the public was very much interested in prehistory and archaeology?

And in the next few decades other archaeological books were best-sellers. Lyell's *Antiquity of Man*—'a trilogy on the antiquity of man, Ice and Darwin,' as a reviewer called it in *The Saturday Review*—was first published in February 1863. A second edition was called for in the following April, and a third in the succeeding November. As William Pengelly declared, with joy, 'three editions of a bulky scientific work in less than a few months.' We have already referred to the publication in 1865 of *Prehistoric Times* by Lord Avebury; this too was published by John Murray, was a good seller, and went on selling for half a century and more.

Of course those were the days when the intellectual world seemed very intimately concerned in the findings of geology, archaeology, and biology. Darwin's *Origin of Species* came out in 1859, and it was in the following year that the exciting debate took place in the British Association meeting at Oxford when T. H. Huxley, 'Darwin's watchdog,' as he once described himself, sparred with the Bishop of Oxford, Soapy Sam Wilberforce. Huxley had described the *Origin of Species* as 'a flash of light . . . on a dark night.' Bishop Wilberforce, a man who, to quote William Irvine's joint biography of Darwin and Huxley, 'was one of those men whose moral and intellectual fibres have been permanently loosened by the early success and applause of a distinguished undergraduate career,' turned to Huxley and 'begged to know, was it through his grandfather or his grandmother that he claimed his descent from a monkey?'—the remark which made Huxley slap the astonished knee of the scientist next to him as he muttered, 'The Lord hath delivered him into mine hands,' and to make the famous speech in which he said he would be 'ashamed to be connected with a man who used great gifts to obscure the truth.' And it was the following year and also at Oxford that Benjamin Disraeli said, 'What is the question now placed before society with a glib assurance the most astounding? The question is this—Is man an ape or an angel? My Lord, I am on the side of the angels.'

The early public interest in geology and archaeology was very closely mixed up with religion and with the discussion of preconceived religious notions. Archaeology and geology were popular for two directly opposed reasons: first, they seemed dangerous to accepted thought, therefore notorious, therefore interesting and news; but, secondly, they might lead to a new philosophy of man, therefore famous, therefore also interesting and news. The result was the same from whatever point of view you started; geology and archaeology were interesting. 'In the 1840s,' said G. M. Young, 'the religious world was divided into those who did not know what the geologists were saying and those who did not mind.' By the 1860s it was divided into those who knew perfectly well what the geologists were saying and did mind, and those who also knew well and didn't mind. Many feared the undermining influence of geology and archaeology on the mind; Blomfield would not allow ladies to attend geological lectures at King's College, London.

I think that it was this uncertainty as to whether archaeology was respectable or not, whether it was going to

undermine faith or support it, that was directly responsible for one of the great moments of popular interest in
archaeology in the 1870s. The story of George Smith has
often been told. He was a minor official in the Assyrian
department of the British Museum and had particularly
interested himself in the transliteration of cuneiform. He
published in 1871 *The History of Ashur-bani-pal Translated
from the Cuneiform Inscriptions*. The next year, while working on the broken clay tablets from the Nineveh Library,
he discovered a tablet which contained the statement
that the ship rested on the mountains of Nizur, followed
by the account of the sending forth of the dove, and its
finding no resting place and returning. 'I saw at once,'
said George Smith, 'that I had discovered a portion at
least of the Chaldean account of the Deluge.' He later
discovered further fragments of the same tablet and fragments of a duplicate text. From all this he was able to
piece together a very great deal of the Babylonian flood
story; and this account he read to the Society for Biblical
Archaeology in December 1872. It must have been an
exciting moment coming as it did only just over a decade
since Darwin and Huxley had been saying, or had
seemed to be saying, that the Bible was not true, that
man was descended from an ape, and that geology and
archaeology were disposing of some cherished fundamentals of Victorian religious belief.

Now, if one listened to George Smith, here was archaeology proving the truth of the Flood story; it was
apparently most definitely on the side of the angels. No
wonder that the interest in George Smith's discovery
was enormous. A portion of the tablets recording the
Deluge story was missing and the *Daily Telegraph* offered
£1,000 to equip an expedition led by George Smith to
look for the missing fragment. The fact that Smith himself had never been on an excavation before and indeed
never been in the Near East does not concern us here;
nor is it our concern except in passing to record that by an
amazing stroke of beginner's luck he found the missing
fragment on the fifth day of his excavations. What concerns us here is that the press and the public had this
archaeological interest in the seventies. George Smith
published general accounts of his work in his *Assyrian*

discoveries and his *The Chaldean Account of Genesis.* This latter book, like Layard's *Nineveh,* became a best-seller.

I do not want to dwell any longer on these points of detail but only to insist that in the great formative period of archaeology—the thirty years from 1840 to 1870—there was an enormous popular interest in the subject. This has continued to our time, fanned by excitements like Schliemann's discovery of Troy and Mycenae, Arthur Evans's discovery of Minoan Crete, the discovery of the Sumerian and Indus civilizations, the realization that there had been a great Hittite civilization. Some of us can remember very clearly the thrill of first hearing of discoveries like that of Howard Carter and Lord Carnarvon at Tutankhamen's Tomb, Sir Leonard Woolley at Ur, or the discovery by four schoolboys of the Upper Palaeolithic painted and engraved cave of Lascaux. This interest has been fostered by various agencies of communication—the *Illustrated London News,* for example, which, since 1900 under the editorship of Sir Bruce Ingram, has given constantly a large amount of space to archaeology, and *Antiquity,* a journal founded in 1927 deliberately to bring together the interested public and professional archaeologists, and, in recent years, radio and television programmes of the BBC.

But it is a commonplace that to trace the evolution of a thing is not to explain or indeed understand it. Why has the public this interest in prehistory and archaeology? In the first place the answer is that there is a widespread interest in history, and an interest in prehistory is just an extension of this general interest. 'Man is an historical animal,' wrote Professor Geoffrey Barraclough, 'with a deep sense of his own past, and if he cannot integrate the past by a history explicit and true, he will integrate it by a history implicit and false.' If you begin to exercise your interest in the past and want an authentic account of what happened in the past, there is no reason why your interest should stop with the Victorians or the Tudors or the Carolingians or the Romans or the Ancient Britons or the Egyptians, and should not extend right back to the La Tène Celts, the megalith-builders, the first Neolithic farmers of Jericho and Hasunna and Jarmo, and the Upper Palaeolithic artists of Lascaux and Altamira.

Many have argued that we cannot make the exercise of historical imagination required by prehistory and that once we go back beyond writing, the achievements and the peoples who made these achievements seem remote and almost subhuman. I do not think that this is right and I like to think that a story told by Professor Fleure in the preface to the last volume of *The Corridors of Time* is encouraging and typical. It is a story about his collaborator, H. J. E. Peake, who had created a chronological series in the Newbury Museum designed to show how inadequate are our ordinary school history books with their few remarks on Caesar and the Gallic War and the Anglo-Saxon invasion wiping out the native population. A result of this was shown when a school inspector spoke of things that had happened 'very long ago,' and a Newbury child interrupted him and said, 'Oh, but that was quite lately, in the La Tène period.'

Apart from this general historical reason there are, it seems to me, four special reasons why prehistory is especially interesting in itself to the general public. In the first place, and not to put too fine a point upon it, origins are especially fascinating and the first of everything has a most special interest and attraction. From our childhood we have always wanted to know who first thought of this, who first invented that, and when we have become older and faced with problems of behaviour, life, human relations, the relations of states, property, religion we have liked to turn to questions of origins, and to ask ourselves questions like 'When was war invented?' 'When did man believe in gods?' 'Were the first human beings promiscuous or was monogamy the rule?' 'Is slavery a very old institution?' 'Were there always kings and priests, was there a Golden Age from which modern man has fallen or have we advanced steadily from apes to Victorians, from hand axes to Harwell?' That prehistory cannot supply the answer to so many of these questions is beside the point; it is all the while closely concerned with origins, and allied to the interest in beginnings is the sense of the incredibly remote and ancient which comes from the study of prehistory. The first Pharaohs were five thousand years ago but the artists who painted on the walls of Niaux and Lascaux may have lived twenty thousand years ago, and the makers of Abbevillian hand axes may have lived four hundred thousand years ago. We shall talk later about relevance, but here, when we contemplate the long millennia during which prehistoric man flourished, we feel only too ready to think that the history of the last five thousand years—Egypt, Assyria, Greece, Rome, and the Western world of Modern History—is almost, from a long chronological point of view, insignificant. Origins, and the great remoteness and ancientness of prehistoric man certainly give a glamour, although, as we shall argue, probably a meretricious one, to prehistory.

In the second place, prehistory is interesting to the ordinary man in the street because its sources are so much nearer to the average person and his life than are the sources on which the historian *sensu stricto* relies. The historian works on papers in the Public Record Office, in our national libraries, in college and cathedral muniment rooms, and in the strong-rooms of country houses, county archive offices, and in parish chests. The prehistorian works on material in museums, it is true, and it is also true that this material is often as remote (or more remote) from the general public as documents in record offices; but often, owing to the enlightened policies of museum curators and committees and to enlightened schemes of display, very accessible. The prehistorian also works on material which he finds by that painstaking surgery of the landscape which we call excavation. He works, also, on field monuments which are visible to all—stone circles, lynchets, barrows, megalithic tombs, hut circles, hill forts—these things, the cultural fossils of prehistory which are part of our present-day cultural landscape—the dead, nonfunctional part of the landscape. But, though dead and nonfunctional, they are, unlike the dead documents in a cathedral library, available always for us to see, constant reminders of prehistory as we go to work or drive on holiday. They are marked on our Ordnance Survey maps with an exemplary zeal and thoroughness in a fashion which is the envy of most European countries; there are even special maps of *Ancient Britain* so that these prehistoric sites should not escape us and so that they should indeed

147

become the objects of our holiday planning. And if we are bored with them there are always our children who want to see Stonehenge and Hadrian's Wall and who will not let their questions go unanswered when we drive them past Maiden Castle or Hetty Pegler's Tump and they say: 'What is that? How old? Why was it built, and by whom?'

Because of its strong surviving component in the British landscape, prehistory is ever very much with us. I sometimes wonder whether the differential survival of field monuments in different countries has not had something to do with the differential development of public interest in prehistory in those countries. In France, for example, where in the vineyard-crowded areas of Languedoc and Gascony few field monuments survive, or where in the intensely cultivated Île de France most things have been ploughed away, it is not surprising that in those areas interest in prehistory is as little as it is great in the southern Morbihan, where almost every walk must bring one to a megalithic tomb. But I digress: my point here is a very simple one. A drive from Marlborough to Devizes passes barrows, Silbury Hill, Avebury, Wansdyke. In the face of these constant challenges in the surrounding landscape it would indeed be a strange man who did not, however grudgingly, ask some questions and demand some answers, even if at first he was satisfied with simple answers like Druids and Ancient Britons and at last he turned to Atlantis and Old Straight Tracks.

But it is not only the sources of prehistoric archaeology that appeal to the general public. Its methods are also of great interest; the immediacy and accessibility of the sources are equalled in general interest by the uniqueness and fascination of archaeological method and technique. Air photography, excavation, Carbon-14 analysis, the delicate operation of piecing together broken pottery, and the restoration of a corroded and decayed metal object, the study of bodies found in peat-bogs, the fact that we can obtain historical data by analysing the contents of a prehistoric stomach—all these and many other things have a special fascination by the very remoteness and intriguing nature of the techniques

148

themselves. Archaeological research has a great deal of the nature of detective work in it; indeed, so, of course, has all research, but it is not often, as in archaeology, that the non-specialist can follow all the stages and understand all the moves in this game of research and detection. The great researches in the natural and physical sciences are also full of excitement, but they are often much harder to follow and involve a knowledge of complicated processes and unfamiliar laboratory techniques which the ordinary reader does not possess and cannot easily secure. And, of course, these techniques and methods used by the archaeologist are, in the most strict sense of the word, scientific. Here perhaps, as Angus Wilson has pointed out, lies one of the satisfactions which prehistoric archaeology offers. 'A humane study that increasingly calls upon scientific techniques,' he wrote, 'offers, in however limited a sphere, a resolution of the ominous dichotomy between man's two intellectual approaches.'

I have already referred to the romance of archaeology and to how the ordinary member of the public warms to the stories of adventure, of luck, and of chance in which the chronicle of archaeology abounds. Every undergraduate, if not every schoolboy, knows how the great painted caves of Lascaux in the Dordogne were discovered by chance by four schoolboys out rabbiting in September 1940 in the lightly-wooded hills near the village of Montignac-sur-Vézère (now Montignac-Lascaux, such is the fame of prehistory). The fine gold ornament usually known as the Grunty Fen torc—it is made of a square-section bar of gold grooved to form four leaves, and then twisted, and is four feet in length—was found by accident by a peat-digger working in the fen near Cambridge. Stories like the finding of Lascaux and the finding of the Grunty fen torc are legion; indeed it might be said with justice that a very great number of archaeological finds are made by chance. This aspect of chance discovery, the fact that on holiday or when digging in one's garden or excavating sewer trenches one may come across something which is of archaeological interest, keeps the ordinary person near to archaeology and warms him to prehistory in a way in which I do not think he can be warmed towards history constructed from written sources. After all it is extremely unlikely that one may find a valuable manuscript while digging in one's back garden, but it is quite possible that one may find a hand axe or a palstave.

There are, then, four reasons, as I see it, why prehistory at present is popular and appeals to people even more than ordinary history does—its remoteness and its concern with origins, its immediacy as a challenging part of our landscape, the fascination of its archaeological methods and techniques, and the romance and chance of discovery. But these are surely only reasons for intensifying an interest in prehistory. The basic interest in prehistory as in history is because we want to know what happened in the past and because we want re-created for us the historical contexts of prehistory.

But is finding out what happened in the past sufficient reason for a study of prehistory, as of history, sufficient reason for the maintenance of teachers and researchers into prehistory, as into history? Are prehistorians then no more than chroniclers, or do they study the past as some explanation of the present and some guide to the future? This is an issue that has been debated a very great deal by historians in the strict sense of scholars whose main sources are literary and epigraphical. Professor T. F. Tout, for example, had no doubt that chronicle was the aim: 'We investigate the past,' he wrote, 'not to deduce practical political lessons but to find out what really happened.' Others have been equally forceful on the other side: 'We seek in the end to know "what really happened,"' says Professor Geoffrey Barraclough, 'in order to assess its bearing and meaning for us. For it is simply not true that the past (as is so often stated) exists for itself.' I must say at once that I am in agreement with Barraclough; we do not all the time study the past for itself, not even the remote prehistoric past can be studied in complete detachment. We must study it with an eye on its relevance to ourselves at the present day.

Now I know that here we enter on very debatable ground. There are those who say that prehistory is so far away from us that it can have no relevance at all to the present, that the red deer hunters of Seamer, the flint-miners of Spiennes, and the metal-workers of Hallstatt have nothing to tell us who live so many centuries later and in such a different state of material economy and culture. This is a position maintained by some who are prepared to admit that modern history is relevant to the present—even using modern history in the widest sense of everything that happened since the fall of Constantinople. Scholars have argued that prehistory is so limited by its methods and its absence of literary sources—its reliance on the surviving remains of the past—that it can have little relevance to us anyway; it is argued that its judgments must be so subjective. To quote Barraclough again: 'The history we read though based on facts is, strictly speaking, not factual at all, but a series of accepted judgements.' If this is so for history proper how much more is it so for prehistory or history improper as it is sometimes cynically called. In prehistory, as we have seen in this book, we are always moving from one set of judgements to another, and what is a fact turns out to be what is currently accepted. In all this is there any historical certainty, and do prehistorians really know what is going on in the past? If they really are unsure of what happened in the prehistoric past, what is the point of arguing the relevance of what is uncertain, and anyway, so long ago, to the present?

That is how one group speaks and they can argue a case. Another group of people thinks it unwise and even improper to think about the relevance of prehistory to the present. It is the same group of people which does not want prehistory popularized or vulgarized—but here the issue is one of interpretation not popularization. The same problem faces the historian all the time. It is often said that he should not interpret, should not assess the relevance of what he thinks happened in the past. But he is the person best qualified to do so, and if he does not, then the amateurs and publicists and propagandists will be left in possession of the field. 'If the accurate, judicious, and highly trained fail to draw the lessons of history,' writes C. V. Wedgwood, 'the unscrupulous and unqualified will do it for them.' It must surely be one of the main tasks of the prehistorian to interpret and to assess the contemporary relevance of the facts which the

151

archaeological researches of his colleagues and himself produce. This is, in my view, one of the main spheres in which the idea of prehistory has not yet fulfilled itself. It cannot be pretended that there is anything approaching a philosophy of prehistory; yet it is precisely in this sphere of the philosophical relevance of prehistory to ourselves that prehistory may have most to contribute to the public.

Let us consider very briefly some of these underlying relevancies, and I say very briefly because it has been my concern in this book not to give my idea of the perspective of prehistory but to discuss how the idea of prehistory has developed and changed. I think the first and most overwhelming relevancy is the universality of time and space in early human history. For so long we have thought in the Western world that we were the heirs of the Greek and Roman civilizations as they were of the civilizations of Crete, Mesopotamia, and Egypt; now we see, quite apart from the historians who are insisting very rightly that Eastern Europe and Russia are as much the heirs of the classical civilization of the Mediterranean as the West, and that any evaluation of European civilization which forgets the contribution of the Arabs forgets a great deal, that Greece and Rome, Assyria, Babylon, and Egypt are only some elements in the long and complicated story of the development of man from the Palaeolithic 'savagery' that produced Altamira and Lascaux to the present day. The cities of Mohenjo-Daro and Harappa in Pakistan, of Anyang in China, of Chichén-Itzá and Palenque in Central America are as relevant to our over-all picture of the human past as are Ur and Athens. Whether we be Americans, Russians, Indians, or Chinese, we share a universal human historical heritage. I do not pretend, or imagine, that a recognition of this fact will alter present-day differences but if people really had an awareness of human history it should put present-day differences in a different perspective and one that made for tolerance.

It is the length of the perspective of prehistory which more than any one thing is to me the contribution of prehistory to modern thought. Let us recollect its essentials. Man, as a sentient upright-walking, talking, tool-making animal came into existence some three-quarters to two-thirds of a million years ago. After millennia of brutish life with little surviving material equipment, and a spiritual and moral equipment at which we can only guess, we find him at the end of the Ice Age not only a superb craftsman in flintwork—as witness, for example, Solutrean laurel leaves—but an artist, making beautiful spear-throwers, sculpturing horses and human beings on the walls of his rock-shelter houses and penetrating into the dark depths of deep caves to establish there cult-shrines, where in front of engravings and paintings and even models of animals, magico-religious rites were carried out. And all this art was at least fifteen thousand years ago and possibly as early as thirty thousand years. Somewhere, perhaps at ten thousand years B C, we find man in some localities in the Near East discovering how to cultivate wheat and barley: agriculture has begun—a discovery that may have been made independently in India and South China and as we know now appears certainly to have been made independently in America. At the same time or later, in the same area of the Near East or in neighbouring areas, animals were domesticated, and from these twin bases of cultivation and domestication the peasant village communities of the Old and New Worlds emerged. From the single basis of domestication came into existence the nomad societies of Arabia, North Africa, and Central Asia.

Very gradually as we look into the record of prehistory we see the settled peasant village communities in the Near East, in India and China, and in Central America develop and prosper so that large communities appear which are towns or cities and which have complex trade relationships and a specialization of labour, which can communicate by writing, and have priests and kings or chiefs; to these organizations we must be prepared, in any objective terminology, to give the name civilization.

What is perhaps most dramatic as we reflect on this long process is the length of time which the earlier stages have taken. No one suggests that the so-called Neolithic revolution—the change to a food-producing economy based on cultivation and domestication—started any-where in the world before ten to twelve thousand years ago, and until recently this date would have been given as nearer six to seven thousand years ago. Yet man himself—man by definition as *homo erectus*—came to Europe six hundred thousand years ago. We as food-producers with a life built on villages and cities have only been in existence for one-sixtieth of man's time on earth. Do these figures of thousands of years mean anything to you? Think of the face of a clock, and of the minute hand going round for an hour. Fifty-nine minutes of that hour represents man the food-gatherer, man in the stage of Palaeolithic savagery, man in the Old Stone Age. In the last minute but one we see him painting at Lascaux and Altamira and Niaux, but it is only at the beginning of the last minute that we see him gaining control over the cultivation of grain and the domestication of animals—it is only then that the Neolithic Revolution takes place, and only in the last half-minute that the social, material and cultural changes we call civilization occur. Egypt, Sumeria, Greece, Rome, Christianity, Buddhism, the pre-Columbian civilizations of America—all these have occurred in that last half-minute of man's long life on earth. This does not mean that they are irrelevant: but it does mean, at least to me, that their relative importance is less. You remember the philosophy which George Borrow put into a sentence in *Lavengro*: 'There's night and day . . . sun, moon and stars . . . likewise a wind on the heath, brother.' True, but to me it is a wind that blows from ancient, dimly apprehended, prehistoric heaths, and that tells us that man is very old, and that the present with its ideological conflicts, its threats of destruction by nuclear warfare, on the one hand, and by overpopulation, on the other, is not necessarily the end of existence, an existence that is already sixty times as long as the beginnings of agriculture and nearly a hundred times as long as the inventions of writing and formalized religions. I think there is a relevance to present thought in our knowledge of prehistory even if the philosophical elements of it are only roughly and crudely thought out as yet.

In his *Modern Historians and the Study of History*, a book of essays published in 1955, Professor F. M. Powicke says: 'The function of history is not to trace back the institutions and ways of thought which have survived as though we were at the end and climax of history. It is at least as important to retrieve the treasures that have been dropped on the way and lost, which if restored would enrich our civilization.' Here I think is the final and real justification of prehistory, its relevance to us, and the reason why it has a popular interest. The real justification is not in origins, or techniques, or in perspective, but in pleasure; the pleasure of prehistory is in the recovery of the treasures of man's prehistoric past that have been dropped on the way and lost. Whatever is missing from the record of the prehistoric past, much survives of its achievement in the visual arts, and we can today admire and enjoy the beauty, for example, of the leaping cows at Lascaux, the brilliant simplicity and purity of line of the stylized Cycladic figurines, the assured craftsmanship of the owls and bulls of the Brå cauldron, the architectural mastery of the builders of Stonehenge. We may find Upper Palaeolithic art or the art of the early Jerichoans who moulded features in clay on to human skulls, very remote in time, but they are not remote in spirit or aesthetic understanding, achievement or inspiration. It is the transcendental character of the visual arts that emerges so clearly and perhaps unexpectedly from the study of prehistory. We may not be able to think ourselves back into the rock-shelters of Upper Palaeolithic man or, perhaps fortunately, into the filth and stench that must have existed in the houses at Skara Brae and Little Woodbury, but the artistic achievements of prehistory require no effort of the imagination in their appreciation. The art of prehistoric man is part of the universal heritage of mankind, and it is sad that as yet it occupies only a small part in the formal histories of art. These usually begin with a few reproductions of Upper Palaeolithic art and then turn hastily to the art of the Egyptian and Sumerian civilizations. Admittedly, for a fuller understanding of prehistoric art, we need to know something of the chronological structure of prehistory and the culture of the varying societies that produced the art; we should have an idea of prehistory if we are to see prehistoric art in its chronological and cultural perspective. But even without that we can enjoy the artistic creations of prehistoric man. The treasures of prehistory do enrich our own civilization, and it is the excitement of the discovery and study and appreciation of the enrichment which is to me the main component of the idea of prehistory which we have at the present day.

IX

The New Archaeology:
Prehistory as a Discipline

LEWIS R. BINFORD

The Idea of Prehistory has, since its publication, been my favourite introduction to the history of archaeology. More than any other work it shows that the development of the subject is to be understood more in the history of ideas than as a result of great discoveries and excavations. *Digging Up the Past* was the title of a famous introduction by that great excavator Sir Leonard Woolley who discovered perhaps the most important of all archaeological treasures, outshining in interest even the tomb of Tutankhamun, namely the Royal Graves at Ur. But in reality, prehistory is not something which lurks underground, waiting to be uncovered by the archaeologist's spade. The finds in themselves do not speak to us directly: they are 'voices of silence', as André Malraux once put it, and it is we who must devise a language to allow us to interpret their message.

The prehistoric past is not simply a vast jigsaw puzzle, to adopt another popular image, with the central problem simply that of digging up enough bits to fit together like the sherds of some broken pot – *Piecing Together the Past*, as Gordon Childe entitled his introduction to the methods of prehistoric archaeology. On the contrary, it is we the archaeologists, the prehistorians who have to devise ways of making some kind of sense out of the disordered jumble of artifacts and rubbish, the discarded remnants of human activities which makes up most of the archaeological record.

There is no easy or obvious way to make sense of the past. The material evidence which we find or dig up offers opportunities, but we have to provide the interpretations, the reconstructions, the models, the theories which give them (or restore to them) their meaning. In this way the prehistorian is rather like the natural scientist who tries to make sense of the world of nature. Nothing tells him in advance how the world actually works, just as nothing tells us in advance how we should interpret the prehistoric past. It is a matter of developing ideas, interpretations and theories, and seeing how far they can be sustained in the face of the evidence we dig up. Much of the evidence on which we today base our present view of early human development has been available for a long time. It is *we*, the interpreters, who have changed. And we have done so through a series of developments in our approach, a growth in self awareness. 'Men make their own prehistory', as Glyn Daniel rightly remarked at the end of chapter VI.

Thirty years later, nearly everything which he wrote in the previous chapters still makes sense. We shall review in a moment some of the major advances which have taken place in recent years – revolutionary has sometimes seemed the appropriate word for them. The 'New Archaeology', the application of radiocarbon dating, and the development of the sort of public archaeology which is sometimes called Cultural Resource Management have brought significant changes. Yet many of the underlying issues, the fundamental questions which emerged during the last century, have not been disposed of. Paul Gauguin, painting in his Polynesian paradise, expressed them succintly in the title of one of the most mysterious of his canvases: 'D'où venons nous? Où sommes-nous? Où allons-nous?' Whatever the uncertainties surrounding the third question, the study of prehistory can certainly lay claim to answer the first and to illuminate the second.

The 'New Archaeology'

The most significant advance in the study of prehistory since the first edition of his book comes, as the foregoing discussion might lead one to expect, not as the result of new discoveries in the field, nor yet from the application of some novel technique from the natural sciences. It is, rather, the transformation of our entire view of the subject, of our idea of prehistory as a discipline, comparable in its significance with the major advances made during the nineteenth century, described in chapter 11.

Something of this was perhaps anticipated by Glyn Daniel when he wrote, at the end of chapter v: 'The news of the early dating by Carbon 14 of the first American agricultural communities has come like a tremendous blast of cold wind blowing down the corridors of time where walked scholars who seemed to have arrived at a fixed picture of world prehistory and cultural origins in terms of Neolithic and Urban Revolutions in the Near East'. But radiocarbon dating was only one element, and not the most important one, in the transformation wrought by the cold archaeological winds of the 1960s as they blew down the corridors of time. The 'New Archaeology', as it was called for a while, was not a technical advance: it sprang rather from the need and wish to redefine the nature of archaeology as a discipline.

The principal character in the story of the New Archaeology is Lewis R. Binford, a burly and substantial figure from North Carolina, whose first major article, 'Archaeology as anthropology', published in 1962, may be taken as the take-off point of the New Archaeology. It was followed by a series of further papers, many of them published in the periodical *American Antiquity*, which were at once both highly original in content and almost impenetrable in style, a combination which made them unpalatable to many readers in Britain. Jacquetta

159

Hawkes was one of those who commented adversely on the combination of poor style and indigestible science which she felt characterised much of the work of the time:[1]

> the provision of clear statements in humanistic terms might also serve to check a growing characteristic of much archaeological and related work which I find particularly distressing. This is a combination of extreme precision of detail with endless uncertainty of interpretation. It is experienced at its worst, like walking across coarse scree, in the pages of *Current Anthropology* . . . .

The first substantial volume produced by Binford and his students appeared in 1968, entitled *New Perspectives in Archaeology*. In Britain, the highly original treatise *Analytical Archaeology* by David L. Clarke, a young Cambridge prehistorian, appeared the same year, filled with ideas and techniques drawn from a variety of disciplines. But once again, it was not easy reading. This perhaps contributed to the very unsympathetic response given to it by most of the senior archaeologists in Britain. As the Russian archaeologist Leo Klejn later remarked, in his useful paper 'A panorama of theoretical archaeology' of the British reaction to Clarke's book:[2] 'The "revolution in archaeology" was viewed primarily as a revolt against the "King's English".'

In reality, the new archaeology was trying to do several things at once, and write elegant prose was not really one of them. In the first place, it was endeavouring to break out of the strait jacket of what were generally thought of as well-established procedures. Archaeology had become first and foremost a matter of classification, of taxonomy. The recognition of artifact types and their grouping together into assemblages seemed the primary task of the research worker. Then, it was widely felt, having reconstructed these assemblages and plotted their extent in space and time, one could write some kind of history in terms of the groups of people who originally used them.

In Britain, this interpretive approach was first developed with authority by Gordon Childe. In *The Danube in Prehistory*, published in 1929, he wrote:[3]

We find certain types of remains – pots, implements, ornaments, burial sites, house forms – constantly recurring together. Such a complex of regularly associated traits we shall term a 'cultural group', or just a 'culture'. We assume that such a complex is the material expression of what today would be called a 'people'.

With his assumption that the archaeologist could proceed directly and simply from a classification in terms of 'cultures' to a recognition of prehistoric 'peoples', Childe was taking a bold step, which allowed him to move from merely static description and speak historically, in terms of significant events in prehistory:

The same complex may be found with relatively negligible diminutions or additions over a wide area. In such cases of the total and bodily transference of a complete culture from one place to another we think ourselves justified in assuming a 'movement of people'.

Much later, in his 'Retrospect', which was the last article he wrote before returning to his native Australia to end his own life, Childe said of this approach[4] that it 'aimed at distilling from archaeological remains a preliterate substitute for the conventional politico-military history, with cultures instead of statesmen as actors, and migrations in place of battles.' In each case the procedure seemed to be: first, do the taxonomy, then write the history.

Already in the years following the Second World War, several scholars had become uneasy about this kind of procedure, which always took as its starting point the classification and grouping of artifacts. As Glyn Daniel remarked in the first edition of this book in 1962 (p.134 above): 'Prehistory is only now in the last ten years becoming consciously a historical discipline and realising that its job is writing history and not classifying antiques'. In America, some scholars were thinking along similar lines. Among the first of them was Walter W. Taylor, whose highly original book *A Study in Archaeology* was published in 1948. And in 1958, Gordon Willey and Philip Phillips published their *Method and Theory in American Archaeology*. There they pronounced their famous dictum that 'archaeology is anthropology or it is noth-

161

ing', and advocated what they termed a processual interpretation. This meant that the archaeologist should not
be content with merely reconstructing the past using the
available data, but should in addition make some effort
to explain it, make: 'an attempt to discover regularities in
the relationships given by the methods of culture-histori-
cal integration'. But after this laudable declaration of
intention (even if it is set in rather inelegant terminology,
of which Jacquetta Hawkes would not have approved),
they soon fell back to the traditional problem of the
definition of archaeological units, and the urge to explain
was not followed up further.

Just how fundamental was this assumption that the
first task was to classify is illustrated even by David
Clarke himself. In his *Analytical Archaeology*, he too could
not escape the prevailing preoccupation with defining
units, with classification, with taxonomy. Indeed, in this
particular respect, his book, despite his pioneering use
of the computer to aid the taxonomic enterprise, was still
a fairly traditional one.

Classification always seemed to result in the calcula-
tion of measures of 'similarity'. The argument ran that if
object *a* or culture A was more like object *b* or culture B
than it was like object *c* or culture C, then object *a* or
culture A had probably been 'influenced' by object *b* or
culture B. Inferences about historical relationships were
drawn from rather mechanical measures of similarity,
yet in reality they never seemed actually to approach
those underlying processes which were at work in bring-
ing about change. Instead, the insistence that similarities
were usually the result of contacts, whether direct or
indirect, between cultures, led almost invariably to diffusionist interpretations.

The approach advocated by Binford and his colleagues
was a different one. It was to study the various dimen-
sions of the culture system – whether subsistence, or
technology, or social organisation or whatever, in their
own terms. The focus was on aspects of prehistoric social
life and economy as they once must have been, rather
than simply on the artifacts which have been preserved.
This implied thinking about living societies, not just
about dead objects. There was no obligation to establish

162

a general and enduring classification of artifacts or cultures, although this could still be of help for some chronological purposes. What was needed was to formulate questions about relevant features of the culture system, and to proceed to find data pertinent to them, without insisting on the development of a perfect taxonomy.

All of this implied a departure from the way archaeological research was commonly conducted, and it entailed an overt attack on established procedures, and sometimes on established reputations as well. As David Clarke put it in 1968:[5]

> A whole army of new studies has developed whose implications have diffused piecemeal into archaeology and which increasingly permeate its fabric in a somewhat disconnected fashion. One response to these new developments has been to avoid them by a nostalgic retreat into historiography, another response has faced these innovations and initiated a period of groping experiment, inevitable error and constructive feedback, whilst yet a third response awaits the outcome, inert within carefully encysted reputations – all of these reactions are concurrently in full development.

It is not surprising that some writers of the older generation felt that talk of scholars 'inert within carefully encysted reputations' was rather near the mark, and they were not altogether sympathetic to new arguments expressed in this rather unflattering way.

Binford himself was scarcely tactful. In his *An Archaeological Perspective* he describes Robert J. Braidwood, one of the senior figures of American archaeology, the excavator of the important Near Eastern site of Jarmo, and one of Binford's early critics, in the following terms:[6]

> Braidwood is a tall, handsome man. He presents an impressive professional image, the Sir Mortimer Wheeler of Rolling Prairie, Indiana. His coats are always tweed, he wears woven single-colored ties, and his shirts are lumberjack plaid. He speaks in a melodious, deep condescending tone of voice. Above all, Braidwood is a gentleman: He sips Cherry Heering, rides the commuter train, and entertains under the spreading trees of his country

home. Archaeology is like a detective story, full of mystery and romance. It reveals the upward struggle of man toward civilization. Only a gentleman at the end of such a progressive line could understand the character of the struggle and recognize when man and 'culture' were ready for that first great step away from our crude forebears – the appearance of agriculture.

Binford's heavy sarcasm may have won some adherents, but such writing understandably alienated many of the older generation of scholars, some of whom also wore tweed coats and had no objection to an archaeology 'full of mystery and romance'. There were clearly underlying differences here of style and outlook of a fundamental nature. This is relevant when one is seeking to understand both the new archaeology and some of the reactions to it.

The second basic approach of the new archaeology was in some ways a more constructive one than the simple rejection of much of the work of the older generation, with its excessive dependence upon classification. The new aim was to operate by processes of reasoning which could be made explicit, so that the whole logic and framework of thought could be openly discussed. This required the deliberate development of archaeological theory, and the recognition that an explanation should not be accepted on the strength of the reputation of the scholar proposing it, but only after the development of alternative analyses, and 'by rigorous testing of deductively drawn hypotheses against independent sets of data.'[7] It is in this rather basic sense that the new archaeology set out to be 'scientific'. Not by the use of computers or sophisticated laboratory analyses, although both were also advocated, but by the adoption of the more rigorous processes of reasoning commonly employed (or thought to be employed) in the natural sciences. Naturally reference was made to the work of contemporary philosophers of science – in the United States mainly to Carl Hempel and in England to R. B. Braithwaite.

The third concern of the new archaeology was to *explain* what happened in the past, not simply to achieve some historical reconstruction of the sequence of past events, or to describe more fully the way of life of prehistoric groups. Such explanation implied a willingness to generalise, to study culture process, to seek, in the words of Willey and Phillips, writing already in 1958:[8]

> an actual convergence with cultural anthropology and the possibility of an eventual synthesis in a common search for cultural causality and law.

This statement expresses well the intentions of what has come to be known as the 'processual approach', and processual archaeology is now a better term than 'new archaeology'. For, after all, the whole 'new' approach to the subject is now some 25 years old.

Processual archaeology implies an inquiry into how cultural systems work, and how they change. It implies considering them as functioning, living systems, and the lessons of modern anthropology are thus highly relevant. One line of approach is the study of the economy, especially of food production and food gathering, since the food residues found in archaeological sites – the broken bones, the carbonised grains – offer ample material. The economic approach in archaeology, as pioneered by Grahame Clark (and discussed in chapter VII) is an important precursor. A further emphasis today is on the investigation of social organisation. The pessimism of Childe about the limitations of the archaeological evidence, quoted on pp.125–6, has been replaced by a more pragmatic optimism – that one doesn't know the limitations of the evidence until one has tried to use it. As Binford put it (writing in the style to which Jacquetta Hawkes and the older generation of British prehistorians so much objected):[9] 'data relevant to most if not all the components of past sociocultural systems *are* present in the archaeological record'.

A notable feature in much of the writing of the early new archaeology, and in subsequent processual archaeology, has been an emphasis on the need to make general statements, and thus to speak in terms of explanations and models which would have a bearing on situations at different times and places beyond the one under consideration, yet which would in some ways be comparable to it. This stress on generalisation, the suggestion that one might speak of laws of cultural development – ('Our

165

ultimate goal is the formulation of laws of cultural dynamics'[10]) – led some commentators to describe the processual approach by the rather ponderous jargon term 'nomothetic' (from the Greek *nomos*, law). Bruce Trigger, one of the earliest critics of the new archaeology, contrasted this outlook with that of the historian, which he saw as largely one of detailed description rather than generalisation, and which has therefore been termed 'historiographic'.

Sometimes these critics of processual archaeology seem to be advocating a rather blinkered particularism, with a search for more and more detail about the specific case under review, but yet with no underlying framework of reasoning for comparing that specific case with others which may have been similar in some ways and whose analysis could be relevant to the problem in hand. Sometimes indeed those like Trigger, who contrast the nomothetic, generalising approach of the processual archaeologist with the supposed particularism of the historian, may in fact be selling history short. For certainly the *Annales* school of historians in France (so called after the periodical in which much of their work has been published) seek a more general understanding of the processes underlying the specific events of history. One of the most eminent of them, Fernand Braudel, in his great work *The Mediterranean and the Mediterranean World in the Reign of Philip II* contrasts[11] 'traditional history – history one might say on the scale not of man but of individual men – *l'histoire événementuelle*, that is, the history of events' with two underlying levels of historical reality. Beneath the surface disturbances of events lies 'another history, this time with slow but perceptible rhythms . . . one could call it *social history*, the history of groups and groupings.' Beneath this again lies 'the almost timeless history', the 'history whose passage is almost imperceptible, that of man in relationship to his environment, a history in which all change is slow, a history of constant repetition, ever recurring cycles'. This perception of what Braudel terms the *longue durée* is close in its sympathetic understanding to what the processual archaeologist is striving for. I would suggest that it stands much closer in spirit to much of the new archaeology of the 1960s than does the particularistic, 'historio-graphic' view of history set out by Bruce Trigger in his book *Time and Tradition*, in which that new archaeology is stigmatised as 'nomothetic'.

The new archaeology, as we have seen, had many antecedents in the archaeology of preceding decades, not least in the ecological approach of Grahame Clark and his followers. It does not set its face against the discipline of history, as some have claimed, but it does employ a generalising, processual approach like that of many modern historians. Even its aspirations to scientific rigour had their precursors a century earlier, as described at the beginning of chapter IV. But the perspective which it offered was a new one in its coherence, and in its willingness to go ahead, in the field and in the laboratory and in the study, to undertake work in detail following the tenets of the new outlook. Anyone who doubts the dramatic nature of its impact should turn to the article 'The revolution in archaeology', published in *American Antiquity* in 1971, by Paul S. Martin, a very senior figure in the archaeology of the American Southwest. He wrote:[12]

> Since 1960, my goals and interests have been modi-fied by a trend that is now widespread in American science – a trend that involves a shift from emphasis on particularising to an imaginative era in which anthropologists and archaeologists built a cultural-materialist research strategy that can deal with the questions of causality and origins and laws . . . . . As a result, the bearing, emphasis and procedures of my research have been substantially altered. Thus a conceptual transformation, a revolution has taken place for me . . . . I feel in a better position to make contributions to anthropology. I now regard the use of logic and scientific methods as the minimum acceptable standard for good archaeology.

Further Developments in Processual Archaeology

Already by 1971, processual archaeology had had a major impact in the United States of America. In Britain, David Clarke's *Analytical Archaeology* was attracting consider-able attention, and much work that one can regard as

KENT FLANNERY

processual was being carried out. Mention was made earlier of the ecological approach of Grahame Clark; and his follower in Cambridge, Eric Higgs, was leading a whole generation of research students into the study of the human use of plants and animals. Indeed, it is probably fair to say that the whole field of archaeological science, that is to say the application of the methods of the natural sciences to archaeology, developed earlier in Britain and Europe than in the USA. The application to finds from archaeological sites of trace element analysis (the analyses of elements present only in very small quantities) was first applied in Britain, allowing the recognition of specific characteristics in imported objects. In this way the source of the raw material could be identified, and valuable information obtained about prehistoric trade. The characterisation in this manner of obsidian, a material of volcanic origin, used in the same way as flint, allowed one of the first reconstructions of an early prehistoric trading system, and other materials have been studied in the same way. American archaeologists, some of whom are largely unaware of the European archaeological literature, often assume that the new archaeology, and the rise in the use of scientific methods which accompanied it, was an essentially American phenomenon. It wasn't. Indeed, the clearest expression of the new outlook was offered by David Clarke, three years before his untimely death, in a brilliant article 'Archaeology: the loss of innocence.'[13]

On both sides of the Atlantic, general problems were being examined in new ways, prominent among them the challenging question of the origins of agriculture, and the problem of the emergence of civilisation and of urban life. In practice it was the insistence that research projects should be 'problem-orientated', should be concerned with posing a series of questions which could be tackled using a coherent research design, that had the most impact. Of course this outlook was not altogether new. In his *Autobiography*, published in 1939, the historian R. G. Collingwood (whose *The Idea of History* inspired the title for the present work) insisted[14] that 'knowledge comes only by answering questions'. He wrote of 'the logic of question and answer', and urged 'a Baconian revolution – the revolution which converts a blind and random study into one where definite questions are asked and definite answers insisted upon'. It is ironic, perhaps, that one element of the 'revolution in archaeology' should go back to the sixteenth century and the days of Francis Bacon, and doubly so that it should have been advocated by Collingwood, one of the most particularistic of 'historiographic' historians. But ultimately what counts when any new outlook is advocated is the implementation of the basic ideas, the practice not the preaching. And it was Binford, in his 'A consideration of archaeological research design' and in later work who insisted that appropriate and, where possible quantitative, methods must be used in archaeology. This was the starting point for the application of sampling theory in archaeology and for the significant developments, for instance in field survey (to be reviewed in the next chapter) which followed. The emphasis on the appropriate application of quantitative methods led Binford to the use of factor analysis, and David Clarke to the application of computerised seriation procedures. But it was not the use of the computer itself which was significant here, so much as the processual aims of the project in question.

The subsequent development of processual archaeology has led in a number of directions. In the first place, the systems approach, already foreshadowed by Binford and Clarke, has developed in a coherent and productive way. Of course, simply to divide the society as a whole, regarded as a system, into a number of subsystems and to consider these in terms of 'feedback' and other such novel concepts does not achieve much in itself. But it does lead the way towards understanding how a culture system can always be changing (for instance as individuals die and other people are born), yet in certain cases remain very little changed – the situation which system analysts term 'homeostasis'. Systems thinking does try to work in a coherent and structured way with the problems about why things change, and why other new social forms come into being. It is concerned with innovation and creation as well as with stability. A consistent attempt to apply the approach to the development of complex society in the Aegean was made in 1972 in *The Emergence of Civilisation, the Cyclades and the Aegean in the Third Millennium BC*, and others have followed.

Critics of this approach have quite reasonably remarked that sometimes all that seems to be happening is that the same old explanations are being dressed up in a pretentious new terminology. But some of these concepts really do allow us to think about the behaviour of whole societies in a new and coherent way, just as in biology they permit a fresh approach to the understanding of the organism as a whole, while not losing sight of its constituent parts. These concepts are among the *Tools for Thought* which the theoretical biologist C. H. Waddington advocated in his useful book of that name.

This use of ideas familiar in other sciences permits the application of techniques of analysis and interpretation which they have developed. For instance, simulation studies in economics have allowed the behaviour of whole economic systems to be modelled and predicted. This entails the construction of a specific model for the system as a whole, and the use of a computer to calculate its behaviour through time, using the rather complex interactions which the model assumes. This technique has been used in archaeology to discuss both the collapse of Classic Maya civilisation, and the rise of complex society in the Aegean. It should be said at once that neither simulation is a very impressive one when compared with the much more complex reality. But as a way of thinking about the way change took place in the past, these simulations are quite interesting.

Since the 1960s and early 1970s, processual archaeology has greatly diversified, with different workers exploring various directions of research.[15] Not all of them have been entirely successful, and some have led to confusion. For instance, some of the second or third generation of new archaeologists resolved, perfectly reasonably, to make the theoretical basis of the subject more sound and more explicit by applying to it more carefully the procedures then current among philosophers of science. Unfortunately, as it now turned out, the philosophy of science of the day did not provide altogether appropriate guidance. The archaeologists in question, John Fritz and Fred Plog, turned to the writings of a leading philosopher, Carl Hempel, whose work was then widely accepted. This led them, and, shortly afterwards, the authors of *Explanation in Archaeology: an Explicitly Scientific Approach*, to argue that *all* valid explanations must be framed in the form of universal laws. That really was an altogether 'nomothetic' approach, to use the terminology favoured by Bruce Trigger. In fact these authors failed actually to produce any meaningful, nontrivial laws relating to past human behaviour, but this did not prevent quite a number of research workers from following their example. Their outlook has, not unreasonably, been described by some critics as 'scientistic' (implying too slavish a dependence on the procedures of the hard sciences). But the philosophy of science has itself moved on over the past fifteen years, and this 'law and order' approach is no longer so vigorously advocated there. Indeed, I think it is fair to say that the Philosophy of Science has so far proved to be a poor guide in the development of theoretical archaeology. Later philosophers have merely criticised the hapless Fritz and Plog for their 'positivistic' shortcomings. In reality these came from following too attentively the precepts of the previous generation of philosophers of science.

A rather more productive trend has been the development of a Marxist or neo-Marxist brand of archaeology. Owing more to French anthropologists than to traditional east European Marxists, they stress, as one might expect, the social divisions within societies, and see change as the result of 'contradictions' between different groups within the community, or between social structure on the one hand (in Marxist jargon the 'relations of production') and the technical basis of society (the 'forces of production') on the other. Their great strength has been a willingness of think in social terms, considering divisions within society, as well as looking at the society as a whole, and also to consider long-term behaviour. Sometimes, however, their rather sweeping statements about the behaviour of society seem a substitute for the detailed, hard analysis of the data which must be part of any satisfactory explanation. Indeed, sometimes, like their exemplar Karl Marx, they give the impression of knowing what the answer ought to be (in conformity with Marxist principles) even before they manage to find it. In such cases their discussion can look more like a demonstration of the soundness of these general principles than a serious attempt, in the spirit of the science, to reach out and discover something until that time unknown.

Other workers have moved away from what they see as the materialism or 'functionalism' of both the Marxist and the mainstream processual approaches, arguing that human thought and human intention must be given their due weight. Some have termed this line of thought 'structuralist' or 'post-structuralist'. There is no doubt that by stressing the need to consider the way humans use symbols, they are exploring an area which many processual archaeologists have neglected. The distinguished American anthropologist Leslie White many years ago stressed that human behaviour is distinguished by the human ability to use symbols, and the philosopher Ernst Cassirer spoke of man as an *animal symbolicum*. Ian Hodder in his recent book *Symbols in Action* has emphasised the need to think in this way and has used the observation and study of the use of 'material culture' (i.e. artifacts) in living non-urban societies to aid

172

the interpretation of prehistoric material. What is less clear, however, among the writings of many of the structuralists and post-structuralists is precisely how they propose to elucidate the meanings of the prehistoric symbols which they wish to interpret. It is one thing to study the use of symbols in a society when you can ask those who are using them what they mean, another to attempt such a study for the prehistoric period. What is needed here is a more coherent methodology. My own view is that a cognitive archaeology, in which we try to study how humans have used concepts and symbols, is a feasible goal. But it is one which is not to be attained simply by the proclamation of good intentions. To study the use of symbols is not, however, the same thing as claiming to arrive at the meanings which these things had for their prehistoric makers.

In any case, all these -isms – positivism, structuralism, functionalism, Marxism – are part of the critical re-examination of the nature of archaeology which is still continuing, in the wake of the new archaeology. Although each proceeds from a different standpoint, they belong, together with mainstream processual archaeo-logy, to that critical re-examination which followed the 'loss of innocence' of the late 1960s and early 1970s. All those involved are struggling to meet the challenge of devising appropriate ways of making the 'voices of silence' speak. And for all of them, the 'idea of prehistory' is no longer something obvious and straightforward: its clearer formulation is a necessary first step if progress is to be made.

Although there are still traditionalists of an older gen-eration, and with them plenty of younger colleagues, who remain virtually untouched by the conceptual revo-lution (the 'young fogeys' as Kent Flannery has termed them), the various groups mentioned above do in general share this acute sense of problem. They wish to develop appropriate and productive methods to allow the use of the material remains from the remote past in an effective way in order to make warranted statements about what happened and why.

These are the people whom one sees today at the annual conference of the Society for American Archaeology in the United States, or of the Theoretical Archaeology Group in Britain. The liveliest discussions there are about theory and about methods rather than simply a review of the finds themselves. Sometimes one or two of their number, suffering from a surfeit of theory, will issue a rallying call to abandon all the talk, all the theorising, and to return to the trenches. Kent Flannery recently urged such a return to the hard realities of fieldwork in his entertaining paper 'The Golden Marshalltown'.[16] There the pretensions of some fashionable contemporary theorists are castigated, and the merits of the traditional virtues of hard digging and hard drinking reasserted. But in reality, Flannery knows, as every thinking archaeologist knows, that behind any application of practical archaeology, there must indeed be an idea of prehistory, a notion of how we are to set about making sense of the prehistoric past. It is all too easy to advance the slogan 'Don't bother me now, I'm digging', but much less so to see what to do with the finds. That is the lesson of this book. It was also, in a revealing and informative way, the lesson of the new archaeology.

REFERENCES
1. Jacquetta Hawkes (1968) The proper study of mankind. *Antiquity 42*, 258.
2. L. Klejn (1977) A panorama of theoretical archaeology. *Current Anthropology 18*, 12.
3. V. G. Childe (1929) *The Danube in Prehistory*. London, v-vi.
4. V. G. Childe (1958) Retrospect. *Antiquity 32*, 70.
5. David L. Clarke (1968) *Analytical Archaeology*. Methuen, London, xiii.
6. Lewis R. Binford (1972) *An Archaeological Perspective*. Academic Press, New York, 11.
7. Lewis R. Binford (1968) Archaeological perspectives, in L. R. and S. R. Binford (eds), *New Perspectives in Archaeology*. Aldine, Chicago, 13.
8. G. R. Willey and P. Phillips (1958) *Method and Theory in American Archaeology*. Phoenix, Chicago, 3.
9. L. R. Binford (1962) Archaeology as anthropology. *American Antiquity 28*, 218-19; L. R. Binford (1958) Archaeological perspectives, in L. R. and S. R. Binford (eds), *New Perspectives in Archaeology*. Aldine, Chicago, 22.

10. L. R. Binford (1968) Archaeological perspectives, in L. R. and S. R. Binford (eds), *New Perspectives in Archaeology*. Aldine, Chicago, 27.
11. Fernand Braudel (1972) *The Mediterranean and the Mediterranean World in the Reign of Philip II*, vol. I. Collins, London, 20.
12. Paul S. Martin (1971) The revolution in archaeology. *American Antiquity 36*, 1-8.
13. David L. Clarke (1973) Archaeology: the loss of innocence. *Antiquity 47*, 6-18.
14. R. G. Collingwood (1939) *An Autobiography*. Clarendon Press, Oxford, 104.
15. J. M. Fritz and F. T. Plog (1970) The nature of archaeological explanation. *American Antiquity 35*, 405-12.
16. K. V. Flannery (1982) The Golden Marshalltown. *American Anthropologist 84*, 265-78.

DAVID CLARKE

X

Towards a World Prehistory

WILLARD LIBBY

Archaeology, especially prehistoric archaeology, has since its inception been a subject almost universal in its scope. The methods of the prehistorian can be applied as effectively in one land as in another. And for the very early periods of prehistory we are dealing with developments which are common to all humankind, and relate to the origins of us all. Yet several things have worked together in recent years to make this underlying unity in some ways much more evident, and indeed very much more real.

The development of radiocarbon dating is one of the most significant unifying factors. It means that we can now all work on a single time scale which is the same from continent to continent, something which was quite impossible earlier. Then there are further scientific methods which permit from area to area that the same sort of questions be asked and answered by the same technical means. Moreover, and as a result largely of the new interests of processual archaeology, there is a whole range of further questions which are now of very great interest, undergoing investigation from continent to continent.

In practical terms, the most striking development of recent years has been the vast increase in the amount of fieldwork which is carried out, most of it using public money. A perception of our prehistoric past now forms one element of our idea of the environment. Those people and groups who are acutely aware of the damage suffered by our environment in the modern world, of the pollution of natural resources, and of the destruction of the vegetation and wildlife of whole areas of the globe are also keenly conscious of the enormous damage being done to the vestiges of the human past. These are also seen as basic cultural resources, and so the whole field of cultural resource management has developed. In Britain and elsewhere, rescue archaeology – the investigation of threatened sites before their destruction – is now a major public concern, and an expensive one. Archaeology has become a big spender.

Perhaps more important than any of these, however, is the manner in which, in almost every country of the world, people have come to see themselves as the product of their past, and the past as something in a sense personal to them. Every nation of the world now has its own prehistory. And while the more recent history of some of those countries only recently freed from colonial rule may have been one of strife, of conflicting ideologies, the period before colonial rule often represents for such a nation a time of authentic cultural integrity. It is from this pre-colonial (and often prehistoric) past that national identities are forged. At least one nation state – Zimbabwe – is named after a great prehistoric site, lying within its territories, a monument which is rightly seen to symbolise the achievements of the inhabitants at a period before foreign influences predominated.

These then are the developments, coming in the aftermath of the New Archaeology and in some cases much influenced by it, which have helped to shape the new

and much enlarged role which the study of prehistory
has now taken at an international level of our view of the
world.

1. The Radiocarbon Revolution

The development of radiocarbon dating must rank as
one of the most important advances – some would say
the most significant single step – in our study of the
prehistoric past. Willard Libby, the American research
chemist who developed the technique in 1949 and thus
made his great contribution to archaeology, received the
Nobel Prize for it in 1960. The method has already been
summarised in chapter IV and some of its consequences
considered in chapter V. But thirty years ago when these
were first written, the full impact of radiocarbon dating
had not yet been felt. In the first place, the precision of
the method was not then very great, and it was in addition necessary to destroy quite a large quantity of organic
material in order to obtain a measurement. Today, laboratories can date a sample weighing just a couple of
grams to within about sixty years with fair reliability. The
new accelerator mass spectrometer method, pioneered
at Oxford and at other laboratories in the United States
and in Europe, now allows radiocarbon dates to be obtained on samples containing only a fraction of a gram of
carbon.

The major revision in our thinking about dating the
past came, as far as Europe in particular was concerned,
with the correction of the radiocarbon time scale by
means of tree-ring dating. It turned out that one of the
basic assumptions underlying the radiocarbon dating
method, as it was first applied, had not been correct. The
assumption had been that the proportion of radiocarbon
in the earth's atmosphere had always been constant. But
we know now that fluctuations in the amount of cosmic
radiation reaching the earth have caused it to vary. So it
was necessary to have a means of checking this factor.

The long tree-ring sequence of the Californian bristle-
cone pine (*Pinus aristata,*) extending back beyond 5000
BC, has allowed the correction of the radiocarbon time
scale in a most convenient way. Wood samples taken
from tree rings of known age (as established by tree-ring

C. WESLEY FERGUSON

counts) were dated in the radiocarbon laboratory. It turned out that before about 1000 BC the radiocarbon dates showed a discrepancy: they were more recent than the true calendar dates (i.e. the tree-ring dates) by up to 700 years. Subsequently a well-chosen series of radiocarbon measurements on tree-rings of known age has allowed a calibration curve to be built up, thus permitting the correction of all radiocarbon dates. It depends on that splendid tree-ring sequence from California, established by Wes Ferguson of Tucson, Arizona, which has been corroborated by the entirely independent sequence for Irish bog oak established by the Belfast radiocarbon laboratory. All of this means that radiocarbon dates for prehistoric Europe, like radiocarbon dates anywhere, have to be set earlier than had initially been thought. The effect of the adjustment in Egypt and the Near East is to bring the radiocarbon dates (after calibration) into much better correspondence with the traditional historical dates in those areas, which are derived from the historical records of their early kings.

In Europe the effect upon the existing chronologies was very different. Far from supporting traditional views about chronology, the calibration showed that many of

179

the assumptions which had been made about links between Europe and the near East or Egypt were completely wrong. Many of the things seen in early Europe,
like the megalithic tombs, turned out to be very much
earlier than the fairly similar things in the Aegean or the
Near East which had sometimes been taken to be their
original inspiration. That was distinctly awkward for the
traditional archaeological view, which had nearly always
argued that the European developments had been
derived from the Aegean and the Near East, following
diffusionist assumptions.

All of this has meant that many of the innovations in
the European prehistoric past which, following the
'modified diffusionism' of Gordon Childe (see chapter
v) were supposed to be derived from the Near East, must
now be set earlier than their eastern prototypes. Much of
European prehistory has had to be rewritten as a result.
So such recent books as *Prehistoric Europe*, by Champion,
Gamble, Shennan and Whittle, or *The Mycenaeans and
Europe* by Anthony Harding, tell a very different story
from such standard classics as Gordon Childe's *The Dawn
of European Civilisation* or Stuart Piggott's *Ancient Europe*.

When, in chapter v, Glyn Daniel discussed the origin
of the impressive megalithic tombs of north-western
Europe, he could not know that calibrated radiocarbon
dates would soon push the megaliths of Brittany back as
far as 4500 BC, or take New Grange in Ireland back to 3000
BC, so that comparison with Mycenae in 1600 BC or with
the earliest built collective tombs in the Aegean, the
round tombs of the Mesara around 2500 BC, would soon
no longer carry much weight. This is one consequence of
the radiocarbon revolution. Along with it has been the
further development of important ideas already present
in embryo when Glyn Daniel wrote (p.91): 'megalithic
architecture may have arisen independently in the west
Mediterranean in several different places', and (p.92) 'It
now looks as if we must accept the independent origin
of some megalithic architecture in Denmark'. Indeed we
must! We now see more clearly – and this applies not
only to megalithic architecture and copper metallurgy
but to all kinds of innovation – that major developments
can occur independently anywhere that the social and

economic conditions are right. That of course still leaves the archaeologist with the crucial task of analysing those conditions. It now means that we need no longer be surprised to see agriculture or cities developing in the Americas altogether independently of comparable happenings in the Old World. The lesson that we have learnt in Europe applies with equal force in all parts of the world: that in studying prehistory we must expect radical innovation. This new perception of human creativity is, in effect the 'cold wind blowing down the corridors of time' which Glyn Daniel was to experience at the end of chapter 11. But perhaps in reality it is a much milder, more pleasant and invigorating breeze.

In any case, the experience has made the prehistorian much readier to accept the possibility of local innovations in all areas of the earth. And the availability of radiocarbon dates from all the continents - allowing for the first time a chronology to be built up which is not dependent upon evidence of cultural contacts, has put the entire discipline of archaeology upon a new footing. It is not by coincidence that the first edition of Grahame Clark's important synthesis *World Prehistory* was published in 1961, in the immediate aftermath of the radiocarbon revolution. Such a work would simply not have been possible ten years earlier.

2. The Tools for the Job

The idea of prehistoric archaeology as a discipline like those of the sciences, with explicit procedures for its interpretive reasoning, was discussed in chapter 1x. In a sense, of course, the entire story of this book reflects precisely that process. But there can be no doubt that the great step forward in terms of self-awareness, of 'loss of innocence', came with the new archaeology.

In practice, however, what counts in the progress of a discipline is not solely the general outlook, the aspirations, the meta-archaeology. It is also the ability of the practitioner to generate new data, and to handle those data in effective ways so as to substantiate or disprove the general theories and models which are under discussion, and to help build new ones. We are talking here less about general theory than about what used to be

GORDON WILLEY

called the methodology of the subject, or today, in the jargon of processual archaeology, 'middle range theory'. In reality, I believe, it is not very easy to distinguish theory from method or the 'middle range' from the upper reaches. What one can say is that there have been several developments, some arising from progress in the natural sciences, and others in response to questions thrown up by processual archaeology, which have greatly added to the armoury of investigative tools at the disposal of the prehistorian. The same questions and the same research techniques are now seen as applicable in every part of the world, and these too have contributed to the development of world prehistory as a discipline. They can be briefly reviewed under five headings.

Intensive Survey. Aerial photography has been recognised as a fundamental research tool of the archaeologist since the First World War. Today it is supplemented by satellite photography, to which is credited the first detection of the extensive irrigation systems of the Maya civilisation of Mesoamerica. This whole field of activity is now often termed 'remote sensing'. The more sophisticated techniques of today, including photogrammetric plotting and digitised mapping, are natural developments from the earlier work.

The greatest change in survey activity has come however mainly from changes in the way fieldwork is conceived and conducted. It has of course always been the practice for archaeologists to go out and prospect for sites to dig. Many of the early classics of archaeology, like George Dennis's *Cities and Cemeteries of Etruria* (published in 1848, and still useful as a field guide) or Squier and Davies's *Ancient Monuments of the Mississippi Valley* (another pioneering work, published in the same year) were based on thorough topographic investigation and the careful mapping of standing monuments. All of this goes back in its origins to the earliest days of topographic survey, such as that in England by Leland and Camden, back in the sixteenth century. It was put on an altogether different and more systematic basis, however, in the 1940s and 1950s by Gordon Willey's systematic work, published in 1953 as *Prehistoric Settlement Patterns in the Viru Valley in Peru*. Here the sites were first located through the study of aerial photographs, and were then visited and mapped. The aim was not simply to locate new sites to excavate, but instead to recover the entire settlement pattern, or rather the sequence of settlement patterns through time. In the Old World, a work of comparable importance was *Land Behind Baghdad* by Robert M. Adams, published in 1965, where aerial photographs provided the starting point for a detailed analysis of early Mesopotamian settlement patterns.

In Greece, too, mention should be made of R. Hope-Simpson's systematic survey of sites of the Mycenaean period (the Late Bronze Age) with the aim of identifying the locations mentioned by Homer in his Catalogue of Ships in *The Iliad*, in which all the cities sending ships to the way of Troy are listed. Hope-Simpson could not rely on aerial photography for this unsuitable terrain, and so visited likely locations on foot: good coastal sites, and potential strongholds. Reference should also be made to the energetic reconnaissance by James Mellaart in Turkey at about the same time, resulting in the discovery of such important sites as Haçilar and Çatal Hüyük, which on later excavation proved to be of the greatest significance for the understanding of early farming origins. In

ROBERT M. ADAMS

Western Turkey and in northern Greece, David French also conducted thorough reconnaissance, with very careful publication of the surface finds, setting new standards of accurate reporting.

All of these surveys, however, proceeded by visiting either sites already known or readily visible (in the case of settlement mounds), or detected from the study of aerial photographs, or by investigating locations thought to be suitable for the kind of site in question. None of these came from a strategy of walking complete areas of countryside with the aim of recording all surface traces of human activity. It was seen as clearly impracticable to walk over the entire surface of an area, even with a large team of fieldwalkers, so that such an enterprise seemed entirely inappropriate.

The solution came through the implementation of a *sampling strategy*. Sampling is, of course, a standard procedure in the natural sciences, where it has long been realised that in order to study a question, such as the range of heights and weights of human individuals in the population, it is not necessary to study and measure everyone. The part can serve for the whole. Of course, it is necessary to devise a good sampling design. The range of settlement types in an area, and indeed the settlement pattern can be studied in the same way. With an appropriate project design, it may be adequate for a survey team to walk over about one tenth of the total surface area in the region in question, and in so doing to be able to say something meaningful about the pattern of settlement. These ideas were set out by Lewis Binford[1] in his article 'A consideration of archaeological research design' in 1964. This was followed by a rapid application of these principles in the field in the late 1960s and early 1970s, especially in the United States, so that the idea of intensive survey (i.e. by total fieldwalking) of a carefully selected sample of the total land surface became well established. The general approach was already well discussed in *Sampling in Archaeology*, edited by James W. Mueller in 1975. Of course, sampling is relevant to many more problems than field survey, but it is there that it has made its largest impact.

It is fair to say that field archaeology, in the sense of studying such earthen monuments as burial mounds and field systems, has been a feature of British archaeology since the nineteenth century and indeed earlier: it was effectively exploited by O. G. S. Crawford in Britain in the 1920s, and the Ordnance Survey (the national British topographic survey) for which he worked, has established a good record of illustrating field monuments on its maps. But the notion of fieldwalking – of trudging systematically up and down ploughed fields looking for scatters of flint and other debris – in a systematic way, following a coherent sampling strategy, has only come more recently to Britain. In practice this has been perhaps the most significant development in archaeological methodology of the past fifty years. Previously, to undertake an archaeological field project nearly always implied excavation – although here one should certainly refer to the splendidly detailed topographic surveys undertaken in Britain by the Royal Commissions on Historical Monuments. Now, on the other hand, much of the most interesting information comes from intensive topographic survey. Much of the highly productive work in Mexico, in the Teotihuacan area, for instance, or in Oaxaca, has been on such a basis. This lead has since been followed

185

in the Mediterranean (on the Melos survey by John F. Cherry and elsewhere), in Britain and beyond.

This seems a particularly good example of a situation where the questions came first, questions about settlement patterns, and where the research methods were appropriately devised to answer them. Bacon and Collingwood would have approved.

Formation Processes. A second focus of interest of contemporary archaeology has been to understand very much more clearly precisely how archaeological sites came to be exactly how they are. How did the various artifacts and other indications of human activity come to be where they were ultimately found? What natural processes did they undergo, after falling out of use by their owners?

These seem, at first sight, rather obvious questions which one would have imagined to have been exhausted long ago. They were, of course, much discussed, albeit in a very general way, when the issue of the Antiquity of Man, reviewed in chapter 11, was discussed. Indeed, the early debates on the Biblical Flood, and its possible reflection in the archaeological record, were really arguments about formation processes. Very often in the history of archaeology we find that some of the really fundamental questions were quite vigorously discussed in the nineteenth century, but then left and neglected for many years.

What is really at issue here is essentially the notion of archaeological *association.* Just because two or more artifacts, or an artifact and some animal bone, are found together, does this indicate that they were in reality associated, i.e. in use together? This deceptively easy question in reality finds no simple answer.

In the field of Pleistocene geology, and in dealing with the palaeolithic period in general, a whole discipline of 'taphonomy' has arisen – the study of how things came to be buried. For archaeology, Michael Schiffer[2] treated this subject well in 1972 in an article entitled 'Archaeological context and systemic context', distinguishing between 'cultural transforms' by which human activity initially forms the archaeological record, and 'natural transforms' by which the material remains of that activity are preserved (or not) to make the archaeological record which we find today. He developed these ideas in an influential book, *Behavioral Archaeology*, published in 1976. The same issues have been tackled, although in a rather different way, by Lewis Binford in his *Bones: Ancient Men and Modern Myths*, published in 1981, where he questions whether the bones and stone artifacts found together in various Lower Palaeolithic deposits of Africa really belong together, and in doing so, questions many widely accepted interpretations. Some of the questions raised by the study of formation processes belong in the field of geomorphology, or 'geoarchaeology'. But others related to the rather different issue of precisely how human behaviour comes to be reflected in the material remains discovered by the archaeologist. It is here that ethnoarchaeology becomes very relevant.

Ethnoarchaeology. When one looks at modern archaeology, which is, after all, supposed to focus on past societies, it seems paradoxical that so many archaeologists now seem to spend their time among living communities, and studying what is called their 'material culture'. That they should need to do so at all is to some extent an adverse reflection on contemporary anthropology, which sometimes seems so caught up with kinship systems and the symbolism of modern groups, that it has little time for collecting the artifacts which they make, or for studying the details of the construction of their houses, or in short doing all those things which were so efficiently done by the traditional ethnographer some seventy and more years ago.

But of course the problems are different. The modern social anthropologist is largely interested in belief systems of the groups which he or she is studying. And they can, after all, be investigated by question and answer as well as by observation. The archaeologist's motivation in studying such groups of people, and in noting how they use artifacts, and how the material record is formed, is very different. The archaeologist, in studying these people, is really studying tomorrow's archaeology – the formation processes by which the actions and indeed the beliefs of the people in question come to be embodied in, and partly reflected in, their material culture, and how these do indeed become

187

buried and preserved for hypothetical future archaeologists. What we are interested in, of course, is largely the behaviour of past populations. We study the material culture and the formation processes of today in the hope of understanding those of yesterday.

That is not to say that the modern archaeologist is seeking to work by analogy – to claim that just because something happens in a living society, it probably did so in a past one. On the contrary, by observing the living case, the archaeologist hopes to gain new insights, formulate ideas about what the past may have been like, so as to test these by further reference to his own archaeological data.

The literature on ethnoarchaeology is now extensive: much of it relates to recent groups operating with hunter-gatherer economies, since it is here that insights can best be gained into the palaeolithic period, which is after all the most remote from us today. The field is well surveyed in two edited volumes, by Richard Gould (*Explorations in Ethnoarchaeology,* 1975) and by Carol Kramer (*Ethnoarchaeology,* 1979). It has proved one of the most fruitful directions of recent archaeological research. Again, its relevance is worldwide. And once again, the questions came first, thrown up by progress in processual archaeology. The research methods have followed.

The physical sciences and archaeology. The enormous contributions made by the physical sciences to archaeology have been very evident over the past forty years. F. E. Zeuner in his *Dating the Past,* first published in 1946, and one of the very first books exclusively dedicated to archaeological science, was concerned mainly with the details of stratigraphic successions in various parts of the world: the approach was largely geological, as it had been since the early days of the last century, as discussed in the first part of chapter II. When Zeuner was writing, the great contributions to dating made by the various radioactive clocks were only then beginning to be felt. Now, in addition to radiocarbon dating, we have the use of methods based on other radioactive isotopes for the early periods, such as potassium/argon dating. In addition there is the important technique of thermoluminescence dating, as well as a series of other methods.

While accurate dating has been the most significant gift offered by physics and chemistry to archaeology, there have been other contributions. In the field of archaeological prospection, the proton magnetometer is a valuable instrument. Resistivity surveying, perhaps the earliest major application of physics to archaeology, is still useful, and other methods are being developed.

The study of materials has been another specialism of great help to archaeology in at least two ways. In the first place, as mentioned in the last chapter, the study of prehistoric trade has become a very fruitful undertaking, thanks to the various means now available for characterising the raw materials traded – whether obsidian or flint, or other stones, or metal or whatever. The process of characterisation involves the identification, by appropriate analytical means, of particular properties (usually chemical properties) which are specific to a particular source of the material in question. In this way an artifact can be traced back to the source of its raw material. This is not the place to review in detail all the techniques available. Those based on geology and petrology have been available for some time, but have generally been applied systematically only more recently – for instance in the work by David Peacock and his students in the University of Southampton on sourcing the clay and other materials used in prehistoric pottery. The other analytical techniques of trace element analysis are of more recent origin, some of them, such as neutron activation analysis, dependent on post-war developments in nuclear physics.

Developments in the study of materials have also led to a much greater understanding of the precise way in which artifacts are made. This is the case, for instance, for metal artifacts, where a whole range of techniques of metallographic examination allow the entire history of manufacture of the tool or weapon to be investigated. In recent years there have been great advances also in understanding how stone tools were actually made, by various refinements in the techniques of flaking. Experimental archaeology is particularly useful where techniques of manufacture (and of use) are concerned. Many of the advances in our understanding of lithic technology

189

have come through experimental archaeology, by trial and error, by the investigation of the effects of heating the raw material and so on. Indeed, some of the most interesting results in understanding how materials were used in early times have come not from any very sophisticated technical examination, but from the sympathetic investigation of just how the materials can most effectively be used with rather simple technical means.

The progress in applying the physical sciences to archaeology can best be gauged by looking at the periodical *Archaeometry*, which since 1958 has been published by the Research Laboratory for Archaeology and the History of Art at Oxford. It is a considerable record of achievement.

The life sciences and archaeology. The life sciences have a much longer history of collaboration with archaeology than do the physical sciences. Food residues from prehistoric sites have been routinely examined since the excavations at the Swiss Lake Villages more than a century ago, and the study of human skeletal remains from excavations goes back considerably further.

It was, however, the development of pollen analysis during the first half of this century, first in Denmark, then in Britain and elsewhere, which allowed a new approach in archaeology. It now became possible to think more coherently about climatic change, and to develop a coherently environmental approach, in which Grahame Clark was one of the leading pioneers, as discussed in chapter VII.

Some of the principal advances of recent decades have come from very simple and pragmatic developments in recovery procedures: notably from water sieving and flotation. These techniques were developed for the Old World in the Near East, where Hans Helbaek, the botanist who had worked with Robert Braidwood on his pioneering excavations at Jarmo, systematically recovered large quantities of carbonised grain from excavations in the Deh Luran plain of southern Iran, in the project directed there by Frank Hole. In the United States the technique was systematically applied by Stuart Struever. It led to a very great increase in the quantity of material found, not just of plants but of small bones and of such

190

HANS HELBAEK

other residues as otoliths, by whose study fish species may be determined.

All of this has led to a great increase in the possibilities of the thorough quantitative analysis of early food residues, and of other environmental remains. In consequence, it is possible to reconstruct prehistoric diet rather comprehensively on many sites. Developments in related disciplines, such as the study of minute land snails, and of insect remains, allow the accurate reconstruction of the micro-environment of the site, or even of specific areas within the site.

It is perhaps fair to say that the study of early subsistence has been one of the growth industries of archaeology in recent years. For instance, in Britain there are several specialists working full time on the analysis of animal bones from archaeological excavations, and a similar situation is found in many parts of the world. What we see here is another notable tendency in the growth of contemporary archaeology and archaeological science: the trend towards specialisation. As the discipline has developed, and the number of practitioners has grown, special skills are needed, and the field becomes divided into a number of smaller specialist sub-

191

disciplines. Although this may carry some disadvantages, it does ensure the high quality of much of the specialist and technical work which is carried out. Of course, new techniques are being developed all the time. This is not the place to review them in detail: many will be found in the pages of the *Journal of Archaeological Science*. It is sufficient to note that the much greater range of techniques available has itself enlarged the scope of prehistory as a discipline.

3. Public Archaeology and Cultural Resource Management

Processual archaeology, as we have seen, has re-shaped the way we conceive of prehistoric archaeology. And a whole series of new research methods have become available through the applications of the natural sciences, as well as of computing and statistical methods. But other factors have in fact affected the practice of archaeology even more radically. The practice of prehistory is, after all, what prehistorians and other archaeologists actually do. To a great extent, now, they tend to be public employees, involved in rescue archaeology to serve publicly defined ends. This represents a shift, over the past two decades, in the practical basis, the funding, the infrastructure, of prehistory and one whose importance cannot be over estimated. To a large extent this growth of public archaeology is a world-wide phenomenon.

In most countries, the notion that the preservation of the relics of antiquity was a public responsibility emerged during the nineteenth century. In Denmark, the systematic protection of the nation's monuments may be said to have begun in 1807, when the Crown Prince signed recommendations including the following:[3] 'Prehistoric monuments which are situated on farmland and are too large and bulky to be shifted, must be divided into two groups: those which merit preservation through royal proclamation, and others of lesser importance which the landowner or tenant may be authorised to use as he sees fit.' In England, a system of state protection began in the year 1882 with the passing of the Ancient Monuments Protection Act. A few monuments were at once designated as protected by being placed upon a published schedule, and the list of scheduled monuments has now grown to number about 13,000. The Act also empowered the Commissioners to accept gifts or bequests of major monuments, which thereby passed into official guardianship. There are now some 400 guardianship monuments in England. Most other nations, then or subsequently, adopted comparable measures. Some, like Greece and Italy, set up a full-scale national Antiquities Service to regulate archaeological matters. But in general, these measures were most effective with the truly outstanding monuments – with Stonehenge in England (donated to the nation in 1918), with Mycenae in Greece, with Chaco Canyon in the south-western United States. They did not in general make effective provision for the very numerous but less obvious archaeological sites, some of them prehistoric, which were continually being destroyed either through urban development or changing agricultural practice.

The radical changes over the past twenty years may probably be traced back to two underlying causes. The more specific of these is the much clearer public awareness of archaeology, whose origins were reviewed in chapter VIII. In England it owes much to Glyn Daniel himself, both in his role as editor of the periodical *Antiquity*, and especially as Chairman of the highly successful television programme *Animal, Vegetable, Mineral?* which was produced for the BBC by Paul Johnstone. Sir Mortimer Wheeler and Glyn Daniel became public figures, TV personalities: they were in fact voted 'Television Personality of the Year' in the years 1954 and 1955 respectively. Comparable developments in public interest are seen in other countries: for instance in France where the monthly magazine *Archéologia* has a wide circulation.

The second more general factor underlying the growth of public archaeology was probably the growing public interest in conservation, and the resultant willingness of national governments to intervene in areas of concern which had not previously been their preserve. Health and welfare came first, and amenities followed. For instance, a United States Supreme Court decision in 1954 indicated that cities had a right to be beautiful just as much as they had to be safe or healthful.

Out of these perceptions has emerged a widespread

MARTIN BIDDLE

recognition that the remains of a nation's past are part of its heritage, and should be preserved for posterity. It is felt too that it is part of the public duty either to prevent the destruction of any significant parts of that historic heritage which may be threatened, or at least to intervene to ensure that damage is minimised, and that what has to be destroyed is at least properly recorded and published. In Britain, the activity of investigating threatened sites is known as rescue archaeology. It developed during the late 1960s, through widespread public concern prompted by such committed archaeologists as Martin Biddle, then as a government response to it, with the establishment of a national budget for rescue. Today, English Heritage, the government-funded body responsible for these concerns in England, spends about 6 million pounds per year on rescue archaeology, and this sum is greatly increased by the contributions of local authorities and of developers. Much of this expenditure goes into major urban projects, like those of Winchester (initiated by Biddle), York and London, which are concerned mainly with the Roman, Saxon and Medieval periods. But in the countryside, where changing farming techniques, especially deep ploughing, have caused widespread

194

destruction, rescue archaeology is responsible for the excavation of many prehistoric sites also. Rescue archaeology has now become the prime source of information about the prehistoric period in Britain.

Similar observations can be made about many other countries. In the United States, the subject is discussed in terms of Cultural Resource Management. This is a much better expression than rescue archaeology, since it implies a more active role in averting threats to sites, rather than simply excavating them when protective measures fail. The Archaeological and Historic Preservation Act of 1974 authorised any Federal agency of the us government to spend money on CRM, and State governments likewise contribute to a total national budget which has been estimated at more than a hundred million dollars per year. But it should be noted that in the United States, the protection is fully effective only on publicly owned land or on publicly funded projects. Private developers on private land are free to do very much as they choose, and in this respect the United States of America lags behind many other nations.

Naturally the position varies from country to country. In the socialist states of eastern Europe and in China, all archaeology is state-regulated, and rescue archaeology has been practised with great effectiveness, for instance in Bulgaria, for more than thirty years. It should be noted too that the notion of state-financed archaeology is not in itself a new one – public archaeology was already under way in the 1930s when the Autobahn system was created in Germany, and the WPA projects were implemented in the United States.

The effects of all this activity have been very substantial. Previously the majority of professional archaeologists worked in universities or museums. Now most are employed by national or regional authorities: they are administrators almost as much as they are research workers. Many problems have appeared in consequence, often related to the task of publishing the vast mass of accumulated data. In the United States, because the original legislation was not well drafted, there is no formal obligation to publish the results of salvage excavations. As a result, while the better-run projects, conducted in the main by well-organised archaeological units, are very well and fully published, a great many of those undertaken on public money escape publication altogether (although almost invariably some sort of written statement is filed with the local State Historic Preservation Officer). By contrast, in Japan, the results are in general well published. But there the quantities of publications which result are so considerable that there is a serious problem in assimilating the great mass of published information that results.

Inevitably conflicts of interest occur. Often they are between private developers, on the one hand, seeking to minimise delay, and professional archaeologists, working to preserve sites, or at least a record of them for posterity. Sometimes, however, the development is itself undertaken by a national or regional agency, and serious difficulties can then arise. Increases in scale always bring difficulties, and probably no country has yet succeeded in developing a completely satisfactory CRM programme or in assimilating the fund of new information which it generates.

Another very serious problem is the deliberate looting of archaeological sites for the antiquities of high commercial value which they contain. In many countries this is now big business, and precious information about their past is being lost through wanton destruction. The irony here is that it is the same public awareness of the past which funds CRM that ultimately underwrites the enterprises of the looter. The private collector, and especially those public museums which pay large sums of money for antiquities of doubtful provenance, bear a heavy responsibility here. When the Metropolitan Museum of Art in New York is willing to pay several million dollars for a Greek vase, a magnificent work decorated by the painter Euphronios, whose provenance is doubtful (allegedly from an unspecified private collection in the Near East but rumoured in the press to be from more recent and 'unofficial' excavations in Etruria), what hope is there of preventing the continuing orgy of destruction? The international antiquities market is now one of the principal causes of archaeological destruction in the world at large.

Despite the painful losses to our common heritage of the information once associated with these wantonly looted objects, the flow of information today, much of it from public archaeology is now enormous. The prehistorian now has to face an unprecedented availability of data. As in other sciences, problems of data handling and data processing sometimes seem to swamp the capacity of the researcher to assimilate and interpret all the work that is undertaken.

4. Archaeology and Identity: the Uses of Prehistory

'Every age has the Stonehenge it deserves – or desires.' This apposite remark, made by Jacquetta Hawkes[4] in 1967 following an illuminating controversy on the possible use of Stonehenge in prehistoric times as a sort of computer and eclipse-predictor, applies with equal and more general force to the prehistory which each age constructs for itself. The whole purpose of this book has been to show that there is no single, given 'idea of prehistory', but that the methods of the prehistoric archaeologist have developed over the years, and will no doubt continue to do so. There is, then, no single, universally valid view of the past.

In recent years this point has been much taken up by a number of archaeologists, influenced by developments and controversies in the philosophy of science, and seeking to apply the ideas of such modern thinkers as Feyerabend and Habermas. These criticise the now traditional notion of science, as set out, for instance by Sir Karl Popper, with its attempt to be 'objective', or at least to achieve a picture of the world which is subject to correction by empirical data. Such a view of science, they argue, is 'positivistic', since there is in reality no such thing as a completely objective observation. Any observation is made by an observer, with the influences of his or her own in-built biases and preconceptions. In consequence, it is argued, the data themselves are 'theory-laden' and even 'value-laden'. These arguments are applied by such critics with even greater force to the disciplines that deal with human affairs, such as sociology or history or prehistory. They argue, as an alternative to the positivism of the sciences, for a 'hermeneutic' (i.e. interpretive)

197

approach, where the role of the observer – the historian or prehistorian – in actively creating the kind of picture of the past which he or she may prefer, is fully acknowledged.

It should be noted that what distinguishes the two modern positions, the scientific and the hermeneutic, is not any disagreement about the source of the picture of the past, the idea of prehistory, which we create for ourselves. Both sides agree that our picture of the past, like our picture of the natural world (including any laws or models that explain it), is a product of the human mind, of the human imagination if you like. The hard scientist, as much as the interpretive historian preoccupied by 'critical theory', will accept that the various elements in our picture of the world are constructs, and therefore, in a sense, thought. The scientist, however, aspires to a methodology where comparison of his theories with the real world will allow them to be corrected or to be rejected when they fail to work. As R. B. Braithwaite[5] put it in his *Scientific Explanation*: 'L'homme propose, la nature dispose'. For the prehistorian the archaeological record plays the role that 'la nature' does for the natural scientist.

In general in this book we have taken the view that prehistoric archaeology is an evolving discipline, which follows the same general rules of inquiry as do the natural sciences. But this is not to deny the powerful role that the observer himself has in determining the kind of prehistory that is written. This applies not only to the personality of the observer, and to the time and social conditions in which he lives, but to his whole range of beliefs. This approach to the 'sociology of knowledge' of our subject is doubly relevant when we consider the various uses to which archaeology is put.

That each age gets the Stonehenge, or the prehistory, that it deserves is, in a sense, inevitable. For this book has already illustrated rather clearly how the prehistory written in each period reflects the preoccupations and limitations of its writers. What we have not perhaps stressed, as much as the adherents of a critical theory approach would wish us to do, is how far the beliefs of the time reflect the social conditions then prevailing.

Several writers have commented, for instance, that the general ideas about the evolution of culture which were current in the second half of the nineteenth century, and well into our own, were to a large extent a product of the self-satisfaction or complacency of the western capitalism of the time. As noted in chapter III, the archaeologists of that time often saw the present world as the result of continued progress from earlier eras, and viewed western man as the culmination of that process, in a line along which the inhabitants of other continents had not yet, in general (as they saw it), progressed so far.

It is, no doubt, possible to study history in these terms, and to set the prehistory written at a given time within the context of its general intellectual climate, and valuable insights may perhaps be derived from the exercise. Initial attempts by archaeologists to work in this vein, have however, been disappointingly naive. Bruce Trigger, for instance, has written:[6]

> Since the late 1960s the security of the middle class in both Britain and America has been seriously eroded by a chronic and deepening crisis that has been exacerbated by repeated failures of American foreign policy. These events produced increasing pessimism about the ability of human groups to control their destiny and a pronounced decline in optimism about technological development. . . . These shifting attitudes laid the groundwork for a conceptual reorientation of archaeology that began in the United States and Britain in the late 1960s.

This seems, however, a rather vague analysis of the causes of the new archaeology or its immediate aftermath. Critical theory here seems distinctly un-critical. Recent history is delineated with a distinctly broad brush, by a series of sweeping generalisations. So too is recent archaeology. The two resultant outlines are then asserted to be causally related. But the author's cavalier approach to recent and accessible data hardly encourages confidence in his judgements of other people's historiography. Yet although we may find this particular application of the 'sociology of knowledge' approach rather unpersuasive, there is no doubt that a keen awareness of the Zeitgeist can offer useful insights into the prehistory which results from it. Jacquetta Hawkes's article about Stonehenge, 'God in the machine', to which reference was made earlier, is a good case in point. She plausibly suggests that the enthusiasm of our own age for computers and for scientific interpretations predisposes workers like Sir Fred Hoyle, when contemplating Stonehenge, to see it with the eyes of twentieth-century scientific man, to think, as it were ahistorically, indeed anachronistically, and to come up with explanations and theories which illustrate his own thought rather more than they offer insights into the thinking of the neolithic Briton.

Political preconception too can colour the way in which models of the past are reconstructed. It is perhaps no coincidence that Marxist archaeologists see prehistoric societies, just as they view contemporary ones, in terms of 'contradictions' and class struggle. For them, hierarchically organised societies, such as the chiefdoms which some writers have seen in later prehistory, are exploitative organisations, controlled by the elite to further their own sectarian interests. But such writers can suggest, perhaps with justice, that the opposite view, put forward by many in the Anglo-American tradition, is likewise coloured by general preconceptions. The notion that chiefdom societies function, in large measure by using the economic process of redistribution whereby the institution of chieftain is economically adaptive, and in the long run beneficial to the system as a whole, does look rather like a prehistoric version of the ideal modern western economy. There is, perhaps, an element there of 'What's good for General Motors is good for America'. The two opposite interpretations of 'rip-off' and of benevolent paternalism do, to some extent, represent different prior preconceptions. This does not, of course, mean that either is entirely untrue, and indeed the two interpretations are not entirely incompatible.

So far we have spoken about preconceptions which, implicitly or explicitly have a major bearing about the way we interpret the prehistoric past. But it is important to realise that this is not an issue without relevance to our own time. How we interpret our past governs in large measure how we see ourselves, and how we see ourselves in turn determines our future actions.

The most obvious example of this is not so much at the personal level, however, as the national one. It is the case that most nations use the image of their own past to bolster up and consolidate national identity. The Marxists, again, will often impose a cynical interpretation on such activities, showing how rulers manipulate symbols to reinforce their own dominant position. And clearly there is no doubt that symbols frequently do act as a means of propaganda, serving first to engender and then to reinforce belief in the legitimacy of an existing social order. The Marxists, however, generally tend to assume that this is a self-serving exercise in manipulation: they sometimes forget that those responsible for propagating a belief system may themselves believe it. Nor is it necessarily justifiable to assume from the outset that the system is in fact not a valid or true or effective one.

In England, much of the national symbolism in use relates to kingship and to the high antiquity of the British constitutional system: the Stone of Scone, Magna Carta, the Crown Jewels, the Battle of Hastings and the rituals of kingship are among the most obvious emblems whose frequent invocation constitutes one of the most evident public uses of our past. The prehistoric past is not greatly employed in the symbolising of British nationhood, mainly because our prehistory is indeed today rather remote from us, separated by a gap of some two millennia.

In other parts of the world, however, written records were not in use until very recent centuries. Often, moreover, they were not used to record what seemed and still seems of greatest significance to the indigenous groups of the lands in question. With the demise of colonial government, these now have to devise their own symbolisms of nationhood. It is here then that prehistory comes into its own in its role as the recent past. It is, moreover, often seen as the true and legitimate past: the past which, often idealised somewhat, shows the original way, the proper style of life and conduct, before the intrusion of alien government and alien customs with the imposition of colonial power.

The interesting question very soon arises as to how

such nations, with a very different view of the past and with a very different idea of prehistory, are to view the procedures of prehistoric archaeology. When we survey, as we have done in these pages, the complex sequence of discoveries and intellectual movements which has led to our own western view of the nature of prehistoric archaeology as a discipline, it is hardly surprising that other groups, with different intellectual histories, may see the subject differently. Nor are we talking here about nations with only a short experience of literacy: it is rumoured, for instance, that the Iranian authorities at present have rather limited interest in the archaeology of the pre-Islamic period on the grounds that enlightenment is not likely to be found in the study of a period prior to the birth of the Prophet.

The problems faced by the archaeologist in the developing world have been well discussed recently by a number of workers. In general, two polar views emerge. One is that the methods of archaeology, as practised in the west, in eastern Europe and in many other countries with long, literate histories such as India and China, have a general validity. Such methods ought to work to the benefit of societies in the developing world also, in the sense that any valid and, so far as may be possible objective, knowledge about their past is of interest and of value.

The opposite view has been well expressed by Daniel Miller[7] in an interesting paper 'Archaeology and Development'. He insists with reference to that:

> Archaeology arises solely out of the colonial structure. There is nothing in most traditional societies that in any way parallels it. Its methodology, paradigms, and context are all unprecedented.

The logic of such observations has been carried further by some members of the 'hermeneutic' school who will argue that one person's beliefs are just as good as another's and that the picture which western prehistoric archaeology may produce, when applied, for instance, in Australia, has no more validity than does a local and traditional aboriginal reconstruction of the past, whether based on myth, on inspirational experience or whatever. The authors of the present work incline more towards the former position than to the subjective, hermeneutic. But rather than attempting to pronounce a verdict on what is at present a lively and interesting debate, it is perhaps more appropriate to move towards a broader and open-ended conclusion for our review of the history of prehistoric archaeology.

We have seen that it is up to us, and that applies to any group with an interest in the past, to formulate our own idea of prehistory, and to seek to reconstruct the past by appropriate means. The decision as to what are in fact appropriate means is not an easy one. We would certainly argue that the developments reviewed in these pages do indeed lead towards a view of what such means may be. But the decision as to precisely what constitutes valid science or objective knowledge is not to be settled by an *ex cathedra* pronouncement, not even when the *cathedra* in question is the Disney Chair of Archaeology in the University of Cambridge. The whole history of science may be seen as the development of an answer to such questions, and to the devising of ways by which theory and data can be related. The natural sciences, although they have indeed grown up partly in the western intellectual tradition, have an applicability and relevance which goes very much further. We would certainly hope and claim that something of the same can be said for many of the insights offered by the development of prehistoric archaeology.

Such methods, applied in every part of the world, and applied by the researchers of each nation with the aim of genuinely increasing our shared knowledge of the past, do indeed offer the hope of a real world prehistory, where the achievements of each area can be properly documented and set into a broader picture. The research conducted in Africa, for instance, in recent decades, has completely revolutionised our knowledge of human origins. This is of relevance to us all, in establishing a collective human identity, which is something which we all need to perceive clearly, just as much as we do our separate national and ethnic identities. That, in the last analysis, is why it is necessary to have an Idea of Prehistory: to know who we are; to be able to give at least some coherent answer to those questions posed by

COLIN RENFREW

Gauguin: 'Where do we come from? Where are we? Where are we going?'.

REFERENCES

1. L. R. Binford (1963) A consideration of archaeological research design. *American Antiquity 29*, 425-41.
2. M. B. Schiffer (1972) Archaeological context and systemic context. *American Antiquity 37*, 156-65.
3. K. Kristiansen (1984) Denmark, in H. Cleere (ed.), *Approaches to the Archaeological Heritage.* Cambridge University Press, 21.
4. J. Hawkes (1967) God in the machine. *Antiquity 41*, 174.
5. R. B. Braithwaite (1953) *Scientific Explanation.* Cambridge University Press, 368. 'Man proposes a system of hypotheses: Nature disposes of its truth or falsity.'
6. B. Trigger (1981) Anglo-American archaeology. *World Archaeology 13*, 149-50.
7. D. Miller (1980) Archaeology and development. *Current Anthropology 21*, 726.

Recommended Reading

No authoritative and definitive history of archaeology and prehistory has as yet been published. Adolf Michaelis, *A Century of Archaeological Discoveries* (London, 1908) deals with discovery, mainly in classical lands, up to the beginning of the twentieth century. This is a translation of his *Die archäologischen Entdeckungen des neunzehnten Jahrhunderts* (Leipzig, 1906); and Friedrich von Oppeln-Bronikowski's *Die archäologischen Entdeckungen im 20 Jahrhundert* (Berlin, 1931) takes the story on another thirty years. Bibliographical details of many of the earlier works on the history of archaeology are given in Glyn Daniel, *150 Years of Archaeology* (London, 1975), and are not repeated here, but special mention must be made of H. J. E. Peake, *The Study of Prehistoric Times* (Huxley Memorial Lecture for 1940), *J. R. Anthrop. Inst.*, 1940, 1. More recent studies of the general history of archaeology include Kenneth Hudson, *A Social History of Archaeology* (London, 1981), the papers in Part I of *Antiquity and Man* (eds John D. Evans, Barry Cunliffe and Colin Renfrew; London, 1981), and a number of works by Glyn Daniel: 'From Worsaae to Childe: the Models of Prehistory', *Proceedings of the Prehistoric Society*, 1971, Part 2, 140–53; *150 Years of Archaeology* (London, 1975); *A Short History of Archaeology* (London, 1981); and Glyn Daniel (ed.), *Towards a History of Archaeology* (London, 1981). Volume 13 of *World Archaeology* (1981–1982) contains a series of useful articles on the development of archaeology in different parts of the world.

For more popular accounts of the history of archaeology see W. H. Boulton, *The Romance of Archaeology* (London, n.d.), Brian M. Fagan, *Quest for the Past* (Reading, Mass., 1978), and C. W. Ceram, *Gods Graves and Scholars* (New York, 2nd edition, 1967), and *The March of Archaeology* (New York, 1958). The general story of archaeology through the discovery of lost cities can be read in Marcel Brion's *La Résurrection des Ville Mortes* (Paris, 1948), and more popularly in Herman and Georg Schreiber, *Vanished Cities* (New York, 1958) and Leonard Cottrell's *Lost Cities* (New York, 1958).

The story of Mesopotamian archaeology is well told in Seton Lloyd's *Foundations in the Dust* (London, revised edition 1980); see also E. A. W. Budge, *The Rise and Progress of Assyriology* (London, 1925). The work of the British School of Archaeology in Iraq over the half-century up to 1982 is described in John Curtis (ed.), *Fifty Years of Mesopotamian Discovery* (London, 1982). For Egypt, see F. Gladstone Bratton, *A History of Egyptian Archaeology* (London, 1967), and for the Aegean, Sir John Myres, *The Cretan Labyrinth* (Huxley Memorial Lecture for 1933), *J. R. Anthrop. Inst.*, 1933, 269. Schliemann's career and his discoveries at Troy and Mycenae are the subject of Emil Ludwig, *Schliemann: The Story of a Goldseeker* (London, 1931), Robert Payne, *The Gold of Troy* (New York, 1958), and Leo Deuel, *Memoirs of Heinrich Schliemann* (London, 1978). For the recent debate over the authenticity of 'Priam's Treasure', see David A. Traill, 'Schliemann's "discovery" of "Priam's Treasure"', *Antiquity*, 1983, 181–86, and 'Schliemann's mendacity: a question of methodology', *Anatolian Studies*, 1986, 91–8; and in reply Donald Easton, 'Priam's Treasure', *Anatolian Studies*, 1984, 141–69, and 'Schliemann's mendacity—a false trail?', *Antiquity*, 1984, 197–204.

Geoffrey Bibby's *The Testimony of the Spade* (New York, 1956) deals with the development of European prehistory, and is especially good on Northern archaeology. A more recent account of Scandinavian archaeology is Ole Klindt-Jensen, *A History of Scandinavian Archaeology* (London, 1975). For France, Colin Simard's *Découverte Archéologique de la France* (Paris, 1955) deals mainly with the story of Palaeolithic discovery, as does the Abbé Breuil's *The Discovery of the Antiquity of Man: Some of the Evidence* (being the Huxley Memorial Lecture for 1941, delivered in 1946), *J. R. Anthrop. Inst.*, 1945, 21. Fuller accounts of the development of French archaeology are R. Lantier, 'Un Siècle d'Archéologie Protohistorique', *Congrès Archéologique de la France*, 1935; and A. Laming-

Emperaire, *Origines de l'Archéologie Préhistorique en France* (Paris, 1964). The development of German archaeology is well described in J. H. Eggers, *Einführung in die Vorgeschichte* (Munich, 1959), and lands further east are now covered by Karel Sklenář, *Archaeology in Central Europe: the first 500 years* (Leicester, 1983).

The development of archaeology in the New World is the subject of Gordon R. Willey and Jeremy A. Sabloff, *A History of American Archaeology* (San Francisco, 2nd edition, 1980). For Central America, Ignacio Bernal, *A History of Mexican Archaeology* (London, 1980) may also be consulted.

For the origins of British archaeology, see Sir Thomas Kenrick's *The Druids* (London, 1927), *British Antiquity* (London, 1950), and 'The British Museum and British Antiquaries', in *Antiquity*, 1954, 132; H. B. Walters, *The English Antiquaries of the 16th, 17th and 18th Centuries* (London, 1934); and the following works by Stuart Piggott: *William Stukeley. An Eighteenth Century Antiquary* (London, 2nd edition, 1978); 'Prehistory and the Romantic Movement', *Antiquity*, 1941, 269 and 305; 'Stukeley, Avebury and the Druids', *Antiquity*, 1935, 22; 'The Ancestors of Jonathan Oldbuck', *Antiquity*, 1955, 150; 'William Camden and the *Britannia*' (Reckitt Archaeological Lecture for 1951), *Proc. Brit. Acad.*, xxxvii, 199; 'Antiquarian Thought in the Sixteenth and Seventeenth Centuries', in Levi Fox (ed.), *English Historical Scholarship in the Sixteenth and Seventeenth Centuries* (London, Oxford University Press for the Dugdale Society, 1956). The three last items are reprinted in a collection of essays by Stuart Piggott entitled *Ruins in a Landscape: Essays in Antiquarianism* (Edinburgh, 1976).

Valuable for the topographical aspects of the early antiquaries is E. G. R. Taylor, *Tudor Geography* (London, 1930), and *Late Tudor and Stuart Geography* (London, 1934). Dr Joan Evans's *A History of the Society of Antiquaries of London* (London, 1956), and her *Time and Chance* (London, 1943) are mirrors of British archaeology seen from the standpoint of one Society and one family. Also may be consulted E. Moir, 'The English Antiquaries', *History Today*, 1958, 781, and G. E. Daniel, 'Who are the Welsh?' (Rhŷs Memorial Lecture for 1954), *Proc. Brit. Acad.*, xl, 145.

Stanley Casson, *The Discovery of Man* (London, 1939) is a general survey of the development of archaeology and anthropology. For the history of anthropology see A. C. Haddon and A. H. Quiggin, *History of Anthropology* (London, 1934), T. K.. Penniman's *A Hundred Years of Anthropology* (London, 2nd edition, 1952), R. H. Lowie, *The History of Ethnological Theory* (New York, 1937), and Marvin Harris, *The Rise of Anthropological Theory* (London, 1969). A more popular survey is to be found in H. R. Hays, *From Ape to Angel* (New York, 1958).

For the early history of geology see Sir Archibald Geikie, *Founders of Geology* (London, 2nd edition, 1905); A. C. Ramsay, *Passages in the History of Geology* (London, 1848 and 1849); H. B. Woodward, *History of Geology* (London, n.d.) and *History of the Geological Society of London* (London, 1907); and, more recently, Roy Porter, *The Making of Geology; Earth Science in Britain 1660–1815* (Cambridge, 1977). Works about individual geologists include T. G. Bonney, *Charles Lyell and Modern Geology* (London, 1901); Mrs Elizabeth Oke Buckland Gordon's *The Life and Correspondence of William Buckland* (London, 1894); *The Great Chain of History: William Buckland and the English School of Geology (1814–1849)* by Nicholaas A. Rupke (Oxford, 1983); Katherine M. Lyle's *Life, Letters and Journals of Sir Charles Lyell* (London, 1881); P. Chalmers Mitchell, *Thomas Henry Huxley* (London, 1913); A. Ledieu, *Boucher de Perthes* (Paris, 1885); and L. Aufrère, *Essai sur les premières découvertes de Boucher de Perthes et les Origines de l'Archéologie Primitive (1838–1844)* (Paris, 1936).

The impact of scientific discoveries upon religious beliefs in the decades before Darwin is well told in C. C. Gillespie's *Genesis and Geology* (Volume LVIII of the Harvard Historical Studies, 1951, reprinted as a Harper Torchbook, New York, 1959), with an excellent bibliography. Invaluable here also is Andrew D. White, *A History of the Warfare of Science with Theology in Christendom* (New York, 1896). A. O. Lovejoy's *The Great Chain of Being* (Cambridge, Mass., 1936), and some of the essays in *Ideas and Beliefs of the Victorians* (Foreword H. Grisewood, London, 1949) are germane to the discussion. The idea of progress itself was studied by J. B. Bury in his *The

Idea of Progress (London, 1920). See also this same author's *Darwin and Modern Science* (London, 1909). Among works on Darwinism and evolution published around the centenary of *The Origin of Species* Loren Eiseley, *Darwin's Century* (New York, 1958), William Irvine, *Apes, Angels, and Victorians* (New York, 1955), and S. A. Barnett (ed.), *A Century of Darwin* (Cambridge, Mass., 1958) may be mentioned. Also of interest here J. W. Judd, *The Coming of Evolution* (Cambridge, Eng., 1910), and Francis C. Haber, *The Age of the World: Moses to Darwin* (Baltimore, 1959). For a recent account of the genetic basis of Darwinian evolution see Richard Dawkins, *The Blind Watchmaker* (Harlow, 1986). The early disputes about the antiquity of man and human evolution are discussed in Peter J. Bowler, *Theories of Human Evolution. A Century of Debate 1844–1944* (Oxford, 1987), and Donald K. Grayson, *The Establishment of Human Antiquity* (New York, 1983).

On Elliot Smith see Warren R. Dawson (ed.), *Sir Grafton Elliot Smith: A Biographical Record by His Colleagues* (London, 1938) and Chapter x of Lowie's *History of Ethnological Theory*.

For contrasting views on the Indo-European problem, see Marija Gimbutas, 'Proto-Indo-European culture: the kurgan culture during the 5th to the 3rd millennia B C', in G. Cardona, H. M. Koenigswald and A. Senn (eds), *Indo-European and Indo-Europeans* (Philadelphia, 1970); and Colin Renfrew, *Archaeology and Language: the puzzle of Indo-European Origins* (London, Cape, 1987).

Childe's contribution is well covered by three recent biographies: Bruce G. Trigger, *Gordon Childe: Revolutions in Archaeology* (London, 1980); Barbara McNairn, *The Method and Theory of V. Gordon Childe* (Edinburgh, 1980); and Sally Green, *Prehistorian. A Biography of V. Gordon Childe* (Bradford-on-Avon, 1981). See also Childe's Presidential Address to the Prehistoric Society, 'Changing Methods and Aims in Prehistory', *Proceedings of the Prehistoric Society*, 1935, 1–15, and the First Gordon Childe Memorial Lecture, by Grahame Clark, 'Prehistory since Childe', *Bulletin of the Institute of Archaeology*, 1976, 1–21.

A number of biographies and autobiographies of other leading figures of 19th- and 20th-century archaeology may be cited here: A. H. Layard, *Autobiography and Letters* (London, 1903); H. Pengelly, *A Memoir of William Pengelly* (London, 1897); M. W. Thomson, *General Pitt-Rivers: evolution and archaeology in the nineteenth century* (Bradford-on-Avon, 1977); E. A. Wallis Budge, *By Nile and Tigris* (London, 1920); Sir Flinders Petrie, *Seventy Years of Archaeology* (London, 1931), and Margaret S. Drower, *Flinders Petrie. A Life in Archaeology* (London, 1985); C. Breasted, *Pioneer to the Past: The Story of James Henry Breasted, Archaeologist* (New York, 1943); Sir Leonard Woolley, *Spadework* (London, 1953); O. G. S. Crawford, *Said and Done* (London, 1955); Sir Mortimer Wheeler, *Still Digging* (London, 1955), Grahame Clark, *Sir Mortimer and Indian Archaeology* (New Delhi, 1979), and Jacquetta Hawkes, *Mortimer Wheeler: adventurer in archaeology* (London, 1982); L. S. B. Leakey, *By the evidence: memoirs 1932–51* (New York, 1974) and Sonia Cole, *Leakey's Luck: the life of Louis Seymour Bazett Leakey 1903–1972* (London, 1975); Mary D. Leakey, *Olduvai Gorge: My Search for Early Man* (London, 1979), and *Disclosing the Past* (London, 1984).

On the methodology and techniques of archaeology prior to the advent of the New Archaeology, the following may be consulted: Sir Mortimer Wheeler, *Archaeology from the Earth* (Oxford, 1954); O. G. S. Crawford, *Man and His Past* (London, 1921); V. Gordon Childe, *A Short Introduction to Archaeology* (London, 1956), *Piecing Together the Past* (London, 1956), and *Social Evolution* (London, 1951); J. G. D. Clark, *Archaeology and Society* (London, 3rd edition, 1957); Stuart Piggott, *Approach to Archaeology* (Cambridge, Mass., 1959); Sigfried de Laet, *Archaeology and Its Problems* (London, 1957); R. J. C. Atkinson, *Field Archaeology* (London, 2nd edition, 1954); O. G. S. Crawford, *Archaeology in the Field* (London, 1953); G. R. Willey and P. Phillips, *Method and Theory in American Archaeology* (Chicago, 1958); and W. W. Taylor, *A Study of Archeology* (American Anth. Ass., Mem. 69, Menasha, 1948).

The fresh outlook sustaining the New Archaeology, and leading towards subsequent developments is well exemplified in L. R. Binford's *In Pursuit of the Past* (London, Thames and Hudson, 1983), and in the article by

David L. Clarke, 'Archaeology, the loss of innocence', *Antiquity*, 47, 1973, 6–18.

The two most influential early statements of the New Archaeology are: D. L. Clarke, *Analytical Archaeology* (London, Methuen, 1968), and L. R. and S. R. Binford (eds), *New Perspectives in Archaeology* (Chicago, Aldine, 1968).

Applications of such approaches are seen in C. Renfrew, *Approaches to Social Archaeology* (Edinburgh University Press, 1984) and K. V. Flannery (ed.), *The Early Mesoamerican Village* (New York, Academic Press, 1976). Positions critical of the supposed scientism or positivism of some of these approaches are taken by B. Trigger, *Time and Tradition* (Edinburgh University Press, 1978), and I. Hodder (ed.), *Symbolic and Structural Archaeology* (Cambridge University Press, 1982).

The systemic approach to culture change is used in C. Renfrew, 1972, *The Emergence of Civilisation, the Cyclades and the Aegean in the Third Millennium B.C.* (London, Methuen, 1972). Many of the concepts of change underlying much thinking in processual archaeology are set out in the book (which is not directed specifically at archaeology) by C. H. Waddington, *Tools for Thought* (Frogmore, Paladin, 1977). Mathematical models and simulation studies are used in three edited works: I. Hodder (ed.), *Simulation Studies in Archaeology* (Cambridge University Press, 1978); C. Renfrew and K. L. Cooke (eds), *Transformations, Mathematical Approaches to Culture Change* (New York, Academic Press, 1979); J. A. Sabloff (ed.), *Simulations in Archaeology* (Albuquerque, University of New Mexico Press, 1981).

The notion of 'explanation' in archaeology and related issues are discussed in some of the above, and in P. J. Watson, S. A. LeBlanc and C. L. Redman, *Explanation in Archaeology* (Columbia University Press, 1971); M. B. Schiffer, *Behavioral Archaeology* (New York, Academic Press, 1976); M. H. Salmon *Philosophy and Archaeology* (New York, Academic Press, 1982); and C. Renfrew, M. J. Rowlands and B. A. Segraves (eds), *Theory and Explanation in Archaeology* (New York, Academic Press, 1982).

The radiocarbon revolution is based on the technique

of radiocarbon dating, set out by its inventor: W. F. Libby, *Radiocarbon Dating* (Chicago University Press, 1955). More recent developments in this and other physical techniques are reviewed in M. S. Tite, *Methods of Physical Examination in Archaeology* (London, Seminar Press, 1972). The two radiocarbon revolutions and the archaeological significance of the method are discussed in C. Renfrew, *Before Civilisation, the Radiocarbon Revolution and Prehistoric Europe* (Harmondsworth, Penguin Books, 1976); and in C. Renfrew, *Problems in European Prehistory* (Edinburgh University Press, 1979); and T. Champion, C. Gamble, S. Shennan and A. Whittle, *Prehistoric Europe* (London, Academic Press, 1984). Its impact is well seen in Grahame Clark, *World Prehistory* (Cambridge University Press, 3rd edition, 1983).

Current developments in archaeological methods and techniques are discussed in the series edited by M. B. Schiffer, *Advances in Archaeological Method and Theory* (New York, Academic Press). Other relevant journals are *Archaeometry*; the *Journal of Archaeological Science*; and the *Journal of Field Archaeology*. Although no longer up-to-date, the edited volume by Brothwell and Higgs is still useful: D. Brothwell and E. Higgs (eds), *Science in Archaeology* (London, Thames and Hudson, 2nd edition, 1969). A broader survey of archaeological methods is given in C. Renfrew and P. Bahn, *A Handbook of Archaeological Method* (London, Thames and Hudson, forthcoming).

Recent thinking about the life sciences and archaeology is exemplified by E. S. Higgs (ed.), *Papers in Economic Prehistory* (Cambridge University Press, 1972); E. S. Higgs (ed.), *Palaeoeconomy* (Cambridge University Press, 1975); and G. Bailey (ed.), *Hunter-Gatherer Economy in Prehistory* (Cambridge University Press, 1983).

Public archaeology and Cultural Resource Management have been discussed by: C. R. McGimsey, *Public Archaeology* (New York, Seminar Press, 1972); H. Cleere (ed.), *Approaches to the Archaeological Heritage* (Cambridge University Press, 1984).

The notion of 'objectivity' is called into question, and the active political implications of archaeology are brought out in: M. Spriggs (ed.), *Marxist Perspectives in*

Archaeology (Cambridge University Press, 1984); D. Miller and C. Tilley (eds), *Ideology, Power and Prehistory* (Cambridge University Press, 1984); and P. J. Ucko, *Academic Freedom and Apartheid: the Story of the World Archaeological Congress* (London, Duckworth, 1987).

The following works give a general introduction to the principles and practices of archaeology today: Frank Hole and Robert F. Heizer, *An Introduction to Prehistoric Archeology* (New York, 3rd edition, 1973); Robert J. Sharer and Wendy Ashmore, *Fundamentals of Archaeology* (Menlo Park, 1979); Philip Barker, *Techniques of Archaeological Excavation* (London, new edition, 1982); Kevin Greene, *Archaeology: an introduction* (London, 1983); and Brian M. Fagan, *In the Beginning. An Introduction to Archaeology* (Boston, 5th edition, 1984).

Index

Adams, Robert M., 183, 184
aerial photography, 72-3, 182, 183
agriculture, 'origins' of, 95, 153
Aldrovandi, Ulisses, 29-30
Altamira, 49-50, 51-2
Americas, 59, 85, 93-5, 96, 181, 182
analysis, *see* interpretation
Andersson, J. G., 62
Andrae, W., 110
animals, bones of extinct, 29, 31-6 *passim*
anthropology, 42-3, 61, 74, 83, 100-1, 106, 121, 187-8
antiquarianism, 6-9
  'new', 134
archaeology, 4-6, 70-3
  and taste, 65
  definitions, 70-2, 134, 161-2, 163
  discoveries of, 62-3, 68, 140-2, 145
  ecological approach, 167, 168-9, 190-1
  finance for, 177, 194, 195
  history of, 6, 8-9, 62-70, 110-11
  Marxist, 172, 173, 200
  'new', 159-60, 163, 164-71, 174, 177-8, 182
  public interest in, 143-5, 148-50 (*see also under* prehistory)
  relationship to prehistory, 5-6, 68, 157-8, 160, 174
  scope, 176
  sources, *see* sources
  specialisations in, 69, 191-2
  techniques, 66-70, 72-3, 148-9, 158, 160, 164-5, 168-71, 176-92
  use of other sciences, 187-90
  whether a science, 44, 61-2, 67, 149, 171, 198, 203
  see also excavations *and* prehistory
art, 49-50, 51-3, 101-2, 153, 155-6
  and society, 125, 155-6

artifacts, 29-32, 34-7, 187-8
  studying manufacture of, 189-90
  tracing material sources of, 189
Ashmolean Museum, 7, 13, 30
association, 29-36 *passim*, 186-7
assumptions, 4, 124-6, 129-30; *see also* ideology
Atlantis, 88, 94
Aubrey, John, 13, 71, 116
Avebury, Lord, *see* Lubbock, Sir John
Aztecs, 94

Bachofen, J. J., 123
Bagford, John, 31
Balme, Edward, 8
Banerji, E. D., 62
Barraclough, Geoffrey, 132, 145, 150, 151
barrows, 8-9, 19
Bastian, Adolf, 81-2
Becker, Professor, 91-2
Bede, 10
Bellamy, Mr, 88, 89
Benedict, Ruth, 104
bias, *see* assumptions *and* ideology
Biblical dating, *see under* dating
Biddle, Martin, 194
Birkbeck, George, 138
Binford, Lewis R., 159-60, 162-4, 165-6, 169, 170, 185, 187
  picture of, 157
Blackwell, Thomas, 17, 18
Bochart, Samuel, 12
bodies, preserved, 45, 101, 119
bones, human, found with bones of extinct animals, 31-6 *passim*; *see also* human remains
Borrow, George, 154
Botta, P. E., 140-1, 142

Boulainvilliers, Comte de, 104
Braidwood, Robert J., 163-4
Braithwaite, R. B., 164, 198
Braudel, Fernand, 166
Breasted, J. H., 92, 133
Breuil, H., 52, 74
Bridgwater, 8th Earl of, 23
Bridgewater Treatises, 23, 24, 28-9
British, early ideas of origins of,
    11-15
Brongniaert, Alexandre, 25
Bronze Age, 76
Brougham and Vaux, 1st Baron,
    138
Browne, Sir Thomas, 22, 50
Bryant, Arthur, 126
Buckland, Miss, 82, 89, 105
Buckland, William, Dean, 23, 26,
    28, 33-4, 37
Burgon, J. W., 42
Burkitt, M. C., 75, 89, 137
Burnett, James, *see* Monboddo,
    Lord

Camden, William, 6, 110
Carbon-14 dating, *see under* dating
Carleton, Dr, 13
Carnarvon, Lord, 63
Cartailhac, Emile, 52
Carter, Howard, 63, 145
Cassirer, Ernst, 172
Casson, Stanley, 19
Catherwood, Frederick, 59
cave paintings, *see* Palaeolithic art
'Ceram, C. W.' (Kurt Marek), 137
Chamberlain, Houston Stewart,
    106-7, 108
Chambers (publishers), 139
Chambers, Robert, 139
Champion, T., 180
chance
    in archaeological finds, 149-50
    as explanation, 33-4, 35
Charles I, King, 6
Cherry, John F., 186
Childe, V. Gordon, 75, 76-7,
    88-93 *passim*, 134, 158, 180
    Dawn of European Civilisation,
        75, 77, 88-9, 180
    on interpretation, 113, 124-6,
        160-1, 165

picture, 115
    praised in USSR, 113
    *The Prehistoric Communities of
        the British Isles*, 76-7
    What Happened in History?, 92,
        131, 132
Christianity and ideas of pre-
    history, 9-12, 21-3, 143, 144
Christy, Henry, 51, 80
Churchill, Winston (17th
    century), 11
Churchill, Winston (20th
    century), 126
'civilization', 95-6, 133-4
Clapham, Sir Alfred, 5
Clark, Grahame, 68, 135, 165,
    167, 168, 181, 190
    defining archaeology, 134
    on ethnography, 122
    on political use of prehistory,
        112
    picture, 123
Clarke, David L., 160, 162, 163,
    167, 169, 170, 175
classification, 20-1, 23-4, 64-5,
    75-8, 120
    as basis, 160-2
    geological, 25
    racial, 103
    see also under prehistory
        (systems in)
climate, 190
Cluver, Philip, 110
Cocherel, Abbé of, 30
Cocherel, tomb at, 30
Coffey, George, 16
Coleridge, S. T., 58
collectors, 6-9, 65; *see also*
    antiquarianism *and* looting
Collingwood, R. G., 169
colonialism, 177, 201, 202
Columbus, Christopher, 93, 94
comparisons, ethnographical,
    121-3, 124, 162
complexity of cultures, 75, 77,
    88-9, 98
conservation, 192-5
Conybere, W. D., 25, 27, 28
Conyers, Mr, 31
Coon, Carleton S., 93, 131, 132,
    139

215

Crawford, O. G. S., 70-1, 72, 76, 129, 130, 185
CRM, *see* Cultural Resource Management
cultural change, theories of, 53-60, 81-2, 89-100; *see also* diffusionist theories *and* evolutionism
Cultural Resource Management, 158, 195, 196
cultural sequences, 73-8
culture(s), 74-5, 161, 162
    comparisons between present and past, 121-3, 124, 187-8
    complexity, 75, 77, 88-9, 98
Cunnington, William, 9, 66
Curle, James, 67
Curtius, Ernst, 110
Cuvier, Georges, 24-5

Daniel, Glyn, 136, 158, 159, 161, 180, 181, 193
Danneil, 110
Darwin, Charles, 23, 24, 27, 80, 142-3
dating, 20-1, 31, 32, 35, 37, 43-4, 61, 153-4, 178-81, 188
    Biblical, 9-11, 21-3, 37, 42-3
    Carbon-14, 44, 69, 95, 96, 159, 176, 178-80
    other scientific methods, 188
    tree-ring, 178-9
Davies, E. H., 183
Dawkins, Boyd, 61
Dawson, Warren, 79, 83, 84
Denmark, 192
    museums, 20-1, 23-4, 38
Dennis, George, 142, 183
diffusionist theories, 54-6, 90-6, 180; *see also* hyperdiffusionist theories
Dilke, Wentworth, 140
Disraeli, Benjamin, 143
distribution graphs, 74
distribution maps, 71
Douglas, Rev. James, 8
Drayton, Michael, 7
Druids, 12-14, 88
Dugdale, Sir William, 30

ecological approach, *see under* archaeology

economics, 135, 165, 170
education, 138-9, 146; *see also* universities
Efimenko, 113
Egyptian art, 101-2
Egyptocentric hyper-diffusionism, 83-8
Ehrenburg, 122
Engels, Friedrich, 112-13, 114, 123
epochs, 74; *see also* dating *and under* prehistory (systems)
Ericsson, Leif, 94
Esper, Johann Friedrich, 33, 35
ethnoarchaeology, 187-8
ethnography, 74, 86, 121-3, 124, 187-8
Evans, Sir Arthur, 60, 62, 76
Evans, Joan, 31-2, 65
Evans, Sir John, 35-7, 64-5
evolution, 47, 143, 144
evolutionism (social/cultural), 47-53 *passim*, 56, 58-60, 75, 77, 81-2, 90, 95-6, 123-4, 199
    and Soviet prehistory, 114
excavation(s), 8-9
    documentation/publication, 66-7, 69-70, 195-6
    only a start, 134
    techniques, 66-70
    see also archaeology
exhibitions, 48; *see also* museums

Falconer, H., 35
Fellows, Sir Charles, 142
Ferguson, C. Wesley, 179
Feyerbend, P. K., 197
finance, 177, 194, 195, 196
Flannery, Kent, 168, 173, 174
Fleure, H. J., 92-3, 129, 130, 133, 146
Flood, the, 24-6, 144
food, 190
Foote, Samuel, 8
Fosbrook, T. D., 139
fossils, 25, 27, 29, 119
Fox, Sir Cyril, 67, 68, 70, 71, 129-30
Fox, J. P. Bushe, 67
Frederick VI of Denmark, 192
Freeman, Williams, 71, 72

216

French, David, 184
Frere, John, 23, 31-2
Fresnel, Mr, 141
Fritz, John, 171
Frobenius, Leo, 74

Gamble, C., 180
Gauguin, Paul, 158-9, 203
Geoffrey of Monmouth, 11
geography, 127-9, 130-1, 133
geology, 74, 129, 186, 189
    history of, 24-9, 34
    public interest in, 143
Gilliéron, 43
Gladstone, W. E., 1, 45-6, 49, 61
Gobineau, Comte de, 104-8 passim
Gould, Richard, 188
Gradmann, Robert, 129, 130
Grant, Madison, 108
Greenwell, Canon, 66

Habermas, Jürgen, 197
Hall, H. R., 62
Hamilton, Sir William, 7
Harding, Anthony, 180
Haverfield, Professor, 3
Hawkes, C. F. C., 68, 69, 76, 89
Hawkes, Jacquetta, 159-60, 162,
    165, 197, 200
Heine-Geldern, 87
Helbaek, Hans, 190, 191
Hempel, Carl, 164, 171
Hesiod, 9
Higgs, Eric, 168
Himmler, Heinrich, 109
history, 2-3, 131-5, 145, 166-7
    sources, 147, 150
    systems of, 3, 9, 10-11, 22-4,
        38-40 (see also Three Age
        System)
    see also prehistory
Hitler, Adolf, 107, 112
Hoare, Sir Richard Colt, 9, 19-20,
    38
Hodder, Ian, 172-3
Holmes, Rice, 56, 76, 77, 88
Homer, 45, 46, 183
Hope, St John, 67
Hope-Simpson, R., 183
Horner, Mr, 43
Hoyle, Sir Fred, 200

human remains, 45, 101, 102, 103,
    190
    and remains of extinct animals,
        32-6 passim
Hutton, James, 26-7
Huxley, T. H., 80, 142-3
hyperdiffusionist theories, 54-6,
    77-90 passim, 92
    and racism, 105-6

ideology, 4, 103, 109-14, 172-3,
    197-203
    see also racism
Incas, 94
India, 99
influence, 162
Ingram, Sir Bruce, 63, 145
interpretation, 69, 157-8, 160-3,
    165-73, 180-1, 187, 197-203
invasions, 99
Irvine, William, 143

Jackson, Wilfred, 84
Jacob, Sir Ian, 137
Jevons, 123
Jews, 103, 107
Johnson, Samuel, 18-19, 21
Johnstone, Paul, 193
Jones, Inigo, 13

Kemble, John, 39
Kendrick, T. D., 11, 76
Kent's Cavern, 33-4, 35
Kidd, John, 28-9
Klejn, Leo, 160
Koldewey, Robert, 110
Kossinna, Gustav, 97, 110, 111
Kramer, Carol, 188

Lane-Fox, A. H., see Pitt-Rivers,
    General A. H.
Langhorne, Daniel, 11
language(s), 15, 17-18, 43, 98-100,
    103
Lartet, Édouard, 51, 80
Lascaux, 50
Layard, Austen Henry, 141-2
LeBlanc, S. A.
    Explanation in Archaeology, 171
Leo xiii, Pope, 132
Letourneau, Charles, 131

217

Lhwyd, Edward, 71, 116, 117
Lhwyd, Humfrey, 6
Libby, Willard, 69, 176, 178
Lightfoot, John, 10, 21, 22, 24
Lisch, Friedrich, 110
Lister, Martin, 116
London, finds in, 31, 136
looting, 196-7
Lost Tribes of Israel, 12, 87-8, 94
Lovejoy, Arthur, 18
Lowie, R. H., 81, 86, 92, 131
Lubbock, Sir John (Lord
     Avebury), 2, 39, 55, 57, 80
   Prehistoric Times, 2, 39, 41-2, 44,
     55, 56, 134, 142
Lucretius, 9
Lyell, Sir Charles, 23, 24, 27-8, 31,
     37, 39, 43, 80, 142
Lyte, Sir Henry Maxwell, 132
Lyttelton, Charles, Bishop, 8, 31

Macalister, Alexander, 75, 82-3
MacCurdy, George Grant, 75, 89
MacEnery, J., 33-4, 35
Mackinder, Halford, 130
McLennan, John Ferguson, 123
McQuedy, Mr, 57
Malraux, André, 157
maps, 71, 147, 182-3, 185
Marek, Kurt ('C. W. Ceram'), 137
Marshall, Sir John, 62-3
Martin, Paul S., 167
Marx, Karl, 172
Marxism, 123-4, 172, 173, 200,
     201; *see under* U S S R
Master Race theories, 77, 90
   see also hyperdiffusionist
     theories *and* racism
materials
   study of, 189-90
   see also sources
Mayan civilization, 59, 61, 94, 182
Mechanics' Institutes, 138-9
media, 137, 138, 139, 145
megalithic tombs, 90-2, 180
Mellaart, James, 183
Mercati, Michele, 30
'Merton, Ambrose' (W. J.
     Thoms), 140
Middle American civilization, *see*
     Americas

Miller, Daniel, 202
Mitchell, Arthur, 50-1
Mitford, John, 140
Molyneux, Thomas, 15
Monboddo, Lord, 17-19, 57
Mongait, 113
Montelius, Oscar, 46-7, 55-6
Montfaucon, Dom Bernard de, 30
Morgan, Lewis H., 58-9, 113, 123
Morlot, A., 43
Mortillet, Gabriel de, 43, 48-9, 51,
     52, 73, 77, 89
Mueller, James W., 185
mummification, 83, 85
Murray, John (publisher), 142
museums, 7, 13, 20-1, 23-4, 30,
     38, 65, 134, 146
   and looting, 196
   see also exhibitions
Mussolini, Benito, 111-12
Mycenae, 55

names, 119-20
nationhood, 117, 201-2
Nature, 1
Nazism, 104, 105, 107-8, 109-10,
     112
Neanderthal man, 37
Nennius, 11
New Grange, 15, 19-20, 91, 180
Newton, Sir Isaac, 117
Nicholson, Bishop, 13
Nilsson, Sven, 41, 57
Nyerup, Rasmus, 20-1, 38

Obermaier, Hugo, 74
O'Neil, B. H. St J., 68
Opport, Gustav, 141
d'Orbigny, A.D., 25
Ordnance Survey, 147, 185
origins, interest in, 3, 95-6, 146-7,
     203
Ó Ríordáin, Sean, 68
Osborn, Henry Fairfield, 108-9
Oxford English Dictionary, 1

Palaeolithic art, 49-50, 51-3, 69,
     153, 155
   disbelief in, 52-3
Paley, William, 23, 24
parallelism, 53

parallels, ethnographic, 121-3, 124, 162
Paviland, 34
Pazyrik, 45
Peacock, David, 189
Peacock, Thomas Love, 17
Peake, H. J. E., 92-3, 133, 146
Pengelly, William, 35, 37, 139, 142
periods, classification of, *see under* prehistory (systems)
Perry, W. J., 15, 56, 77, 84-8, 90, 92-3, 94, 105
Perthes, Jacques Boucher de Crêvecoeur de, 34-5, 37
Petrie, Sir Flinders, 49, 65, 66, 67
Phillips, C. W., 68
Phillips, Philip, 161-2, 165
photography, aerial/satellite, 72-3, 182, 183
Piggott, Stuart, 13-14, 16-17, 68, 89
Pitt-Rivers, General A. H. Lane-Fox, 63-4, 65-7, 69, 81
Plog, Fred, 171
Plot, Robert, 13, 30
politicians, 103, 109, 114
    see also Nazism
politics, 177
    see also ideology
pollen analysis, 190
Popper, Sir Karl, 197
pottery, 7, 189
Powicke, F. M., 155
Pownall, Thomas, 15-16, 18, 57
preconceptions, *see* assumptions
prehistory
    attitudes to, 3-4, 18-19, 45, 52, 78, 87-9, 126-7, 131-4, 136-40, 143-50, 177
    complexity, 77-8
    definitions and use of term, 1-2, 134-5, 202-3
    early ideas of, 9-23
    late Victorian ideas of, 41-59
    limitations, 100, 103, 119-21, 124-6, 134, 151-2, 161-3, 165 (*see also* interpretation)
    reasons for studying, 150-6
    relationship to archaeology, 5-6, 68, 157-8, 160, 174

revolutions during, 92, 96, 153-4
revolutions in study of, 63-4, 67, 91-2, 159-60, 180-1 (*see also under* archaeology (history of *and* 'new'))
sociology of, 198-200
sources, *see* sources
status, 3-4, 61
systems in, 46-7, 54, 57, 73-8, 113-14 (*see also* Three Age System)
techniques in, 118-19, 121-5, 127-9, 134
whether a science, 116-19, 158, 164, 167, 198, 203
see also archaeology
Prestwich, Sir Joseph, 28, 35, 36, 37, 43
Price, Sir John, 11
Prichard, James Cowles, 42-3
primitivists, 16-19, 57
processual archaeology, *see under* archaeology ('new')
Prout, William, 23
public attitudes to prehistory, *see under* prehistory
public responsibility, 192-6
publication, 66-7, 69-70, 195-6
Pumpelly, R., 62
pyramids, 90

race, 100-5
racism, 103-10, 111; *see also* 'Master Race' theories
Radford, C. A. Ralegh, 68
radiocarbon dating, *see under* dating (Carbon-14)
Raglan, Lord, 56, 77, 87-8, 105
Ratzel, F., 74
Rawlinson, George, 42, 141
recovery techniques, 190-1
Redman, C. L.
    Explanation in Archaeology, 171
Reinach, Salomon, 55
relationships, *see* comparisons
religion, 75
    see also Christianity
Renfrew, C., 204
    The Emergence of Civilisation, 170
rescue archaeology, 194-5

retrogression, 51, 60
Richmond, Ian, 68
Rosenberg, Alfred, 107-8
Rowlands, Henry, 11-12
Russia, *see* USSR

Sahni, Daya Ram, 62
Sammes, Aylett, 12, 13
sampling, 184-5
Sautuola, Marcelino de, 49, 51-2
    daughter of, 49, 52
Schaafhausen, H., 37
Schiffer, Michael, 186-7
Schliemann, Heinrich, 44, 45, 55,
    63, 67, 111
Schliemann, Sophie, 45
Schmerling, P. C., 33
Schmidt, Hubert, 62
Schneider, Hermann, 109
science(s)
    and specialisation, 69
    philosophy of, 164, 171, 197
    whether archaeology and
        prehistory are, *see under*
        archaeology, *and under*
        prehistory
scientific method(s), 86, 89-90,
    164, 170, 171, 188-9
Scottish primitivists, 16-19, 57
Sedgwick, Adam, 25-6, 28
sequences, cultural, *see* cultural
    sequences
Shennan, S., 180
Sherwood, Robert, 11
similarity, *see* comparisons
simplicity, desire for, 87-9, 114
Smith, Charles Roach, 140
Smith, George, 144-5
Smith, Sir Grafton Elliot, 15, 56,
    77, 79-88 *passim*, 90, 92, 105
Smith, William, 25, 27
societies, *see* cultures
societies, learned, 7, 8, 116
sociology, 198-200
Sollas, W. J., 121
Somme deposits, 34-7, 43
sources, 4-6, 124, 125, 147, 150,
    158
    accessibility, 147-8, 149-50
    inadequacy, 57
    protection of, 192-5

Spanuth, Jürgen, 88
Spencer, Herbert, 47, 48, 80, 123
Spengler, O., 50
Squier, E. G., 183
Stalin, Joseph, 112
state, 177, 192-6, 201-2
Stephens, John Lloyd, 59
Stone Age
    dating, 43
    origins of idea, 38-9
stone tools, 189
Stonehenge, 13, 197, 200
structuralism, 172-3
Struever, Stuart, 190
Stukeley, William, 13-14
surveying, 182-6
    resistivity, 189
    see also photography
Sybel, H. von, 111
symbols, meaning of, 172-3, 201
systems, *see under* prehistory
systems approach, 170

tails, 18
Tallgren, A. M., 112
taphonomy, 186
taste, 7, 65
Taylor, W. W., 135, 161
Tennyson, Alfred, Lord, 51, 60
terminology, 1-3, 7, 39, 70-1, 74-5
Thomas, Mr, 141
Thompson, R. Campbell, 62
Thoms, W. J. ('Ambrose
    Merton'), 140
Thomsen, Christian Jurgensen,
    22, 24, 38-9, 54, 123
Three Age System, 24, 46, 54, 58,
    73, 110
Times, The, 1
Toland, John, 13
Tollund man, 45, 101, 119
tools, 29-32, 34-7, 189
topographic surveying, 185-6
Tournal, 32-3
Tout, T. F., 150
Toynbee, Arnold, 50, 132-4
Tradescant, John, 6-7
Trevelyan, George, 126, 127
Trigger, Bruce, 166, 167, 171, 199
Troy, 45
Twyne, John, 12, 13

220

Tylor, Sir Edward, 1, 50, 58, 61, 79-81, 123

uniformitarianism, 27-9, 37
universalism, 131-4, 152
universities, 3-4, 26, 61, 81, 143
Ussher, James, Archbishop, 10, 21, 22, 24, 43, 61
USSR, 112-13, 114, 124, 126

Vaisey, Mr Justice, 136-7
Vallancey, Charle, 15-16
Vincent of Beauvais, 10

Waddington, C. H., 170
Wagner, Richard, 106
Walpole, Horace, 7-8, 16
war, 63, 67
Ward, John, 68
Watson, P. J.
  Explanation in Archaeology, 171
weapons, 30, 32
Webb, John, 13
Wedgwood, C. V., 151-2
Wedgwood, Josiah, 7
Wells, H. G., 139
Wheeler, Sir R. E. Mortimer, 67-8, 130, 193

Whewell, W., 23
White, A. P., 10
White, Leslie, 172
Whitehouse, W. E., 129, 130
Whittle, A., 180
Wilberforce, Samuel, Bishop, 143
Willey, Gordon R., 161-2, 165, 182, 183
Williams, V. Nash, 68
Wilson, Angus, 149
Wilson, Daniel, 1, 3, 39
Wilson, J. T., 82
Winckler, Hugo, 62
Windmill Hill, 139
'Woodland-Men' and 'Land-Workers', 16, 18, 57
Woolley, Sir Leonard, 62, 70, 157
Worsaae, Jens Jacob, 54, 55, 56
Wright, Thomas, 39
writing, 15-16, 94
Wynne, William, 11

Young, G. M., 138, 143

Zimbabwe, 177
Zeuner, F. E., 188